'This volume makes a ʒ   f qualitative
research by offering a coɩ   of heuristic
inquiry.
   The book fills a critical g   ↲ theoretical
discussions to showcase the   ↲ristics across diverse
disciplines. The case studies pɩ   ↲g art and design, documentary-
making, indigenous studies,   ↲otherapy, and social care, effectively
demonstrate the versatility and rigour of this often-misunderstood approach.
   The book's strength lies in its balanced perspective. It emphasises the
potentiality of heuristic research and its unique value in fostering personal
discovery, enhancing creativity, and navigating uncertainty as essential
aspects of the research process. The inclusion of chapters on heuristic inquiry
in AI and time-limited contexts further broadens the scope and relevance of
the book.
   Heuristic Enquiries: Research Across Disciplines and Professions is a valuable resource for researchers across disciplines, particularly those seeking to
deepen their understanding of epistemology. Through its engaging case studies and insightful discussions, the book not only illuminates the power of this
methodology but also encourages a more nuanced understanding and appreciation of its role in advancing qualitative research.
   Welby Ings and Keith Tudor are accomplished and recognised scholars in
their respective fields and their research and academic activities consistently
demonstrate their deep understanding of complexity.'
   Sérgio Nesteriuk Gallo, *Professor of Postgraduate Design, Anhembi*
Morumbi University, São Paulo; Deputy Coordinator in Architecture,
Urbanism, and Design at Coordination of Superior Level Staff
Improvement, Brazil

'This endorsement is written with the highest regard for the editors Welby Ings
and Keith Tudor each of whom are formidable and prolific authors in their
own right. As the driving force behind this publication, they have applied the
power of their combined intellects to engage trans-disciplinary and cross-
cultural contributing scholars and to curate skilfully a thorough, multi-
perspectival, yet highly accessible insight into the many dimensions of
heuristic inquiry.
   This book establishes the invaluable potential of heuristic inquiry to quantitative and qualitative research across fields as diverse as allied health, AI, the
arts, computer science, education, mathematics, and psychology. First drawing
in and grounding the reader through an engaging, insightful introduction to
heuristic inquiry, the book leads us on a journey of discovery through an array
of disciplinary perspectives. Contributing authors, from across various disciplinary fields and cultures, provide multifaceted insights into how heuristic enquiry

can enable researchers to traverse unchartered fields and unpredictable ground, engage with challenging questions and complex subjects, immerse in speculative exploration, discover new paths and insights, and illuminate new knowledge.

Providing an invaluable reference for scholars across diverse disciplines, this book will prove an especially valuable guide to scholars engaged in emergent fields, such as creative practice research, as well as scholars incorporating indigenous knowledges, ontologies, and epistemologies into their research projects. It not only explains why heuristic enquiry is of value, and how it can be deployed in a wide range of research settings, it also provides diverse exemplars of its application in practice.'

Professor Jillian Hamilton, *Interactive and Visual Design, School of Design, Queensland University of Technology, Brisbane, Queensland, Australia*

'Can literature and the visual arts be part of legitimate research? Can good research involve the very person of the researcher? This remarkable book sets out to illuminate the many ways that heuristic research "invites us to enquire about ourselves, others, and the world". Starting with the history of heuristics evolving approaches in exploring personal and phenomenological knowledge, this rich, engaging, and substantial book significantly adds to heuristic inquiry in the fields of psychotherapy and social care. It also goes far further, describing heuristic research from cultural thinking outside traditional Western constructs such as spiritual dimensions that are a feature of Māori research, and the Persian concept of illuminative thinking, to contemporary visual arts practice, documentary-making, and comparative study of heuristic inquiry in artificial intelligence and in artistic research. This will be a go to resource for anyone interested in exploring this exciting and expanding area.'

Del Loewenthal, *Emeritus Professor of Psychotherapy and Counselling, University of Roehampton, London, United Kingdom, and Chair of the Southern Association of Psychotherapy and Counselling, UK*

'This book is destined to become a "go to" resource for anyone wishing to conduct heuristic research whatever their context and scope of interest. After "Gathering In", an opening that sets the frame for the collection, Chapter 1 offers a concise overview of the evolution and current theoretical understanding of qualitative and quantitative heuristic inquiry. What follows is a banquet of culturally and topically diverse studies which lead the reader into the rich complexity of contemporary human science research.

The various authors effectively demonstrate what more human research can reveal when it engages life holistically on its own terms, refusing to reduce, dominate, or control the dynamic collaborative and participatory process. Studies consider an interesting range of theoretical and applied questions. One work, for instance, explores commonalities and divergences between a Western framework such as Moustakas' heuristic inquiry and aspects of Persian thought, illustrating how such an exploration allows for deeper understanding of both. There is an exploration of what is meant by the term "good care". Another author offers a heuristic study of the experience of psychotherapy for someone diagnosed with schizophrenia. The final section of the book widens the aperture even further by bringing applications and reflections from disciplines beyond psychology making heuristic inquiry more contemporary, pluralistic, and relevant to today's challenges.

It is this diversity in topics addressed while remaining within a well-defined heuristic discipline that marks this book as extraordinary. By providing an overview, examples of research in practice, as well as avenues for further exploration as it does, the book offers the would-be researcher a practical multidimensional view of where they might focus and how they might design their own inquiry. Inspiring and useful!'

Maureen O'Hara, *Professor of Psychology, National University,*
La Jolla, California, United Sates of America

HEURISTIC ENQUIRIES

Heuristic Enquiries provides an illuminating exploration of heuristic research by offering case studies of heurism in theory and practice across a number of disciplines, including art and design, psychology, psychotherapy, social care, social geography, and indigenous studies.

Heuristic research is a major method and methodology in qualitative research, emphasising the value of discovery, whether of the self, or the self with others. It is also misunderstood, misrepresented, and, in certain disciplines or fields, marginalised. This volume offers a major contribution to heuristic research by offering case studies of heuristics from specific disciplines, interdisciplinary practices, and professional contexts. The book is introduced with a review of the evolution of heuristic inquiry and includes chapters that discuss a comparative study of heuristic inquiry in AI and in artistic research, heuristic research in a time-limited context, and heuristic supervision.

This unique book is a comprehensive overview of the relationship between research and practice for postgraduate and doctoral research students, as well as academics, researchers, and practitioners.

Welby Ings is a Professor of Design at Auckland University of Technology, New Zealand, and is an award-winning designer, filmmaker, and writer.

Keith Tudor is Professor of Psychotherapy at Auckland University of Technology, New Zealand. A qualified social worker and psychotherapist, he now works primarily as an academic.

HEURISTIC ENQUIRIES

Research Across Disciplines and Professions

Edited by Welby Ings and Keith Tudor

Routledge
Taylor & Francis Group

LONDON AND NEW YORK

Designed cover image: Cover illustration by Elizabeth Hoyle

First published 2025
by Routledge
4 Park Square, Milton Park, Abingdon, Oxon OX14 4RN

and by Routledge
605 Third Avenue, New York, NY 10158

Routledge is an imprint of the Taylor & Francis Group, an informa business

British Library Cataloguing-in-Publication Data
A catalogue record for this book is available from the British Library

ISBN: 978-1-032-83097-1 (hbk)
ISBN: 978-1-032-83095-7 (pbk)
ISBN: 978-1-003-50775-8 (ebk)

DOI: 10.4324/9781003507758

Typeset in Optima
by SPi Technologies India Pvt Ltd (Straive)

CONTENTS

CONTRIBUTORS

Guy Cousins is a practicing psychotherapist working in private practice in New Zealand. His research dissertation explores the impact of attending boarding school on the adult psyche.

Akbar Ghobakhlou, a PhD graduate from Otago University, is a machine learning and artificial intelligence expert at Auckland University of Technology. His research centres on practical uses of intelligent technologies like monitoring, visualisation, and predictive models. His interests cover data mining, machine learning, image processing, smart sensors in precision agriculture, and environmental monitoring.

Maurice Hamington is a Professor of Philosophy and Affiliate Faculty of Women, Gender, and Sexuality Studies at Portland State University, USA, who writes about the theory and application of feminist care ethics. His latest book is *Revolutionary Care: Commitment and Ethos* (Routledge, 2024). For more information on his scholarly activities, see mhamington.com

Elizabeth Hoyle is a senior lecturer in the School of Communications at Auckland University of Technology, Aotearoa, New Zealand. She teaches screenwriting, screen production, and live-to-air broadcast. Currently working towards the completion of a practice-led doctorate, she is translating the narratives of grief using documentary and animation.

Alana Humphris is a dedicated psychotherapist based in Auckland, New Zealand. She completed her Master of Psychotherapy in 2023. With a background in crisis support, she brings compassionate expertise to her practice.

Alana is committed to fostering mental wellbeing and empowering her clients.

Anna Kingi is a student of psychotherapy at Auckland University of Technology, New Zealand. Anna currently works in integrated primary mental health services, and is most interested in psychoanalytic psychotherapy and mind–body approaches to healthcare.

Hossein Najafi is a senior lecturer in art and design at AUT, working on the integration of practical artistry with academic research. His studies explore the intersection of media aesthetics, narrative form, and cognitive psychology, utilising technologies such as Motion Capture and Deep Learning. He is also dedicated to mentoring VFX students, many of whom have contributed to notable film projects.

Elizabeth Nicholl is an existential-analytic psychotherapist and is a member of the Southern Association for Psychotherapy and Counselling (SAFPAC) in the UK. She completed her PhD in 2019 at the University of Roehampton, London. Elizabeth is also employed in the education sector, working for a counselling and psychotherapy awarding organisation.

Luke Oram is a psychotherapist (PBANZ) based in Auckland, New Zealand. His clinical experience involves working in public health settings and prison populations as well as leading men's groups for over ten years. Also a musician and writer, he likes to think of therapy as an act of story and metaphor. He is particularly interested in archetypal psychology, dreamwork, and spirituality.

Tangaroa Paora (they/them) is of Muriwhenua descent. Their PhD thesis explores gender role differentiation in Indigenous Māori performance. Tangaroa is a lecturer in Te Ara Poutama (Faculty of Māori and Indigenous Studies at AUT) and their research, academic, and community engagements focus on Kapa Haka (Māori Performing Arts) and finding spaces for the elevation of gender fluid contributions to communities.

F. Derek Ventling has been involved in all aspects of art and design: industry, pedagogy, and research. Born in the USA, raised in Switzerland, he is at home in New Zealand, where he independently thinks and practises.

GATHERING IN

Keith Tudor and Welby Ings

Oneroa

It was early summer, and, on the beach, small waves crawled along the sand—turning shells and debris, they took things away and left others in their wake. Gathering, turning, moving. In te reo Māori (the Māori language), this place is called Oneroa. It refers to a long expanse of sand. If you look up from the shoreline, depending on which way you turn, you can see farmland, or a city, or sweeps of gnarled Pōhutakawa trees. It is a place of great beauty.

On the hill above the shoreline is a retreat, a cluster of buildings that across many years has provided shelter for researchers seeking silence and focus. Here, a small group of us had gathered for four days: computer scientists, designers, educators, filmmakers, indigenous scholars, and psychotherapists; people from diverse disciplines and from different cultures, whose homelands are scattered across the globe.

We were connected by a common thread. We had all employed heuristic inquiry as an approach to research and we shared a common commitment to understanding its depth and applications. We were seeking a variation of perspectives and insights that had not been brought together before. We were researchers with situated experiences of a complex and deeply enabling approach to research.

This book is the result. It is a commitment to the new generation of researchers who are considering the nature and application of a heuristics as a unique approach to inquiry.

DOI: 10.4324/9781003507758-1

Heuristics

Heuristics is all about discovery. From its origins in the Greek word εὑρίσκω, meaning 'to discover', heuristic research invites us to enquire about ourselves, others, and the world. McLeod describes it as 'a powerful discovery-oriented approach to research' (2003, p. 97) and, while we agree with this, we would go further and suggest that heuristics is not simply an approach to research, it *is* research. Whilst the focus on the personal, subjective, interior, and self-search in some forms of heuristic research has led to certain criticisms of its self-referential nature, there has always been a strong sense that the discoveries made in such research (the findings) need to look outward (Moustakas, 1990; Sela-Smith, 2002). As Rogers puts it: '*What is most personal is most general*' (1961/1967, p. 26, original emphasis).

Unlike some other approaches to research, heuristics may be both a methodology and a method (see Tudor, 2023). Some heuristic researchers argue that it doesn't prescribe a methodology; indeed, Douglass and Moustakas state that, 'As a conceptual framework of human science, heuristics offers an attitude with which to approach research, *but does not prescribe a methodology*' (1985, p. 42, emphasis added). What this means is that part of the process of heuristic research is the discovery of its underlying methodology. As Ings puts it: 'heuristics is not a prescribed methodology but [rather] a paradigm inside which disruption and illogic might profitably function' (2011, p. 80). For other heuristic researchers, there is a natural synergy between the heuristic method and existential philosophy (e.g., Douglass & Moustakas), while others view phenomenology as a philosophical and methodological base for their method, such as Patton (2002) who considers heuristics as a form of phenomenological inquiry, and Mihalache (2019) who views it as aligned with transpersonal research. A third perspective is that heuristics is both a methodology and a method, which, in many ways, may be seen in Moustakas' own work in which he defines various *concepts*, such as identifying with the focus of inquiry, tacit knowing, intuition, the internal frame of reference, etc. (Douglass & Moustakas, 1985; Moustakas, 1990) which represent some underlying assumptions of the research, as well as certain *phases of enquiry*, i.e., initial engagement, immersion, incubation, illumination, explication, and creative synthesis, which suggest a certain *method* to the enquiry. Whilst this has been discussed in the literature, what hasn't been acknowledged is the impact of these discussions on the discipline of the researcher, which is partly why, in deciding the focus and scope of this book, we wanted to invite colleagues from different disciplines to contribute their thinking about method and methodology, which, as you the reader will see, represents different views across quantitative and qualitative approaches to research.

With regard to language, in heuristic research, the use of 'enquiry' or 'inquiry' tends to shift depending on the disciplinary focus of the writer, or whether they are referring to a formal or informal use of heuristics (see also

Tudor, 2023). This book encompasses both uses, according to the authors' preference.

The project

Although we are from different backgrounds and disciplines, as editors we came together over our mutual interest in heuristics (see Chapter 10). However, we both had experience with, and a commitment to, interdisciplinary and transdisciplinary working, and in fostering the next generation of researchers and writers.

Early on in our thinking about this project, we had the idea of gathering contributors together, and providing them with board and lodging so that they could have the space to reflect, think, and write. Initially, the coronavirus pandemic and national and international travel restrictions delayed and then somewhat changed the project so that, in the end, some of us gathered together, across four days at the end of 2023, at the Vaughan Park Retreat Centre, Long Bay, Auckland, Aotearoa New Zealand, while those who for various reasons couldn't attend, wrote and submitted drafts of their chapters before the event.

In establishing the kaupapa (purpose) of the project, we discussed the sense and feel of what we sought to enable. We wanted something that would be helpful; something that would have been useful to us when we first considered the potentials of heuristic inquiry. We thought about the importance of the theoretical, practical, personal, general, rigorous, creative, inspiring, and stimulating. We wanted the book to represent what Sultan refers to as 'embodied relational writing' (2019, p. 198), and to demonstrate both affection and empathy for the reader. We hope that we have achieved this – but recognise that you, the reader, will be the final judge.

Before we introduce the book we would like to acknowledge people and entities who supported the project:

- For funding the residential writing retreat, the Faculties of Design and Creative Technologies and of Health and Environmental Sciences at Auckland University of Technology.
- For hosting this event and looking after us so well for the three days of the retreat, the staff at Vaughan Park Anglican Retreat Centre, Auckland.
- For their excellent chapters, all the contributors.
- For their contribution to Chapter 10, Akbar Ghobakhlou, Elizabeth Hoyle, Alana Humphris, Anna Kingi, Luke Oram, Tangaroa Paora, and Derek Ventling.
- For her interest in and support of the project, Eleanor Taylor at Taylor & Francis (UK).
- For her fine copy-editing of the manuscript, Angie Strachan.

- For the cover image, Elizabeth Hoyle.
- For the finished product, the production team at Taylor & Francis (UK).

The book

In true heuristic fashion, the final version of the book reflects an emergent process of discovery. In the journey some contributors have been with us from the beginning, some withdrew, and others joined us. The book proposal was peer-reviewed, and following advice we included another chapter (Chapter 1). As a result, the book has a sense of both looking in (i.e., at the field of heuristic research) and looking out to the community (i.e., colleagues in different disciplines, research, and publishing).

Following this introduction (the gathering in of you, the reader), we begin by looking back on the evolution of heuristic inquiry across both quantitative and qualitative approaches. The co-authorship of this chapter represents researchers across these different approaches, traditions, or paradigms and, thereby, provides a plural(istic) view of the history of heuristic research.

We have called the next section of the book 'Stepping forward'. In each of the six chapters researchers from different fields present their engagement with heuristic inquiry. These writers come from diverse fields and the chapters unfold commonalities and distinctiveness in each context. The first two chapters examine heuristic inquiry in relation to cultural thinking outside traditional Western constructs. In the first, Tangaroa Paora discusses how heuristic inquiry's flexibility and engagement with the tacit can be extended and applied to spiritual dimensions that are a feature of Māori research. In the next chapter, Hossein Najafi draws resonances between heuristic inquiry and the Persian concept of illuminative thinking. These chapters are important because they demonstrate how the nature of heuristic inquiry can engage with, rather than 'speak over', other ontologies and epistemologies. Like these contributions, the next chapter also discusses heuristic inquiry in relation to creative research. Here, Derek Ventling compares two forms of contemporary visual arts practice: one inside the academy and one conducted as professional practice. This is followed by Elizabeth Hoyle's discussion of heuristic inquiry in the development of biographical and autobiographical documentary making. In this chapter she unpacks and renegotiates Kleining and Witt's (2000) principles for heightening chances of discovery in heuristic inquiry in her practice-led doctoral project. The final chapters in this section of the book present discussions of heuristic inquiry applied in the field of social care and of psychotherapy. In the first, Maurice Hamington writes from a professional context, unpacking how a care heuristic can be employed to improve care habits and help therapists (in the broad sense of the term) to focus on the role of care in human sustenance and flourishing. In her chapter, Elizabeth Nicholl discusses her experience of heuristic inquiry when conducting a study into how people with a diagnosis of 'schizophrenia' experience their personal therapy. The chapter demonstrates how heuristics can be employed as a means of discovering new understandings of a research topic, whereby both the researcher and co-participants gain self-knowledge at the same time.

The third section of the book, 'Reaching across', comprises three chapters. In different ways, these span the field of heuristic research and take up questions, concerns, themes, or reflections that reach across disciplines. In the first of these, Akbar Ghobakhlou and Hossein Najafi offer a comparative study of heuristic inquiry in artificial intelligence and in artistic research. Their contribution echoes and follows on from Chapter 1 and, thus, offers a useful comparison between quantitative and qualitative approaches to research (which, interestingly, identifies more synergies than differences). In the next chapter, four students and their supervisor reflect on the impact of the students having limited time to conduct, write-up, and submit their research, doing so with reference to Moustakas' (1990) phases of heuristic inquiry. This is especially significant in the context of what some of the early heuristic researchers, especially Moustakas (1990) and Sela-Smith (2002), wrote about the importance of having time to do heuristic research. In Chapter 10, we (Keith and Welby) consider the implications of heuristic research for the supervision of that research. At the heart of chapter are reflections from supervisees on which we comment with reference to the small amount of existing literature on the subject. We hope that this chapter will be informative for students and supervisors alike.

In the last section and of the book, 'Facing outwards', we offer some reflections as editors of the book, discussing our approach to the work, its distinctive features, and our aspirations for its use as we move forward as researchers and practitioners to apply and develop the potentials of heuristic inquiry in a productive yet uncertain world.

Welcome

Nau mai (come, welcome), haere mai (come here), piki mai (climb up), kake mai (ascend).

This greeting is in te reo Māori, the first language of Aotearoa New Zealand. It carries a sense of welcome and engagement. In the context of embarking on a voyage, it alludes to gathering and climbing on board te waka (a canoe or sea-going vessel) in order to paddle and sail it together. As editors, we did this with our invitations to the contributors, and we now have pleasure in inviting you the reader to climb into these pages and in this sense to engage with the uncertainty, depth, complexity, creativity, and discovery that is heuristic research.

Welcome to the book.

References

Douglass, B., & Moustakas, C. (1985). Heuristic inquiry: The internal search to know. *Journal of Humanistic Psychology*, *25*(3), 39–55. https://doi.org/10.1177/0022167885253004

Ings, W. (2011). Managing heuristics as a method of inquiry in autobiographical graphic design theses. *International Journal of Art & Design Education*, *30*(2), 226–241. https://doi.org/10.1111/j.1476-8070.2011.01699.x

Kleining, G., & Witt, H. (2000). The qualitative heuristic approach: A methodology for discovery in psychology and the social sciences. Rediscovering the method of introspection as an example. *Forum Qualitative Sozialforschung/Forum: Qualitative Social Research*, *1*. https://doi.org/10.17169/fqs-1.1.1123

McLeod, J. (2003). *Doing counselling research* (2nd ed.). Sage.

Mihalache, G. (2019). Heuristic inquiry: Differentiated from descriptive phenomenology and aligned with transpersonal research methods. *The Humanistic Psychologist*, *47*(2), 136–157. https://doi.org/10.1037/hum0000125

Moustakas, C. (1990). *Heuristic research: Design, methodology and applications*. Sage.

Patton, M. Q. (2002). *Qualitative research and evaluation methods*. Sage.

Rogers, C. R. (1961/1967). 'This is me'. In *On becoming a person* (pp. 1–27). Constable.

Sela-Smith, S. (2002). Heuristic research: A review and critique of Moustakas's method. *Journal of Humanistic Psychology*, *42*(3), 53–88. https://doi.org/10.1177/0022167802423004

Sultan, N. (2019). *Heuristic inquiry: Researching human experience holistically*. Sage.

Tudor, K. (2023). Critical heuristics: From 'I who feels' to 'We who care – and act'. In K. Tudor & J. Wyatt (Eds.), *Qualitative research approaches for psychotherapy: Reflexivity, methodology, and criticality* (pp. 115–132). Routledge.

Looking Back

1

A REVIEW OF THE EVOLUTION OF HEURISTIC INQUIRY

Hossein Najafi, Keith Tudor, and Welby Ings

Introduction

This chapter considers the evolution of heuristic inquiry as a research method and methodology and its application across two key forms of scholarly engagement, quantitative and qualitative research. As a quantitative approach, heuristics is applied in a range of fields including computer sciences, biology, finance, geography, mathematics, psychology, statistics, and physical sciences. As a qualitative approach, it is employed in diverse disciplines from art and design, through education, to nursing, psychology, psychotherapy, social geography, and sociology. The chapter discusses the concept of heuristics and clarifies some distinctions. This is followed by a discussion of the evolution and development of heuristic inquiry in both quantitative and qualitative research.

The concept

The English word heuristics comes from the Ancient Greek word εὑρίσκω, meaning 'to discover', and is related to the word eureka, which comes from another Greek verb *heúrēka* meaning 'I have found it' (a word popularised by Archimedes' discovery regarding volume and density through the displacement of water). Through this connection, the word has been associated with discovery (Douglass & Moustakas, 1985; Hjeij & Vilks, 2023). The etymological roots of heuristic tie it closely to investigative procedures (Pinheiro & McNeill, 2014); similarly, Smith (2022) draws an association between Aristotle's discussion of *epagôgê*, by which one seeks to find but not necessarily prove a general truth, and the nature of heuristic inquiry.

DOI: 10.4324/9781003507758-3

As a noun, heuristics is used to describe an evolutionary mental phenomenon in humans that results in faster and sometimes more optimal decision-making (Hjeij & Vilks, 2023), as well as reflective process of self-discovery. The word is also used to describe how artificial intelligence might replicate or reconstruct similar mental procedures in computer science (Nutakki & Mandava, 2023). Kahneman defines heuristics as a 'procedure that helps find adequate, though often imprecise answers to difficult questions' (2011, p. 97). As an adjective, heuristic is most associated with nouns such as inquiry, framework, method, methodology, and research. We suggest that heuristic inquiry describes a process of exploration and discovery that is used to navigate and make meaning of complex, unpredictable, and/or unknown realms. Given these two forms and uses of the word, we may understand heuristic inquiry as an approach to research that adopts and utilises heuristic mental processes to discover experience and/or to solve problems.

To understand the concept of heuristics better, one may juxtapose it with its antithesis, algorithmic problem-solving. Algorithmic thinking was developed by the Persian mathematician, Al-Khawarizmi (from whose name the term is derived). Seen as a counterpoint to heuristic inquiry, algorithmic procedures for solving a problem (or performing computations) follow an exact set of instructions that involve specified step-by-step actions. Thus, while a heuristic approach involves rules of thumb or educated guesses, an algorithmic approach follows a set of rules or procedures to arrive at a solution. This means that an algorithmic process is more systematic and less prone to human bias than a heuristic approach (Grossman & Frieder, 2004), while a heuristic approach, especially in qualitative research, acknowledges, embraces, and makes meaning of the bias. Knuth defines an algorithm as 'a set of rules that precisely defines a sequence of operations such that each rule is effective and definite and such that the sequence terminates in a finite time' (1997, p. 4). Algorithms are based on logical or mathematical principles, and they ensure accurate and consistent results. Hjeij and Vilks (2023) note that inquiries based on pure logical decision-making, such as rational decision-making in economics (Savage, 1972), or the Aristotelian framework of syllogistic deductive logic (Priest, 2008) are also not considered heuristic. However, Boyer and Merzbach (2011) argue that a reciprocal relationship can exist between heuristics and algorithmic problem-solving.

Hjeij and Vilks suggest that the spectrum of heuristics is very broad, observing that the application of a heuristic 'may require intuition, guessing, exploration, or experience; some heuristics are rather elaborate, others are truly shortcuts, some are described in somewhat loose terms, and others are well-defined' (2023, p. 2). The same authors observe that the broader application of heuristics in research has grown considerably, noting that, while in 1970 the Scopus database located only 20 published articles with the word 'heuristic' in their title, by 2021 this number had increased to 3,783 (Hjeij & Vilks, 2023). In contemporary research, heuristics and heuristic inquiry are used across diverse fields including artificial intelligence (AI) (Kaveh & Mesgari, 2023), artistic research (Ardern & Mortensen Steagall, 2023), computer science (Abdulsaheb & Kadhim, 2023), education (Isroilova, 2023), mathematics (Aghsami et al., 2023), nursing studies (Whybrow & Milligan, 2023), and psychotherapy (Tudor, 2023).

Evolution and application of heuristics in quantitative research

Kleining and Witt (2001) note that the German mathematician Joachim Jungius (1587–1657) was among the first researchers in the Common Era to use the term 'heuretica' formally. Jungius, whose work emphasised the importance of developing methods to solve unsolved problems and find new theorems, categorised learning into empirical, epistemic, and heuristic, with the heuristic category representing the pinnacle of problem-solving and knowledge acquisition.

In 1637, the French philosopher René Descartes published his *Discourse on Method* (2012) in which he advocated mathematical reasoning as a means for advancing knowledge. Descartes outlined a problem-solving approach involving four steps: accepting only true axioms, breaking down problems, organising thoughts from simple to complex, and ensuring thoroughness (Lorenzini, 2023). Descartes also worked on transforming problems into algebraic equations to create a universal science (*mathesis universalis*). However, towards the end of his life he began working on *Rules for the Direction of the Mind* (1701/2022), proposing heuristic rules for scientific inquiry that focused on simplification, geometric representation, and identifying knowns and unknowns. Despite criticism from other philosophers (such as Leibniz) for being overly general, Descartes' methods laid a foundation for addressing the discovery and investigation of complex problems across diverse disciplines.

In 1837, the Czech mathematician and philosopher Bernard Bolzano published his multi-volume work on a *Theory of Science* (Bolzano 1837/2014), in the fourth volume of which he offered a structured approach to invention, with general and specific rules for discovering truths. In this work he emphasised the use of heuristics which talented individuals often unconsciously apply to solve complex tasks.

In his paper on *Truth and Probability*, Ramsey (1926/1931) explored inductive logic as a heuristic habit of the mind. He provided a pragmatic justification for induction, suggesting that mental habits, such as inductive inference, are ecologically rational when they lead to generally true beliefs.

Nine years later, in 1935, Duncker, a pioneer in the experimental study of problem-solving, explored both facilitators and limitations to answering a question. His work on functional fixedness highlighted the challenges of thinking creatively and using objects in unconventional ways. One example of this was the Duncker Candle Problem which was a puzzle whereby one must attach a candle to a wall using only a box of thumbtacks and matches, without dripping wax, a task which was used to test creativity by using objects in unusual ways. Dunker's work was significant because he emphasised the interplay between the internal mind and the external problem structure in successful problem-solving.

In 1945, George Polya, often referred to as the father of modern problem-solving in mathematics, sought to revive the study of heuristics in his book *How to Solve It*. His principles of problem-solving involved understanding the problem, planning, executing, and reflecting on improvement. His work focused on methods like inductive reasoning and analogy (Hertwig & Pachur, 2015) and influenced the development of artificial intelligence (AI).

In 1955, Herbert Simon (renowned for his theory of bounded rationality), suggested in his book *A Behavioural Model of Rational Choice* that decision-making is constrained by limited information, time, and cognitive capacity, arguing that these factors can lead to satisficing, that is, looking for satisfactory rather than optimal decision-making. His collaboration with Allen Newell produced the *Logic Theorist* and the *General Problem Solver* (GPS), which described early AI processes that employ heuristic approaches in decision-making (Newell et al., 1959; Simon & Newell, 1958). However, while the GPS was efficient with sufficiently well-structured problems like the *Towers of Hanoi* (a puzzle with three rods and moveable, different-sized disks), it was not capable of solving complex real-life problems. Consequently, Simon dedicated most of the remainder of his career to the advancement of machine intelligence. The results of his experiments showed that, like humans, certain computer programs can make decisions using trial-and-error and shortcut methods (Estevadeordal et al., 2003). Significantly, Simon and Newell argue that heuristics is used by both humans and intelligent machines. They note that 'Digital computers can perform certain heuristic problem-solving tasks for which no algorithms are available… [and] in doing so, they use processes that are closely parallel to human problem-solving processes' (1958, p. 7). Simon and Newell's approach later evolved into meta-heuristics (a search within the space of solutions for a specific problem) and hyper-heuristics (searching within a heuristic space), underscoring the role of heuristics in complex problem-solving (Mart et al., 2018).

In 1968, at the Chemnitz University of Technology, Johannes Müller introduced *systematic heuristics* to improve efficiency in scientific and technological problem-solving. His approach employed a library of proven solutions for recurring problems and was used to streamline the process of problem-solving from planning to evaluation. Despite the program's early termination (due to ideological conflicts), Müller's methods found success in diverse industrial applications (Banse & Friedrich, 2000).

In *Methodology of Scientific Research Programmes*, Imre Lakatos (1978) presents the concepts of 'negative' and 'positive' heuristics, where a 'negative heuristic' represents the unchallengeable foundation of a research program, while a 'positive heuristic' steers its progress and the forecast of new discoveries. Lakatos' thinking highlighted the significance of concentrating on achievable solutions to intricate problems, by excluding what was less pertinent.

In their influential 1974 publication *Judgement under Uncertainty: Heuristics and Biases*, Tversky and Kahneman introduce three fundamental cognitive heuristics: *availability, representativeness,* and *anchoring and adjustment*. These became cornerstones to understanding human judgment in uncertain contexts (Kahneman, 2011; Tversky & Kahneman, 1974). Their study became a fundamental framework for designing AI procedures (Martínez et al., 2022). Kahneman and Tversky's *availability heuristic* describes a situation where the ease of recalling an event skews our perception of its likelihood, leading to overestimations of risks (such as those from terrorist attacks as highlighted in the media, or misjudgements in business contexts where success stories overshadow numerous failures). Their *representativeness heuristic* is used to assess the likelihood of an object belonging to a certain category based on its similarity to a prototype where statistical reality is overlooked (which often results in errors such as the base rate fallacy; Bar-Hillel, 1980). *Anchoring and adjustment* describe how initial information (or an anchor) can heavily influence subsequent judgments and decisions, even when the anchor is irrelevant, as illustrated in experiments where starting points in a multiplication task significantly affect the outcomes. However, while simplifying decision-making, Kahneman and Tversky's heuristics often lead to systematic biases and errors and demonstrate the complex nature of human cognition and decision-making.

Another quantitative researcher whose work on heuristics has contributed to the field of decision-making is the German psychologist Gerd Gigerenzer. His theory opposes Kahneman and Tversky's heuristics and biases approach. Gigerenzer argues that heuristics are neither irrational nor inferior to the optimisation or probability calculations. Instead, he emphasises the ecological rationality of heuristics, especially in uncertain and complex environments, and introduces the concept of the adaptive toolbox: a collection of mental shortcuts tailored for specific problems (Gigerenzer, 1996; Gigerenzer et al., 2015; Gigerenzer & Gaissmaier, 2011). His research included the *recognition heuristic*, which can lead to more accurate decisions in situations with limited information, and the *take-the-best heuristic* which focuses on the most important cues in decision-making (Gigerenzer & Todd, 1999). In a similar vein, Slovic and his colleagues write about the 'affect heuristic' which proposes that emotion is important in guiding judgements and/or decisions, and, thereby, acts as a 'mental shortcut' in making and acting on such decisions quickly (Slovic et al., 2002, 2004, 2007).

Heuristic inquiry in qualitative research

Although heuristics describes a broad approach to research that adopts and utilises heuristic mental processes to solve problems, when employed in qualitative research, heuristics appears somewhat different. Nevertheless, in both quantitative and qualitative approaches, in a heuristic inquiry the researcher moves away from the application of pre-established formulae and emphasis is placed on heightened levels of flexibility, trial and error, astute questioning, and acceptance that there will be an optimal solution that is discovered rather than guaranteed.

Clark Moustakas, an American psychologist who was a prominent figure in the humanistic psychology movement of the 1960s, began to develop a systematic *qualitative* approach for heuristic studies in the fields of clinical and educational psychology (Moustakas, 1967). In the 1950s, Moustakas' academic career was disrupted by his daughter's serious illness. While he accompanied his daughter throughout this difficult journey (and subsequent recovery), the experience had a profound impact on Moustakas, which then led him to investigate the phenomenon of loneliness in three books: *Loneliness* (1961), *Loneliness and Love* (1972), and *The Touch of Loneliness* (1975). This journey of personal exploration and understanding led to his seminal book, *Heuristic Research: Design, Methodology, and Applications* (1990), in which he elaborated the heuristic method, providing a comprehensive framework and diverse examples for conducting such research. According to Moustakas, reflecting on his own experience, the process of heuristic research has six phases: initial engagement, immersion, incubation, illumination, explication, and creative synthesis (Douglass & Moustakas, 1985; Moustakas, 1990). However, it is worth noting that Moustakas came to these phases a posteriori, i.e., *after* the research; they may not be applicable to all such heuristic projects. We make this point as some heuristic researchers assume that they have to follow these phases (for discussion of which, see also Chapter 8).

Clark Moustakas credited various humanistic psychologists with influencing the development of his heuristic methodology, specifically: Paul Bridgman's (1950) insights into subjective knowledge; Abraham Maslow's (1956) work on self-actualisation; Carl Rogers' (1963) theory of the structure of personality; Eugene Gendlin's (1962) concept of focusing; Martin Buber's (1965) concept of mutuality; Michael Polanyi's (1966) ideas on tacit knowledge and intuition; Sydney Jourard's (1968) work on self-disclosure; and Willard Frick's (1982) theories on identity. Moustakas was also influenced by the writings of Søren Kierkegaard, Edmund Husserl, and Gordon Allport. From this, Moustakas identified a number of concepts that, in effect, provide the methodology underpinning the method, i.e., identifying with the focus of inquiry, self-dialogue, tacit knowing, intuition, indwelling, focusing, the internal frame of reference (Douglass & Moustakas, 1985; Moustakas, 1990), and validation (Moustakas, 1990).

Moustakas' heuristic research approach represents a deeply introspective journey, emphasising the researcher's personal experience and self-discovery. As a process, it involves a conscious engagement with perceptions, intuitions, and knowledge, leading to a deeper understanding of both the subject and the self (Moustakas, 1990). Moustakas argues that questions about the subject of the research as well as methodology arise from inner search, thus requiring the researcher's full commitment and immersion in, openness to, and reflective exploration of the subject of inquiry. This process often involves venturing into unknown territories, the tacit dimension of knowledge, and relying on discovery through illumination (Moustakas, 1990), as well as exploring any resistance to the process (Sela-Smith, 2002). In this process a researcher creates a depiction and/or a narrative that portrays the essence of their experiences, which requires full engagement of self-resources and autobiographical connections (Moustakas, 1990). Finally, Moustakas argues that such an approach demands total presence, honesty, and a commitment to personal transformation, making heuristic research a profound and transformative exploration of human experience.

In 2002 Sela-Smith critiqued Moustakas' research, arguing that his focus had moved away 'from the self's experience of the experience to focusing on the idea of the experience' (2002, p. 53). From her own heuristic self-inquiry and a re-evaluation of Moustakas' work, she identified six key elements in heuristic research: self-experience, inward reach, surrender, self-dialogue, self-search, and transformation. More recently, Tudor (2022, 2023) offers a critique of what he considers to be Sela-Smith's undue focus on the interior and the individual, represented in the phrase 'I-who-feels', and argues in favour of a more exterior and collective view of and focus for research represented by the phrase 'we-who-care – and act'.

Most recently in this tradition, and encompassing the disciplines of education, psychology, social work, and sociology, as well as therapy, Sultan (2018) published a book on *Heuristic Inquiry* in which she emphasises the holistic and embodied nature of this approach to research.

In a separate tradition from that of Moustakas, German sociologist Gerhard Kleining (1982) proposes a qualitative heuristic as a suitable method for social science research. His approach was founded on four principles: the researcher's open-mindedness and willingness to revise preconceptions; the flexible and evolving definition of the research topic; the consideration of a wide variation in research perspectives; and the identification of similarities in data. His work and later writing with Harald Witt emphasises adaptability in qualitative research (Kleining & Witt, 2001).

Heuristics has also been used in geography, in which Thompson understands a heuristic to be 'a practical method that attempts the solution of theoretical, empirical, or interpretative problems, while geographical metaphors are ways of seeing and of framing these problems' (2017, p. 57).

In the last two decades, heuristic inquiry has also been employed as a method for heightening the potential for creative discovery in artistic, practice-led, and ethnocultural studies, notably in the visual arts, film, creative writing, music, and communication design. In examining studies from these fields, Welby Ings (2011, 2014, 2018, 2022) has considered the nature and supervisory implications of immersion, self-care, and critical, aesthetic refinement. His work has also focused on instances where heuristic inquiry is employed to artistically engage with semi-fictional storytelling.

In addition to these applications, heuristic, practice-led ethnocultural studies have also begun to profile in artistic, doctoral, practice-led theses. These studies, emanating from indigenous and culturally specific knowledge systems, transcend conventional research paradigms. Within them heuristic inquiry has been explored as a means of creating bridges between culturally shaped approaches to research and existing methodological writing.

Beginning in 2008, a number of theses associated with Persian and Middle Eastern storytelling and filmmaking began drawing connections between heuristic inquiry and the subjective journey of the artistic researcher who, through the process of artefact creation becomes integrated with their work – see El Noor (2008), Aziz (2009), and Najafi (2023).

Heuristic inquiry was also used by the Chinese film poet Chen Chen in her doctoral thesis, *Bright on the Grey Sea* (2018). Her study involved an exploratory journey into the realms of Chinese poetic wisdom by anchoring itself in the philosophical and aesthetic principles of the *Xiang* system (a layered conceptual framework derived from Chinese poetry), and the concept of *menglong* (akin to mystery or enigma, in Western thought).

Among Oceanic Indigenous scholars, four doctoral candidates have recently embedded heuristic inquiry inside existing culturally-shaped approaches to artistic research. Building on work he began developing in 2016 in 2020, Robert Pouwhare advanced a model he called *Pūrākau* which unpacked how Indigenous Māori scholarship utilises tacit, explicit, and spiritual knowing in a process of creation and reflection. His heuristic framework was later adapted by the choreographer Tangaroa Paora (2023) and the documentary-maker Toiroa Williams (2024), both of whom progressed their research projects through heightened levels of sensitised immersion, customary practice, and the studied-self in the context of collective responsibility.

As these studies were emerging, in 2021, the Samoan composer Igelese Ete employed heuristic inquiry as a framework for developing a *Koneseti* (a form of Samoan narrative opera). His research design moved through processes of *fesili* (questioning), *foafoa* (taking action), *mai totōnu* (inner reflection), and *mai fafo* (external reflection).

Conclusion

Despite divergent trajectories in quantitative and qualitative research, heuristic inquiry exhibits numerous commonalities that bridge these two realms. In both research approaches, heuristics fundamentally rely on instances of human experience as data, a basis which underscores its experiential nature (Russell & Norvig, 2010). Researchers utilising heuristics in either approach demonstrate a willingness to engage with the unknown, and to embrace complexity. This acceptance of, and navigation through, the unknown and the tacit dimension of knowledge is intrinsic to heuristic inquiry, regardless of whether it is quantitative or qualitative (Ings, 2014; LeCun et al., 2015). Central to this, again in both approaches, is the concept of intuition. Traditionally perceived as exclusive to qualitative methodologies (Moustakas, 1990), intuition has also found its place in quantitative realms, manifesting in various heuristic procedures (Johnny et al., 2020; Simon, 1979). Its focus on and facilitation of the recognition of emerging patterns in human behaviour, experience, and society further illustrates the applicability of heuristics across research approaches (Flasiński, 2016; Ventling, 2017). Heuristics requires researchers to prioritise efficient problem-solving and/or discovery over absolute certainty, an approach that is particularly pertinent given the extreme complexity of the questions, issues, subjects, and spaces explored and navigated by heuristic researchers (Lash, 2007; Moustakas, 1961; Russell & Norvig, 2010). Given its emphasis on discovery, heuristic research also tends to reflect on – and in this sense to discover – things about itself, for instance as Sela-Smith (2002) did about Moustakas' (1990) work. There are few frameworks of methodology and/or method that have proved so adaptable and mutable across diverse disciplines and approaches in research.

This chapter has offered a brief outline of the complex development of heuristics as a protean system of inquiry by tracing its presence in different traditions and across a number of disciplines. Initially grounded in philosophy and mathematics, heuristics has evolved and played a pivotal role in diverse fields of inquiry, including artificial intelligence, humanistic as well as cognitive psychology, education, geography, and art and design. Its evolution has been marked by significant milestones, including Herbert Simon's theory of bounded rationality, Moustakas' disciplined self-inquiry, and the groundbreaking work of Tversky and Kahneman on cognitive biases. These developments have not only enhanced our understanding of knowledge inquiry but also underscored the importance of heuristics in human thought.

References

Abdulsaheb, J. A., & Kadhim, D. J. (2023). Classical and heuristic approaches for mobile robot path planning: A survey. *Robotics, 12*(4), 93. https://doi.org/10.3390/robotics12040093

Aghsami, A., Abazari, S. R., Bakhshi, A., Yazdani, M. A., Jolai, S., & Jolai, F. (2023). A meta-heuristic optimization for a novel mathematical model for minimizing costs and maximizing donor satisfaction in blood supply chains with finite capacity queueing systems. *Healthcare Analytics, 3*, 100136. https://doi.org/10.1016/j.health.2023.100136

Ardern, S., & Mortensen Steagall, M. (2023). Awakening takes place within: A practice-led research through texture and embodiment. *DAT Journal, 8*(1), 70–100. https://doi.org/10.29147/datjournal.v8i1.701

Aziz, L. (2009). *Gilgamesh, the hero of Mesopotamia* [Master's thesis, Auckland University of Technology]. Tuwhera Open Access Theses & Dissertations. https://hdl.handle.net/10292/813

Banse, G., & Friedrich, K. (2000). *Konstruieren zwischen Kunst und Wissenschaft* [Constructions between art and science]. Idee-Entwurf-Gestaltung.

Bar-Hillel, M. (1980). The base-rate fallacy in probability judgments. *Acta Psychologica, 44*(3), 211–233. https://doi.org/10.1016/0001-6918(80)90046-3

Boyer, C. B., & Merzbach, U. C. (2011). *A history of mathematics*. John Wiley & Sons.

Bolzano, B. (1837/2014). *Theory of Science* (4 vols.; R. George & P Rusnock, Trans.). Oxford University Press.

Bridgman, P. (1950). *Reflections of a physicist*. Philosophical Library.

Buber, M. (1965). *The knowledge of man*. Harper & Row.

Chen, C. (2018). *Bright on the grey sea: Utilizing the Xiang system to creatively consider the potentials of menglong in film poetry* [Doctoral thesis, Auckland University of Technology]. Tuwhera Open Access Theses & Dissertations. https://hdl.handle.net/10292/11737

Descartes, R. (2012). *Discourse on method*. Hackett Publishing.

Descartes, R. (1701/2022). *Rules for the direction of the mind*. DigiCat.

Douglass, B. G., & Moustakas, C. (1985). Heuristic inquiry: The internal search to know. *Journal of Humanistic Psychology, 25*(3), 39–55. https://doi.org/10.1177/0022167885253004

El Noor, M. (2008). *Narratwist: Alteration in meaning in a short film text* [Master's thesis, Auckland University of Technology]. Tuwhera Open Access Theses & Dissertations. https://hdl.handle.net/10292/408

Estevadeordal, A., Frantz, B., & Taylor, A. M. (2003). The rise and fall of world trade, 1870–1939. *The Quarterly Journal of Economics, 118*(2), 359–407. https://www.jstor.org/stable/25053910

Ete, I. (2021). *Naatapuitea: An artistic interpretation of traditional and contemporary Samoan musical structures, instrumentation and koniseti* [Doctoral thesis, Auckland University of Technology]. Tuwhera Open Access Theses & Dissertations. https://hdl.handle.net/10292/14792

Flasiński, M. (2016). *Introduction to artificial intelligence*. Springer. https://doi.org/10.1007/978-3-319-40022-8

Frick, W. B. (1982). Conceptual foundations of self-actualization: A contribution to motivation theory. *Journal of Humanistic Psychology, 22*(4), 33–52. https://doi.org/10.1177/002216788202200404

Gendlin, E. (1962). *Experiencing and the creation of meaning*. Free Press.

Gigerenzer, G. (1996). On narrow norms and vague heuristics: A reply to Kahneman and Tversky. *Psychological Review*, *103*(3), 592–596. https://doi.org/10.1037/0033-295X.103.3.592

Gigerenzer, G., & Gaissmaier, W. (2011). Heuristic decision making. *Annual Review of Psychology*, *62*(1), 451–482. https://doi.org/10.1146/annurev-psych-120709-145346

Gigerenzer, G., Hertwig, R., & Pachur, T. (Eds.). (2015). *Heuristics: The foundations of adaptive behavior* (Reprint ed.). Oxford University Press.

Gigerenzer, G., & Todd, P. M. (1999). Fast and frugal heuristics: The adaptive toolbox. In *Simple heuristics that make us smart* (pp. 3–34). Oxford University Press.

Grossman, D. A., & Frieder, O. (2004). *Information retrieval: Algorithms and heuristics* (Vol. 15). Springer Science & Business Media.

Hertwig, R., & Pachur, T. (2015). Heuristics, history of. In J. D. Wright (Ed.), *International encyclopedia of the social & behavioral sciences* (2nd ed., pp. 829–835). Elsevier.

Hjeij, M., & Vilks, A. (2023). A brief history of heuristics: How did research on heuristics evolve? *Humanities and Social Sciences Communications*, *10*(1), 1–15. https://doi.org/10.1057/s41599-023-01542-z

Ings, W. (2011). Managing heuristics as a method of inquiry in autobiographical graphic design theses. *International Journal of Art & Design Education*, *30*(2), 226–241. https://doi.org/10.1111/j.1476-8070.2011.01699.x

Ings, W. (2014). Narcissus and the muse: Supervisory implications of autobiographical, practice-led PhD design theses. *Qualitative Research*, *14*(6), 675–693. https://doi.org/10.1177/1468794113488128

Ings, W. (2018). Heuristic inquiry, land and the artistic researcher. In M. Sierra & K. Wise (Eds.), *Transformative pedagogies and the environment: Creative agency through contemporary art and design* (pp. 55–80). Common Ground Research Networks.

Ings, W. (2022). Supervising art and design students who integrate mental health experiences with autobiographical research. *International Journal of Art & Design Education*, *41*(2), 227–241. https://doi.org/10.1111/jade.12410

Isroilova, N. A. (2023). Using the heuristic method – An effective way of organizing research and educational activities of pupils of preschool educational organizations. *European Journal of Innovation in Nonformal Education*, *3*(5), 173–175. https://inovatus.es/index.php/ejine/article/view/1765

Johnny, O., Trovati, M., & Ray, J. (2020). Towards a computational model of artificial intuition and decision making. In L. Barolli, H. Nishino, & H. Miwa (Eds.), *Advances in intelligent networking and collaborative systems* (Vol. 1035, pp. 463–472). Springer. https://doi.org/10.1007/978-3-030-29035-1_45

Jourard, S. (1968). *Disclosing man to himself*. Van Nostrand.

Kahneman, D. (2011). *Thinking, fast and slow*. Macmillan.

Kaveh, M., & Mesgari, M. S. (2023). Application of meta-heuristic algorithms for training neural networks and deep learning architectures: A comprehensive review. *Neural Processing Letters*, *55*(4), 4519–4622. https://doi.org/10.1007/s11063-022-11055-6

Kleining, G. (1982). Umriss zu einer Methodologie qualitativer Sozialforschung [Outline of a methodology for qualitative social research]. *Kölner Zeitschrift für Soziologie und Sozialpsychologie* [Cologne Journal of Sociology and Social Psychology], *34*(2), 224–253. https://nbn-resolving.org/urn:nbn:de:0168-ssoar-8619

Kleining, G., & Witt, H. (2001). Discovery as basic methodology of qualitative and quantitative research. *Forum Qualitative Sozialforschung/Forum: Qualitative Social Research, 2*(1). https://doi.org/10.17169/fqs-2.1.977

Knuth, D. E. (1997). *The art of computer programming* (Vol. 3). Pearson Education.

Lakatos, I. (1978). *The methodology of scientific research programmes: Philosophical papers Volume 1.* Cambridge University Press. https://doi.org/10.1017/CBO9780511621123

Lash, T. L. (2007). Heuristic thinking and inference from observational epidemiology. *Epidemiology, 18*(1), 67–72. https://doi.org/10.1097/01.ede.0000249522.75868.16

LeCun, Y., Bengio, Y., & Hinton, G. (2015). Deep learning. *Nature, 521*(7553), 436–444. https://doi.org/10.1038/nature14539

Lorenzini, D. (2023). Philosophical discourse and ascetic practice: On Foucault's readings of Descartes. *Meditations. Theory, Culture & Society, 40*(1–2), 139–159. https://doi.org/10.1177/0263276420980510

Mart, R., Pardalos, P. M., & Resende, M. G. (2018). *Handbook of heuristics.* Springer. https://doi.org/10.5555/3294115

Martínez, N., Agudo, U., & Matute, H. (2022). Human cognitive biases present in artificial intelligence. *Revista Internacional de Los Estudios Vascos, 67*(2). https://www.eusko-ikaskuntza.eus/eu/riev/human-cognitive-biases-present-in-artificial-intelligence/rart-24782/

Maslow, A. (1956). Self-actualizing people: A study of psychological health. In C. Moustakas (Ed.), *The self* (pp. 160–194). Harper & Brothers.

Moustakas, C. (1961). *Loneliness.* Prentice-Hall.

Moustakas, C. (1967). Heuristic research. In J. Bugental (Ed.), *Challenges in humanistic psychology* (pp. 100–107). McGraw-Hill.

Moustakas, C. (1972). *Loneliness and love.* Prentice-Hall.

Moustakas, C. (1975). *The touch of loneliness.* Prentice-Hall.

Moustakas, C. (1990). *Heuristic research: Design, methodology, and applications.* Sage Publications.

Najafi, H. (2023). *Displacement of self-continuity: An illuminative, heuristic inquiry into identity transition in an animated short film* [Doctoral thesis, Auckland University of Technology]. Tuwhera Open Access Theses & Dissertations. https://hdl.handle.net/10292/15784

Newell, A., Shaw, J. C., & Simon, H. A. (1959). Report on a general problem solving program. *IFIP Congress, 256,* 64. https://bitsavers.trailing-edge.com/pdf/rand/ipl/P-1584_Report_On_A_General_Problem-Solving_Program_Feb59.pdf

Nutakki, M., & Mandava, S. (2023). Review on optimization techniques and role of artificial intelligence in home energy management systems. *Engineering Applications of Artificial Intelligence, 119,* 105721. https://doi.org/10.1016/j.engappai.2022.105721

Paora, T. I. (2023). *Takatāpui – Beyond marginalisation: Exploring Māori gender, identity and performance* [Doctoral thesis, Auckland University of Technology]. Tuwhera Open Access Theses & Dissertations. https://hdl.handle.net/10292/16962

Pinheiro, C. A. R., & McNeill, F. (2014). *Heuristics in analytics: A practical perspective of what influences our analytical world.* Wiley.

Polanyi, M. (1966). *The tacit dimension.* Doubleday.

Polya, G. (1945). *How to solve it.* Princeton University Press.

Pouwhare, R. (2016). *He iti te manu he nui te korero – The bird is small – the story is epic* [Master's thesis, Auckland University of Technology]. Tuwhera Open Access Theses & Dissertations. https://hdl.handle.net/10292/9776

Pouwhare, R. (2020). *Ngā Pūrākau mō Māui: Mai te patuero, te pakokitanga me te whakapēpē ki te kōrero pono, ki te whaihua whaitake, mē ngā honotanga. The Māui narratives: From Bowdlerisation, dislocation and infantilisation, to veracity, relevance and connection* [Doctoral thesis, Auckland University of Technology]. Tuwhera Open Access Theses & Dissertations. https://hdl.handle.net/10292/13307

Priest, G. (2008). *An introduction to non-classical logic: From if to is.* Cambridge University Press.

Ramsey, F. P. (1926/1931). Truth and probability. In R. B. Braithwaite (ed.), *The foundation of mathematics and other logical essays* (pp. 21–45). Routledge & Kegan Paul.

Rogers, C. R. (1963). Toward a science of the person. *Journal of Humanistic Psychology, 3*(2), 72–92. https://doi.org/10.1177/002216786300300208

Russell, S. J., & Norvig, P. (2010). *Artificial intelligence: A modern approach* (3rd ed.). Prentice Hall.

Savage, L. J. (1972). *The foundations of statistics.* Courier Corporation.

Sela-Smith, S. (2002). Heuristic research: A review and critique of Moustakas's method. *Journal of Humanistic Psychology, 42*(3), 53–88. https://doi.org/10.1177/00267802042003004

Simon, H. A. (1955). A behavioral model of rational choice. *The Quarterly Journal of Economics, 69*(1), 99–118. https://doi.org/10.2307/1884852

Simon, H. A. (1979). Rational decision making in business organisations. *The American Economic Review, 69*(4), 493–513.

Simon, H. A., & Newell, A. (1958). Heuristic problem solving: The next advance in operations research. *Operations Research, 6*(1), 1–10. https://doi.org/10.1287/opre.6.1.1

Slovic, P., Finucane, M., Peters, E., & MacGregor, D. G. (2002). Rational actors or rational fools: Implications of the affect heuristic for behavioral economics. *Journal of Socio-Economics, 31*(4), 329–342. https://doi.org/10.1016/S1053-5357(02)00174-9

Slovic, P., Finucane, M., Peters, E., & MacGregor, D. G. (2004). Risk as analysis and risk as feelings: Some thoughts about affect, reason, risk, and rationality. *Risk Analysis, 24*(2), 311–322. https://doi.org/10.1111/j.0272-4332.2004.00433.x

Slovic, P., Finucane, M., Peters, E., & MacGregor, D. G. (2007). The affect heuristic. *European Journal of Operational Research, 177*(3), 1333–1352. https://doi.org/10.1016/j.ejor.2005.04.00

Smith, R. (2022). Aristotle's Logic. In E. N. Zalta & U. Nodelman (Eds.), *The Stanford Encyclopedia of Philosophy.* Metaphysics Research Lab, Stanford University. https://plato.stanford.edu/archives/win2022/entries/aristotle-logic/

Sultan, N. (2018). *Heuristic inquiry: Researching human experience holistically.* Sage.

Thompson, L. (2017). Heuristic geographies. In B. R. Roberts & M. A. Stephens (Eds.), *Archipelagic American studies* (pp. 57–73). Duke University Press.

Tudor, K. (2017). The fight for health: An heuristic enquiry. In K. Tudor (Ed.), *Conscience and critic: The selected works of Keith Tudor* (pp. 143–168). Routledge.

Tudor, K. (2022). Supporting critical self-enquiry: Doing heuristic research. In S. Bager-Charleson & A. McBeath (Eds.), *Enjoying research in counselling and psychotherapy* (pp. 57–79). Springer. https://doi.org/10.1007/978-3-031-13942-0_4

Tudor, K. (2023). Critical heuristics in psychotherapy research: From 'I-who-feels' to 'We-who-care – and act'. In K. Tudor & J. Wyatt (Eds.), *Qualitative research approaches for psychotherapy: Reflexivity, methodology, and criticality* (pp. 115–132). Taylor & Francis.

Tversky, A., & Kahneman, D. (1974). Judgment under uncertainty: Heuristics and biases: Biases in judgments reveal some heuristics of thinking under uncertainty. *Science, 185*(4157), 1124–1131. https://doi.org/10.1126/science.185.4157.1124

Ventling, F. D. (2017). *Illuminativa – The coalescence of light and craft thinking* [Doctoral thesis, Auckland University of Technology]. Tuwhera Open Access Theses & Dissertations. https://hdl.handle.net/10292/7037

Whybrow, D., & Milligan, C. (2023). Military healthcare professionals' experience of transitioning into civilian employment: A heuristic inquiry. *Work, 76*(2), 663–677. https://doi.org/10.3233/WOR-220317

Williams, T. (2024). *Tangohia mai te taura - Take This Rope: Exploring Māori documentary-making approaches to elevate whānau narratives* [Doctoral thesis, Auckland University of Technology]. Tuwhera Open Access Theses & Dissertations. https://hdl.handle.net/10292/17323

Stepping Forward

2

HEURISTIC INQUIRY, *RANGAHAU*, THE EXPLICIT AND THE ESOTERIC

Tangaroa Paora

Recently, heuristic inquiry has been employed in a number of Indigenous Oceanic and Māori artistic research studies, notably Pouwhare (2020), Ete (2021), Faumuina (2022), Paora (2023a), and Williams (2024). This chapter considers how such inquiry might productively support Indigenous, creative research that is developed inside a specifically Māori paradigm, where *rangahau* (gathering, grouping, and forming, to create new knowledge and understanding), is grounded in a cultural perspective that is respectful of *tikanga Māori* (customs) and *āhuatanga Māori* (cultural practices). Specifically, the chapter considers a practice-led, doctoral research project that asked, 'How might an artistic reconsideration of gender role differentiation shape new forms of Māori performative expression?'

The chapter discusses how a heuristic inquiry enabled *mahi* (practice) and reflection to function as a dynamic that enabled knowledge to move fluidly between the realms of *te kura huna* (what is unseen, genealogical, esoteric, or tacit), and *te kura tūrama* (what is explicit and seen). Here, a heuristic inquiry enabled a researcher to turn ideas over, examining them in flexible ways from a multiple variation of perspectives (Kleining & Witt, 2000). In this state, the researcher's trajectory moved from the formless towards a growing sense of meaning and direction, as perceptions and understandings grew and the parameters of the problem were recognised (Douglass & Moustakas, 1985). As an Indigenous, artistic researcher I was also able to navigate both the explicit and the esoteric, to uncover and reveal (Moustakas, 1990), to shift and sift (Douglass & Moustakas, 1985), and to connect creatively what had hitherto been unconnected (Ings, 2011).

The project that formed the substance of the study combined the principles of heuristic inquiry with a *kaupapa Māori* framework (a Māori approach to

DOI: 10.4324/9781003507758-5

research where being Māori, respecting Māori ways of operating in the world, and contributing to Māori knowledge is integrated). Smith (2015) describes this as research 'by Māori, for Māori, and with Māori'. The project explored the lived experience of eight *takatāpui tāne* (Māori men who identify as gay). The term takatāpui does not easily translate as LGBTQI+ or Queer, because it encapsulates a Māori way of understanding people as spiritual and physical beings who have the ability to shift, transform, and be fluid in both gender and sexual preference. The study involved interviewing participants about their sense of identity, and ways in which they experienced being Māori, being performers, and being gay men. Data from interview transcripts was crystallised using *pakiwaitara* (a Māori form of poetic inquiry). These texts were complemented by a series of photographic portraits. This material was then synthesised into a choreographed, oratorical performance that was performed inside a theatrical space called a *Whare Takatāpui* (a house of performed queer stories). The composed work integrated oratory, animation, portraiture, choreography, and sound design into a narrative that located being *takatāpui* in historical and social contexts that had been partially eroded through processes of colonisation.

The dynamics of practice-led inquiry inside a Māori worldview

Methodologically the study sought a productive meeting place between *rangahau* (Māori research) and heuristic inquiry. What distinguished the methodology was the proposition that heuristic inquiry could operate in an epistemological framework where realms of *te kura huna* (esoteric knowledge) and *te kura tūrama* (explicit knowing) coexisted. Within this space a metaphorical structure and dynamic was activated through methods that integrated *tikanga* (customary practices), data gathering, and artistic synthesis (Figure 2.1).

Figure 2.1 shows the dynamic relationship between *te kura huna* and *te kura tūrama*. Within this structure the flow of *mahi* (practice) and reflection on mahi is the dynamic that enables knowledge to move fluidly between the realms of *te kura huna* and *te kura tūrama*. In the diagram, this dynamic is depicted as *Te Ao Hurihuri* (circular air movement).

In Māori understanding, *te kura huna* refers to knowledge that resources an inquiry from the realm of the unseen. Such knowledge may include *taha wairua* (the metaphysical), tacit knowing, *whakapapa* (genealogies), erased histories, the mysterious, and the unknown (Pouwhare, 2020; Pouwhare & McNeill, 2018). However, *te kura tūrama* refers to the realm of the explicit. This may include iterations of research that are overt and tangible, such as documentable data, physical changes, and prototypes of iterative thinking. Joining these realms of the explicit and inexplicit is a *pou tiriao* (an invisible spiritual pillar that connects physical and metaphysical worlds). Conceptually, this pillar is the bridge that contains the *mauri* (life force) of the research. In other words, this is the support column that sustains the living essence of the

RANGAHAU

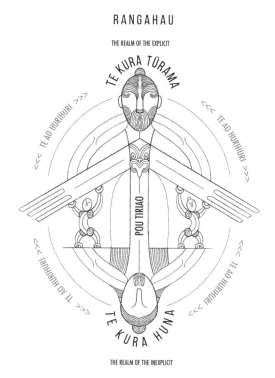

FIGURE 2.1   The project's research design.

Source: Paora (2023).

inquiry: it represents the tenacity and strength of purpose that is necessary when a study navigates what is currently unknown.

Inside this structure, iterative practice is the agency that enables ideas to form and be developed between realms of knowing. For example, researchers may gather information from interviews and existing literature (this knowledge comes from the explicit realm of *te kura tūrama*). However, a researcher may also draw on ancestral, creative processes, inspiration, and an ability to sense 'rightness' from *te kura huna*. Thus, research is guided by what is sensed as much as by what is seen. The process of progressing ideas is not necessarily chronological, because artefacts emanating from an inquiry may cause rethinking about another aspect of the research. Thus, the dynamic of thinking moves within an evolution where iterations of practice, reflection on practice, and revised practice enable the researcher to develop and refine thinking that will eventually become objects or performances that bring storied experience into the world.

The nature of *rangahau*

As Māori, conventionally, we practice *rangahau* as a distinctive way of researching that focuses on revealing and gathering of knowledge. Within this process, a performing artist seeks the essence of ideas and resonances that may lead to creative expressions of identity. *Rangahau* comprises two words, each with a contributing meaning. *Ranga* refers to the gathering of people, items, or materials; it can also mean to raise or pull up by the roots (though in this case it refers to knowledge). *Ranga* may also be associated with collective endeavour, exhumation, and preparation for distribution of past, present, and new knowledge. The word *hau* refers to the vital essence of a person, place, object, or wind. Thus, the livingness and breathing subjectivity of the researcher is implicit and integral to any inquiry. Māori believe that a study cannot exist without a *mauri* (life force), and the presence and resonance of the researcher. In a research project, the dynamic relationship between the researcher and the researched occurs as a flow of reflective *mahi* (practice). Although a researcher may feel the presence of *mauri*, its physicality is not visually evident, rather it is identified through sense.

The nature of heuristic inquiry

As an approach to conducting practice-led artistic research, heuristic inquiry has a rich history of application (Ings, 2011; Najafi, 2023; Scrivener, 2002; Tavares & Ings, 2018; Ventling, 2018; Williams, 2024). Emanating from the Greek word *heuretikos* (to discover), it describes a methodological approach in which the researcher is immersed within the realm of discovery, sensing what feels right and then thinking or examining information in variable ways from multiple perspectives (Kleining & Witt, 2000). Through this process the researcher seeks 'to understand through experimentation, evaluation, and trial and error methods' (Ventling, 2018, p. 126). Ventling also suggests that heuristic inquiry fluidly embraces the subjective and personal and this makes the approach useful to particular forms of artistic research. He notes:

> The intuitive, imaginative artistic practitioner can adapt the heuristic frame-work to an individualistic exploration. Because heuristics does not focus on a pre-determined formula or course of action, it allows continuous changes to concepts, the researcher's position, or even the research design. Particularly in experiential practice-led research, this adaptability may be useful because it heightens chances of discovery and supports the artist/researcher in finding and developing their own meaning.
>
> (Ventling, 2018, p. 127)

His observation resonates with Moustakas' description of heuristic inquiry as

> [an] internal search through which one discovers the nature and meaning of experience and develops methods and procedures for further investigation and analysis. The self of the researcher is present throughout the process

and, while understanding the phenomenon with increasing depth, the researcher also experiences growing self-awareness and self-knowledge.

(Moustakas, 1990, p. 9)

In a heuristic inquiry, Douglass and Moustakas suggest that 'vague and form-less wanderings are characteristic in the beginning, but a growing sense of meaning and direction emerges as the perceptions and understandings of the researcher grow and the parameters of the problem are recognised' (1985, p. 47).

They also suggest that a challenge the heuristic researcher faces is

[to] examine all the collected data in creative combinations and recombi-nation, sifting and sorting, moving rhythmically in and out of appearance, looking, listening carefully for the meanings within meanings, attempting to identify the overarching qualities that adhere in the data.

(Douglass & Moustakas, 1985, p. 52)

Within this practice-led research informed by *rangahau*, the heuristic con-cept and phase of immersion was particularly significant as it trusts – and demands – that the researcher enquires about themselves subjectively in order to discover understanding in and from the realms of *te kura huna* and *te kura tūrama*.

Immersion

Both *rangahau* and heuristic inquiry are predicated on the belief that a researcher pursues a subjective immersion inside a question (or series of questions). Douglass and Moustakas argue that this initial grounding of the self affirms subjectivity. They say, 'Embracing the subjective in this way clears the path for personal knowing, tapping into the nuance and variation of expe-rience, crawling inside the self and eventually making contact with the tacit dimension, the basis of all possible knowledge' (1985, pp. 43–44).

In my work, I am initially immersed inside an idea, but this immersion continues and deepens as the initial question fuses with iterative practice to become a site of deep indwelling, where knowing is both interior and exte-rior. Here, one looks outwards and inwards and decision-making is tied to *tōtika* (a sense of rightness).

This sense of rightness is a significant idea in Polynesian thinking that Faumuina (2022) likens to the Tongan concept of *māfana* (the attractive warmth emitted by an idea or performance that has inherent resonance and harmonious connection). It is something felt rather than seen, but it can be employed by a researcher to sense strong or weak associations and trajec-tories of thought that have the potential for investigation and development.

Within the Māori concepts of immersion there is a phenomenon called *takiwātanga*. This is a complex space and time inside which one's physical, emotional, intellectual, and spiritual dimensions can be immersed and operate in productive ways. Here demarcations between the physical and the non-physical coexist. In such a state the researcher dwells in the world of the present but also in a world that is becoming. Here one can lose one's sense of time, such that meals are skipped, and the breaking of dawn can arrive unexpectedly after hours of intensive problem-solving.

While Douglass and Moustakas (1985) allude to a related idea in their discussion of the 'immersed self', I liken *takiwātanga* to engaging within a space and time where practice itself becomes a world. This is a coexistent state that accompanies the ordinary, external life that I must maintain. I must still go to work, manage my finances, shop for food, and meet family obligations, but alongside this the world of the inquiry becomes deeper than a series of processes; it is a living space. Here I am in very deep levels of experimentation, questioning the self and the research question using trial and error. Being concurrent, the immersive world accompanies me down the shopping aisles and it is positioned beside me in the passenger seat of the car. However, in this immersive, heuristic realm I consciously remain more open, I purposely engage the tacit and the explicit, I descend through layers into very deep levels of knowing and not knowing, working with potentials greater than what can be offered by a prescribed formula. This realm of discovery has a distinctive fluidity, and my 'knowingness' is both rational and beyond rational. I think of this immersion as a space where I choose to let my heart, mind, and *taha wairua* (spiritual self) determine and affirm what is right and what is needed. I am guided by tangible things like the necessary pitch of a sound, the accuracy of a movement, or the communicative clarity of body of text, but I also sense resonance and harmony with the *kaupapa* (subject), and I remain alert to congruencies and patterns that connect ideas in harmonious ways. I do not expect linearity; I understand an inquiry as a complex living entity. In this regard I am reminded of John Wood who suggested that because heuristics is 'concerned with discovery, rather than with proof' it is a more appropriate method for many creative practitioners because it does not involve 'a series of linear, finite questions' (2004, p. 9).

Te Whare Takatāpui

This may sound obscure in discussion, so perhaps to be clearer it is helpful to demonstrate how features common to both *rangahau* and heuristic inquiry contributed to the resolution of the research project *Te Whare Takatāpui*.

This was the title of my doctoral thesis that sought to artistically consider how gender role differentiation in *takatāpui tāne* (Māori gay men) might shape new forms of performative expression. The study gathered data using audio interviewing and photography. This material was then progressed through poetic inquiry into a composed and choreographed performance work that was supported by a book of portraits and poetry.

The study's methodology was underpinned by Kleining and Witt's (2000) principles of holding oneself open to change; actively introducing variations of perspective; dwelling in states of immersion; embracing subjectivity; and using the tacit and the explicit to discover similarities, patterns, and homologies. These principles were embodied through eight methods. The methods were: *karakia* (incantation); *kaitahi* (the ritual of eating together to create unity); *kanohi ki te kanohi* (face-to-face) interviewing; *pakiwaitara* (poetic inquiry); portrait photography; iterative experimentation and self-dialogue; choreography; and production design – methods that offer a distinctive, Māori approach to conducting research, as well as the way in which heuristic principles infused the inquiry.

Methods

Karakia

At the outset of any significant activity, including parts of a research project, Māori evoke an incantation called *karakia*, which forms a connection between the physical and metaphysical realms. In the morning I recite *karakia* to orient myself for the day, and at night to give thanks for the blessings that will accompany with me into the future. *Karakia* stands as both the conduit and foundation for all interactions with people, *atua* (gods), and *whenua* (land). In the process of *karakia*, one creates protection and safe passage for both the researcher and all who share vulnerable knowledge within the research space. Thus, at the outset and sometimes at the close of an interview, it is customary practice to recite *karakia*. One *karakia* I used in this research project is associated with taking care of takatāpui and our place within te ao Māori. It reflected on the creative narrative and how we, as Māori, are seen as descendants of *Ranginui* and *Papatūānuku*.

Kaitahi

In the Māori world, the self is always connected to community, so research about self is always in the context of community, and a community requires the same attention to care and inclusiveness that would be afforded to a singular researcher. In his discussion of this perspective, Williams notes that, unlike heuristic self-search, *rangahau* 'occurs within a collective consciousness that is integral to Māori worldviews. Thus, what is created is rarely singular or individualised, instead *mahi* (practice) is collaborative and interwoven with deep levels of cultural responsibility' (2024, p. 34).

The research question I was exploring involved men making journeys into sometimes difficult pasts so they could bring to light experiences that might help us understand a greater whole. These journeys were understood to be concurrently singular (of the self) and collective (inside a wider community). The study asked these men to travel into layers of memory, so the process needed to be governed by high levels of cultural and personal trust. Therefore, at the outset, before any interviewing or image making occurred, we engaged a practice called *kaitahi*.

Broadly, *kaitahi* means to eat together, but the undertaking is deeper than this. *Kaitahi* is made up of two words, *kai* (food and also actioner) and *tahi* (as one). Here, people *karakia* (recite incantation) and share food, thinking, and discussion. *Kaitahi* helps to shape the safe and compassionate space of a study. In the data gathering phase of the project, *kaitahi* was used to welcome and settle participants before subsequent photoshoots and interviews. Over dinner at the university marae,[1] takatāpui participants, the researcher, crew, supervisors, collaborators, and supporters met as a *whānau* (family). In the grace of *kaitahi*, people felt safe because they shared in a relaxed, hospitable environment positioned within *te ao Māori* (the Māori world).

Kanohi ki te kanohi interviewing

The research was understood as collective but embracing individual journeys into the unknown. Within Māori research practice, there is an understanding that the intimate human experience should avoid dispassionate approaches. This is because it is considered inappropriate to establish alienating distances between participants, especially when working with personal experiences. As a consequence, interviews are, wherever possible, conducted face-to-face. In Māori this is called *kanohi ki te kanohi*, and such interviewing is designed to ensure personal connection in the presence of shared cultural values and practices (including *karakia*). According to Smith (1999), *kanohi ki te kanohi* interviewing is based on five principles:

- *He kanohi kitea* (a face seen, is appreciated)
- *Titiro, whakarongo, kōrero* (looking, listening, and speaking)
- *Manaaki tangata* (sharing and hosting people, being generous)
- *Kia tūpato* (being cautious)
- *Kaua e takahi i te mana o te tangata* (avoiding trampling on the mana of participants).

The interviews were preceded by an orienting discussion (*kōrero*) several weeks before the formal project began. This was followed by time spent recording participants just prior to the photo shoot, where each man talked through personal identity narratives, his beliefs relating to the nature of Māori performance, and the gendering of physical and the esoteric dimensions of *takatāpuitanga* (being Māori and queer).

One of the advantages of heuristic inquiry is the accommodation of flexibility. This enables a researcher to adjust to unexpected circumstances. In this project scheduled interviews and photoshoots faced significant disruption because the inquiry spanned two natural disasters (the 2019–2022 COVID-19 pandemic and a catastrophic cyclone that hit New Zealand between 5 and 11 February 2023). These calamities impacted on some people's ability to travel for face-to-face interviews. Participants fell ill; parts of the country were locked down; and participant's families were impacted by weather conditions. In addition, many facilities inside the university (such as photography studios) were closed.

However, these disruptions were not perceived as challenges, but absorbed into an understanding that time and resourcing are flexible and thus that a study's focus must remain open to change. Kleining and Witt allude to this phenomenon in their second rule for optimising chances of discovery in heuristic inquiries. They observe that: 'the topic of research is preliminary and may change during the research process. It is only fully known after being successfully explored' (2000, p. 2). Accordingly, interviews were delayed and rescheduled, and in rare cases where participants were confined to their homes, an interview was conducted online.

Had the pandemic not occurred, I would have completed the thesis a year earlier, but the project's ethos would not have been the same. An example of this is evident in the final outcomes of the project. I had initially envisaged that there would be nine *takatāpui tāne* in the inquiry. However, in *Irarere*, the book of poetry and photographs that emanated from the inquiry (Paora, 2023c), and in the performed work *Te Whare Takatāpui* (Paora, 2023b), only eight men were physically present. For the ninth participant, Shaun Hindt, there was no photograph, and the poetry I eventually wrote about him was not shaped by his spoken interview. He was a friend I had loved... and he died. Nevertheless, and in a very Māori fashion, Shaun became more present within the project after he passed and he permeated multiple layers of the inquiry. Because of *te kura huna*, he wasn't an absence: his spirit became absorbed into the project. His life and perceptions were mentioned in oratory, he was present in dedications and memories of his unique understanding of being *takatāpui* shaped my thinking as the data gathering was synthesised into creative works.

Pakiwaitara

The fourth method employed in the study was used to interpret the essence of each man's interview. The approach may be described as *pakiwaitara* and it refers to a particular form of iterative experimentation, specifically related to narratives within *te ao Māori* and is akin to poetic inquiry. *Pakiwaitara* enables the researcher to explore ideas and relationships and synthesise recorded interview material into coherent artefacts. The origins of *pakiwaitara* lie in storytelling from non-written realms, including *waiata* (song), *mōteatea* (laments), carvings, and oratory. In the study, these poems formed part of the content of a book *Irarere* that contained portraits of the eight men and a contextualising essay (Paora, 2023c).

In creating these poems, I immersed myself in each man's interview and employed a process of subtraction to elevate the essence of what was communicated. Accordingly, the resulting poems only contained words that were *spoken* by the interviewees. Prendergast (2006) described this method as 'found poetry', involving writers creating new work from existing texts. Gannon defines the approach as 'poetic inquiry' and proposes that through 'the rearrangement, restructuring and editing of existing texts down to their essence, experiences can be simplified and presented in poetic form' (2022, p. 19). Poetic inquiry builds on approaches developed by Szto et al. (2005) and Gannon (2022), who have demonstrated how such an approach to interview data can be used to compress or locate resonance within recorded information. Poetic inquiry describes research that uses poetry 'as, in, [or] for inquiry' (Brown et al., 2021, p. 257). As a method, it encourages creativity and deep engagement with qualitative data. The method is attentive to participant language and it 'can deepen researcher reflexivity, increasing the emotive impact of research, and promoting an efficiency of qualitative expression through the use of "razor sharp" language' (Brown et al., 2021, p. 257). In the last two decades, poetic inquiry has challenged traditional methods of data synthesis.

However, *pakiwaitara* does more than this. Being drawn from recorded speech, the poems are shaped by pauses and emphasis as much as they are by recorded statements. Given that historically *te reo* Māori was an oral and visual language (it operated in realms beyond the written word), these poems were distinguished by their sense of immediacy and personal presence. In them we hear the voice of the speaker because the address is direct and comes straight from what was spoken. The following *pakiwaitara* taken from a 30-minute interview with Gigi Pikinga in December 2021, serves as an example:

Real!
I feel!
I change!

They/Them, Non-binary, He/Him, She/Her, That Bitch.
Enough!

Boy no!
Girl no!
Just changing, being and existing
Growing upwards.

When I was young, I wanted to be in kapa haka.
But I would not take off my t-shirt.
I would not slap my chest.
I refused.
I could hear the girls screaming out those notes
and I thought, 'Gurl! I can sing better than you.'

I grew up engulfed in all things Māori.
We teased each other.
I teased you about your ugly, big black feet
and you teased me because I was a limp wristed girl.
Backhanded acknowledgements.
We all had shit going on.
I was no different.

But I will not be placed in your confinement.
You cannot contain my spirit,
I am the architect of my life.

This 'immediacy of presence' aligns somewhat with Richardson's assertion that poetry can, in certain instances, better represent an individual than verbatim quotation, because poetry provides space for us to encounter a person's 'pauses, repetitions, alliterations, narrative strategies, and rhythms' (1994, p. 522).

Drawing on what I had discovered though the use of *pakiwaitara*, I felt the inquiry asking me questions about the nature of my own voice. It wanted to know how, as a researcher, I might speak to an overview that could connect the photographic portraits and poems taken from the men's interviews. What surfaced began to significantly shape the eventual performance, *Te Whare Takatāpui*.

The oratory in this presentation was developed by standing back from the literature and interviews and finding my 'voice for the voices'. It required that I create a performative voice for the thesis, that moved between *te kura huna* and *te kura tūrama*; between the dark and the light, the lost and the fragmented, the imagined, the recalled, and the tangible. The following excerpt from the *Te Whare Takatāpui* that was performed initially in darkness then progressed into the light, serves as an illustration:

Imagine the night…
The movement of air through the grass.
Papatūānuku.
Above… an eternity of sky
Forever reaching
Ranginui – the father.

…And here
a whare.
Perhaps a whare tapere,
A house of performance.
But more
In the half light,
Unadorned
A whare takatāpui
A house for those erased.
The bachelor sons and maiden aunts
The tungāne and tuāhine
Takakau (who never married)
Who loved their own.

Once,
Before the missionaries
And the condemning laws,
We were treasures.
The tane who cared for the wounded,
The wahine whose voices called through the haka.
We were irarua,
Irarere,
Our genders fluid and uncompromised.

Takatāpui tane,
Who as men gazed up at their father,
The embracing heavens.
Who loved,
Who protected,
…Who cried,
At the grief at separation.
The ancient male.
The first male.
Who did not measure manhood,
On the rugby field or battle ground.
The lover and protector of all things.

But we the takatāpui,
…Our stories were stripped from history.
The bargeboards that showed our love,
Cut in half,
Divided,

And exiled to cities on the other side of the world.
Our papahou
Intimate.
Locked behind glass in museum cases,
In London.
Desecrated,
Eradicated,
Erased…
The traces of our tupuna,
Our whakapapa,
Whispers behind the hand.
Peka – fragments.

But here?
In these half-lit walls,
In the whare takatāpui,
A restored place to stand.
The new poupou.
The pillars that hold up the house.
The takatāpui tane.
The living strength.
A people,
Who will not be silent.

Proud,
Māori,
Eternal,
Protecting….

It had not been my intention to write poetry. At the outset of the research, I thought that I was dealing with interviews, locating themes, and delivering findings, but heuristic inquiry constitutes a journey without a road map and it can cause you to find horizons beyond what you initially imagined. I am reminded in this regard that heuristic inquiry, 'does not focus on an established course of action but on deeply constituted experience, reflective search, sensitive overview and discovery' (Ings, 2011, p. 227).

As I began working with the recorded data from the interviews, I realised that the research was speaking in another voice. It was not the rational, objective voice of conventional European scholarship; it sounded more like the nuanced rhythms and emphases of my ancestors. *Pakiwaitara* being an oral form of communication, began to shape my oratorial compositions that were refined iteratively through rehearsal and reflection. Words were spoken into the darkness, I felt their power and the ways they intruded on space, and from this aural world (rather than from edited rewritings), I refined resonances within the work.

Portrait photography

The fifth method involved portrait photography. While initially the research inquired into the experience of *takatāpui tāne* who adopt gendered performance roles that differ from those of the gender they were assigned at birth, as the project developed the study became concerned with a deeper understanding of each man's gender identity. During the interviews, I watched *and* listened, and I began to consider how I might capture parts of the men's identity in portraiture. Because their interviews often included references to walking in two worlds, a concept of two connected portraits took form. For the shoot, participants were asked to bring clothing that they felt expressed how they felt they were seen (or 'passed')[2] in the common world, and apparel that they felt expressed their inner identity. Photographs of these two states were eventually used to construct a dual portrait (Figure 2.2).

The resulting images were conceived as *poupou* (pillars) that held up the walls of the *Whare Takatāpui*.[3] While one version was evident to the audience, during the performance, as I spoke about each *tāne* the portrait was turned on a pivot to reveal his expression of his *takatāpui* nature.

Iterative experimentation and self-dialogue

Iterative experimentation is fundamental to both heuristic inquiry and *rangahau*, and it is through this process that questions are asked and ideas are formed. In this process, the researcher experiments, watches, listens, and feels for the inherent *tōtika* (rightness) of what is emerging. In this process I was in dialogue with the research question, the self, and data emerging from it (Ventling, 2018). Kleining and Witt note that, in a heuristic inquiry:

> Research procedures are not linear but dialectical. We 'ask' our material 'questions' in a similar way one may ask a person, receiving 'answers' and questioning again. We preferably use 'open' questions... The text should be interrogated from as many different perspectives as possible and the answers analysed... The dialogic procedure is a means to adjust the epistemic structure of the researcher to the structure of the phenomenon and brings it in line with itself.
>
> (Kleining & Witt, 2000, para. 12)

In this study, iterative experimentation and self-dialogue were manifest in rehearsal processes associated with development of the final performance and in

FIGURE 2.2 Dual portraits of Piripi Gordon, Varron Armstrong, and Aniwa Koloamatangi depicting how they present themselves to the world and how they perceive their *takatāpui* identity.

Source: Marcos Mortensen Steagall.

photographing and synthesising participants' stories into *pakiwaitara*. Iterative experimentation was also integral to the development of animated sequences for *Te Whare Takatāpui*. Given that the history of same sex attraction and gender fluidity in Māori history has been largely erased, my original assumption was that we would not see a house, but would only encounter the portraits that formed its walls (these were double-sided photographs of the men in the project). However, as the research progressed, the concept of darkness and lightness and the fluidity between these spaces became increasingly significant. The metaphors surfaced through interviews with numerous participants, because transformation in Māori thinking is often tied to epitomical understandings of light and dark.

Māori hold a deep connection to the natural environment, and we understand that there are spiritual powers moving through space and time that, as humans we cannot easily detect. However, the presence of the spiritual can be sensed and experienced in light and dark. Māori identify this as *te pō* (darkness) and *te ao mārama* (the world of light). Both have a *mauri* or lifeforce that is rendered evident through interaction. Light and dark are not seen as different things; they are part of a dynamic. In Māori cosmology our origins begin in *te kore* (the void) where potential resides. From here we discover *te pō*. The darkness of this space contains essence of the unknown that is evident in *te kura huna*. From here we progress into *te ao mārama*, the realm of light in which we encounter *te kura tūrama*.

Using this principle and a history that has been erased and partially recovered, I conceived a *whare* as a building in an unpopulated landscape. The structure was not heavily adorned, and its presence would be mutable... yet it still needed to belong in the world (Figure 2.3). By animating and dissolving images, I was able to create periods where the fluid nature of the *whare* either gained presence or disappeared in response to phases in my oratory.

Refining this dynamic involved multiple iterations that were shaped in dialogue with modifications to my oratory. Along with the emerging and fading *whare*, I began to consider associated features like the sound of darkness, the intensity of half-light, the space of aural distance, the weight of breath, and the tangibility of a celebrated present.

FIGURE 2.3 Frame grabs from the animated *Te Whare Takatāpui*, appearing and disappearing in an unpopulated, alpine landscape.

Source: Paora (2023).

Choreography

The performance work *Te Whare Takatāpui* was also developed through a process of iterative experimentation. I choreographed three female performers who were proficient with *poi*. Poi is a traditional Māori training tool used by men to strengthen flexibility in the wrists and forearms for weaponry use in combat. In modern use, *poi* has found its way into Māori performing arts as a percussion instrument used by women to showcase feminine strength. I also choreographed an additional sequence that involved two historical manifestations of masculinity that were initially separate then merged in harmony with each other. As these dances took shape, I was able to assess both the physically evident (form, rhythm, timing) in the realm of *te kura tūrama*, and *feel* the mauri of the work rising up from *te kura huna*. It was as the power and force of this energy from the realm of the unseen became manifest that I was able to use *tōtika* (rightness) to sense artistic resonance that edged the choreography incrementally towards a state of resolution.

Production design

These seven methods contributed to an eighth encompassing concern with production design. Production design describes the creation of the physical and spiritual space of the work. The idea of a traditionally designated space for performance has a deep history in *te ao Māori*, that is sometimes referred to as a *whare tapere* (house of performance).

Initially, I considered an open space that was divided by a stage. The physical design for this space was developed through a process of physical and digital model making. This enabled me to think about lighting, sound, movement, and the tone of people's initial encounter with the work. I explored multiple possibilities, experimenting with projection, sound, seating plans, and performance space, such that people experiencing the work might feel physically and spiritually sheltered while encountering what might be relatively new and challenging ideas.

However, as the thesis developed, I began to face the logistics of a performance that I realised might manifest itself in a life beyond the doctoral examination. Participants wanted the research to have agency, potentially featuring in national and regional arts festivals. As a consequence, I needed to design something that had the potential to travel and adapt. Several determinants began to reshape my considerations. Firstly, I needed an interior space that was acoustically neutral, so that sound mixes and the *pakiwaitara* could be discernible in their more subtle registers. Secondly, because I was considering projected backgrounds, the performance would require a darkened environment. Thirdly, I wanted the performance to deal with subtle shifts in concealment and revelation, so the space would need to accommodate a lighting system. Finally, I required some way of displaying the poupou, so they would hang in a stable manner but also be pivotable (Figure 2.4).

FIGURE 2.4   Photograph of the final night of the performance, showing the photographic poupou, the performers, and the positioning of the audience in an intimate space The large screen that featured the animated projections of the *Whare Takatāpui* and alpine landscapes is in darkness behind the performers. A filmed record of the performance is viewable in Paora (2023b).

Source: Paora (2023).

Conclusion

This project bought together two approaches to research, heuristic inquiry and *rangahau*. Increasingly, heuristic inquiry has found resonance with certain Indigenous researchers working in creative fields. However, as a methodology, it has had to be negotiated carefully within contexts that are epistemologically very different from the worlds in which it was developed. Qualities that *rangahau* and heuristic inquiry share, include the personal nature of the inquiry, engaging both explicit and tacit knowledge, pursuing research beyond the provisions of a template; indwelling with the question or issue; and strategically questioning iterative practice. However, dimensions of Indigenous research also embrace principles that generally fall outside of the provisions of Western scholarship. These include the role of spiritual knowing, customary practices, and the studied-self as part of a collective.

This chapter has offered such concepts as expansions to how we conceive heuristic inquiry within an Indigenous framework, which may be helpful as research within the academy moves forward into wider 'common worlds'. In this regard we might be reminded of Hannah Arendt who noted that:

the reality of the public realm relies on the simultaneous presence of innumerable perspectives and aspects in which the common world presents itself and for which no common measurement or denominator can ever be devised. For though the common world is the common meeting ground of all, those who are present have different locations in it, and the location of one can no more coincide with the location of another than the location of two objects. Being seen and being heard by others derive their significance from the fact that everybody sees and hears from a different position. This is the meaning of public life… Only where things can be seen by many, in a variety of aspects, without changing their identity, so that those who are gathered around them know they see sameness in utter diversity, can worldly reality truly and reliably appear.

(Arendt, 1958, p. 57)

Notes

1 *Marae* are meeting grounds that are a focal point for people to gather in tribal, communal capacities. *Marae* typically have a *wharenui* (a meeting house) where discussion and oratorical practices take place, and a *wharekai* (a dining hall) where guests and hosts share food and lift the sacredness that has occurred in the meeting house. *Kaitahi* occurs inside a *wharekai*.
2 'Passing' is a historical term used in LGBTQI+ cultures to describe the preservation of safety by appearing in public in such a way that one's 'queerness' or *irarere* is not identifiable.
3 *Poupou* are Māori carved pillars traditionally depicted as Māori ancestors. They are displayed within *wharenui* (meeting houses).

References

Arendt, H. (1958). *The human condition* (2nd ed.). University of Chicago Press.
Brown, M. E. L., Kelly, M., & Finn, G. M. (2021). Thoughts that breathe, and words that burn: Poetic inquiry within health professions education. *Perspectives on Medical Education, 10*(5), 257–264. https://doi.org/10.1007/s40037-021-00682-9
Douglass, B. G., & Moustakas, C. (1985). Heuristic inquiry the internal search to know. *Journal of Humanistic Psychology, 25*(3), 39–55. https://doi.org/10.1177/0022167885253004
Ete, I. (2021). *Naatapuitea: An artistic interpretation of traditional and contemporary Samoan musical structures, instrumentation and koniseti* [Doctoral thesis, Auckland University of Technology]. Tuwhera Open Access Theses & Dissertations. http://hdl.handle.net/10292/14792
Faumuina, C. (2022). *Asi – The presence of the unseen* [Doctoral thesis, Auckland University of Technology]. Tuwhera Open Access Theses & Dissertations. https://hdl.handle.net/10292/15350
Gannon, E. (2022). *Mindfulness and drawing: A visual poetic inquiry into the representation of mindful drawing experiences* [Doctoral thesis, Auckland University of Technology]. Tuwhera Open Access Theses & Dissertations. https://hdl.handle.net/10292/15415
Ings, W. (2011). Managing heuristics as a method of inquiry in autobiographical graphic design theses. *International Journal of Art & Design Education, 30*(2), 226–241. https://doi.org/10.1111/j.1476-8070.2011.01699.x

Kleining, G. & Witt, H. (2000). The qualitative heuristic approach: A methodology for discovery in psychology and the social sciences. Rediscovering the method of introspection as an example. *Forum Qualitative Sozialforschung/Forum: Qualitative Social Research, 1*(1). https://doi.org/10.17169/fqs-1.1.1123

Moustakas, C. (1990). *Heuristic research: Design, methodology and applications.* Sage.

Najafi, H. (2023). *Displacement of self-continuity: An illuminative, heuristic inquiry into identity transition in an animated short film* [Doctoral thesis, Auckland University of Technology]. Tuwhera Open Access Theses & Dissertations. https://hdl.handle.net/10292/15784

Paora, T. (2023a). *Takatāpui – Beyond marginalisation: Exploring Māori gender, identity and performance* [Doctoral thesis, Auckland University of Technology]. Tuwhera Open Access Theses & Dissertations. http://hdl.handle.net/10292/16962

Paora, T. (2023b). *Te Whare Takatapui* [Filmed performance]. https://openrepository.aut.ac.nz/bitstreams/e99dca96-d83c-41dd-901d-62a000f79c05/download

Paora, T. (2023c). *Irarere.* Ia/AUT Press.

Pouwhare, R. (2020). *Ngā Pūrākau mō Māui: mai te patuero, te pakokitanga me te whakapēpē ki te kōrero pono, ki te whaihua whaitake, mē ngā honotanga. The Māui narratives: From Bowdlerisation, dislocation and infantilisation to veracity, relevance and connection* [Doctoral thesis, Auckland University of Technology]. Tuwhera Open Access Theses & Dissertations. http://hdl.handle.net/10292/13307

Pouwhare, R., & McNeill, H. (2018). Purakau: He mahi rangahau. *DAT Journal, 3*(2), 261–290. https://doi.org/10.29147/dat.v3i2.94

Prendergast, M. (2006). Found poetry as literature review: Research poems on audience and performance. *Qualitative Inquiry, 12*(2), 369–388. https://doi.org/10.1177/1077800405284601

Richardson, L. (1994). Writing: A method of inquiry. In N. K. Denzin & Y. S. Lincoln (Eds.), *Handbook of qualitative research* (pp. 516–529). Sage.

Scrivener, S. (2002). The art object does not embody a form of knowledge. *Working Papers in Art and Design 2.* https://www.herts.ac.uk/__data/assets/pdf_file/0008/12311/WPIAAD_vol2_scrivener.pdf

Smith, L. T. (1999). *Decolonizing methodologies: Research and Indigenous peoples.* Zed Books; Otago University Press.

Smith, L. T. (2015). Kaupapa Māori research – Some kaupapa Māori principles. In L. Pihama, S.-J. Tiakiwai, & K. Southey (Eds.), *Kaupapa rangahau: A reader. A collection of readings from the Kaupapa Rangahau workshops series* (pp. 46–52). Te Kotahi Research Institute.

Szto, P., Furman, R., & Langer, C. (2005). Poetry and photography. *Qualitative Social Work, 4*(2), 135–156. https://doi.org/10.1177/1473325005052390

Tavares, T., & Ings, W. (2018). Navigating artistic inquiry in a creative-production thesis: The narrative and illustrative potentials of realismo maravilhoso. *DAT Journal, 3*(2), 9–42. https://doi.org/10.29147/dat.v3i2.85

Ventling, D. (2018). Heuristics: A framework to clarify practice-led research. *Journal of Design, Art and Technology, 3*(2), 122–156. https://doi.org/10.29147/dat.v3i2.88

Williams, T. (2024). *Tangohia mai te taura - Take This Rope: Exploring Māori documentary-making approaches to elevate whānau narratives* [Doctoral thesis, Auckland University of Technology]. Tuwhera Open Access Theses & Dissertations. http://hdl.handle.net/10292/17323

Wood, J. (2004). The culture of academic rigor: Does design research really need it? *The Design Journal, 3*(1), 44–57. https://doi.org/10.2752/146069200789393599

3

RESONANCES BETWEEN HEURISTIC INQUIRY AND PERSIAN ILLUMINATIVE THINKING

Hossein Najafi

Introduction

This chapter proposes a dynamic interplay between heuristic inquiry and Illuminative thinking, by developing and examining a unique blend of Western and Persian epistemologies. Drawing from a rich corpus of Persian literature and philosophy, particularly the works of philosopher Shahab al-Din Suhrawardi and the poet Farid al-Din Attar, I demonstrate how the ancient philosophy of illuminationism might enrich contemporary heuristic approaches to inquiry, and in doing so, I argue for a culturally dexterous research paradigm which is systematic, shaped by praxis, and capable of engaging with a researcher's intuitive insights. In this chapter I include specific Persian words and provide approximate translations for some key terms as a way of drawing a closer connection between two distinctive realms of thinking.

Research

Mockler (2011) and Wagner et al. (2012) note that a research paradigm emanates from the way a researcher sees the world and that the nature of reality and ways of knowing lie at the heart of research design. They suggest that once a research paradigm is established, then the researcher considers how to study the world through a systematic inquiry by asking certain questions that shape the project's methodology, and then methods that are employed to address specific parts of the study. Mockler (2011) argues that the research's paradigm, methodology, and methods are all linked to the researcher's ontology and epistemology (Figure 3.1).

DOI: 10.4324/9781003507758-6

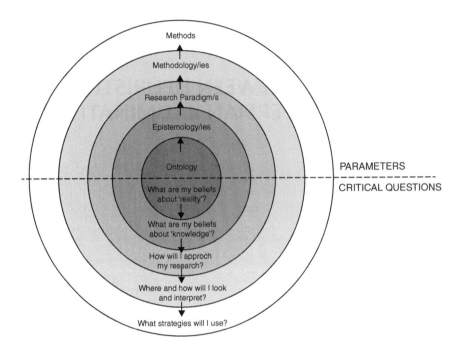

FIGURE 3.1 Relationships within a research design.

Source: Reproduced with permission from (Mockler, 2011, p. 160).

Research paradigm

A paradigm is 'a body of beliefs and values, laws and practices that govern a community of practitioners' (Carroll, 1997, p. 171). Paradigmatically, many of my personal research projects and the master's and doctoral theses I supervise may be understood as artistic inquiries (Klein, 2010) which employ forms of practice-led study. As an Iranian researcher my orientation is influenced by Persian literature and philosophy and as such, what underpins my understandings is partly shaped by اشراق (Ishraq), i.e., illuminationism and by Western approaches to research design. This gives rise to forms of inquiry that we might describe as an illuminationist, artistic, and practice-led.

Artistic research

In 2010, Julian Klein discussed a research orientation he called artistic research. He proposed that if we consider art as a mode of perception, then we can think of artistic research as the mode of a process. In such an orientation, reflection on research occurs inside the artistic experience itself (Klein, 2010).

Most challenges, questions, and problems in artistic inquiries are shaped through the creative endeavours of the practitioner who engages practical methods that emerge from internal experiences (Gray, 1996). Practice may engage a multitude of methods (Haseman, 2006) that are exercised in a process of intervention, creation, and conversion, that may either produce knowledge or heighten understanding (Scrivener, 2000). Barrett and Bolt (2007) suggest that it is through a process of elucidation and clarification that new knowledge emerges, and this moves beyond the artist beyond solipsistic, reflective practice.

Practice-led research

I use the term practice-led research to describe an inquiry that is led through practice. In other words, the researcher employs practice as both an agent of questioning and discovery. In practice-led artistic research, both Hamilton (2011) and Ings (2015) suggest that a dynamic exists between theory and practice, such that as the researcher shapes their work, they in turn are shaped by questioning and discovery. Such research calls theory to itself and theory is questioned and shaped within the researcher's practice. I would argue that, as a consequence, theory merges with the self through an embodiment that invigorates and revitalises the inner voice. This is because practice-led artistic research is, as Gray puts it, 'simultaneously generative and reflective' (1996, p. 10). The relationship between what is interior and what is generated through practice may result in elevating both the self (the artist) and the body of knowledge (Chen, 2018; Ings, 2018; Pouwhare, 2020). This might be likened to the Chinese concept of Zhe Jiang where tenacity leads to reverence, reverence leads to expertise, expertise leads to vision, and vision leads to the researcher not only increasing artistic ability but also becoming a better person (Chen, 2018).

Illuminationism

Over a thousand years ago, Suhrawardi's حكمت الاشراق (*The Philosophy of Illumination*) (1186/2000) shaped Persian literature and architecture by blending Hermetic, Pythagorean, Zoroastrian, Islamic, Platonic, and Neoplatonic symbolism (Nasr, 1964). Illuminationism emphasises the primacy of experience and intuition (Ziai, 1990), knowledge by presence, and the importance of imagination and innovation (Marcotte, 2019). During the same era, Persian poets like Rumi and Attar exemplified and heightened the tenets of illuminationism (Aminrazavi & Nasr, 2013). By retrieving a large corpus of ancient texts, Suhrawardi (1186/2000) was the first scholar to realise that the sources of Persian and Greek wisdom might be related. He sought to reunite Greek and Persian wisdom lost after Aristotle, recognised connections between the two wisdom traditions, and advocated for a universal and perennial wisdom beyond Aristotle's rationalistic approach. His work shaped a new way of conceiving intellectualisation and practice in the Iranian-Islamic world, and his thinking remains delicately manifested in much Iranian-Islamic art and architecture (Rahbarnia & Rouzbahani, 2014). Ziai (1990) and Aminrazavi and Nasr (2013) all suggest that Suhrawardi's legacy still permeates Iranian cultural and academic understanding. Suhrawardi's philosophy of Illumination uses the non-corporal, allegorical ontology of light as an intellectual substrate. His thinking took diverse forms including symbolic and mystical narratives that considered the journey of a soul across the cosmos to, as Nasr notes, a 'state of deliverance and illumination' (1964, p. 59).

Significantly, the philosophy of Illumination considers practice as a mode of intellectual engagement (Ziai, 1990) and places emphasis on intuition and *knowledge by presence*. It also positions imagination and innovation at the centre of its ontology (Marcotte, 2019). Although Suhrawardi's *The Philosophy of Illumination* is considered a seminal text on illuminationism, Dabbagh (2009) notes that Suhrawardi's thinking permeated the work of many intellectuals, artists, and poets of the period. Even Ibn Sina, the most prominent Peripatetic (Aristotelian) philosopher in the Islamic world (known as Avicenna in the West) wrote three treatises on illuminationism towards the end of his life.

In considering the concept of illuminationism in this chapter, I have drawn on the thinking of two philosophers, Ibn Sina and Suhrawardi, and one poet, Attar of Nishapur, a prominent Persian poet and mystic. According to Zwanzig (2009), as an illuminationist, Attar offers an important perspective on self-discovery through his work *The Conference of The Birds* (Attar, 1984). Attar's approach as a practitioner, his storytelling skills, and his elaboration of the gradual progression of internal exploration, may be seen as resonating with heuristic approaches to inquiry as a journey that is undertaken without a pre-set, formulaic template.

Knowing through praxis

Qutb al-Din al-Shirazi (1236–1311), one of the earliest commentators of Suhrawardi, suggests that illuminationism is the intuitive revelation of intellectual lights and their overflow on the self (Berenjkar, 2019). According to Aminrazavi and Nasr, 'both metaphysically and historically, illuminationist (اشراقی) philosophy refers to an ancient pre-discursive mode of thought which is intuitive (ذوقی) rather than discursive (بحثی) and seeks to reach illumination by asceticism and purification' (2013, p. 130). Epistemology is at the core of the *philosophy of illumination* and its definition of knowledge is what differentiates it from the canonical peripatetic tradition; as Suhrawardi notes, knowledge is the 'presence and the emergence of the things to the intellectual self' (quoted in Beheshti, 2015, p. 55). Yazdi suggests that this '*knowledge by presence*' (1992, p. 1) is achieved in the process of self-awareness and the *feeling* of existential states.

Ziai suggests that art and literature become the metalanguage of illumination as the vehicle to achieve knowledge, because in these realms knowledge passes through 'the experienced and the imagined' (1990, p. 216). Ziai also suggests that poetic language and the use of metaphors, allegory, symbolism, and references to myths and legends can function as a way to not only contemplate and internalise the knowledge of things, but also to reach beyond philosophical discourse and reach out to a wider audience.

At the beginning of his book, Suhrawardi (1186/2000) states that:

Although before the composition of this book I composed several treatises on Aristotelian philosophy, this book differs from them and has a method peculiar to itself. All of its material has not been assembled by thought and reasoning; rather, intellectual intuition, contemplation and ascetic practices have played a large role in it. Since our sayings have not come by means of rational demonstration but by inner vision and contemplation, they cannot be destroyed by the doubts and temptations of the sceptics. Whoever is a traveller on the road to Truth is my companion and aid on this path.

(p. 10)

Suhrawardi was a prolific scholar, and his early writings, which use a classical lexicon and literature, are mostly commentaries on Avicenna's peripatetic philosophy. During his long travels through Persia, India, Anatolia, and Syria he met many poets, mystic sages, Gnostics, and Sufis and thereby became acquainted with a large number of ancient texts. As a consequence of these interactions, he gradually elevated his philosophy to illuminationism into which, and especially in his later writings, he integrated a significant range of Hermetic, Pythagorean, Zoroastrian, Islamic, Mystic, Platonic, and Neoplatonic symbolism (Nasr, 1964). As a consequence, there was a shift in his style of writing as he began incorporating poetry and narrative stories into his philosophical writing. Although at this time, Arabic was the official intellectual and scientific language of the Islamic Golden Age, Suhrawardi wrote most of his treatises in Persian, and the titles of his treatises reflect a creative and poetic sensibility: *Treatise on the State of Childhood, Treatise on the Nocturnal Journey, The Red Intellect, The Chant of the Wing of Gabriel, The Occidental Exile, The Language of Termites*, and *The Song of the Simurgh* (Walbridge, 2011).

Even though he prioritised the primacy of experience in the *Philosophy of Illumination*, Suhrawardi does not dismiss reason and rational thinking (Ziai, 1990). While acknowledging and explaining intuitively attained knowledge, Suhrawardi still proposed using rational reasoning and the classical mechanisms of logic albeit in a different order. In other words, the main difference between peripatetic philosophers and Suhrawardi lies in where to begin an inquiry: either one moves from discursive knowledge towards intuition (like Avicenna), or one begins from experience and intuition and then progresses towards the rational and the reasoned (as Suhrawardi suggests).

This is why many scholars consider illuminationism as an example of the fusion of Platonian intuitionism and Aristotelian rationalism (Corbin, 1964; Marcotte, 2019; Nasr, 1964; Walbridge, 2001; Ziai, 1990). Contrary to the peripatetic philosophers, Suhrawardi believes in the primacy of essence over existence. He also rejects the peripatetic notion that we are never able to *know* the essence of things (Beheshti, 2016). He maintains that the sole act of constructing the definition of a thing does not reveal its essence and it is a tautology (تبدیل الالفاظ.). Because of this, Suhrawardi proposes the idea of *illuminationist vision* (مشاهده اشراقی). Here, the researcher opens their inner eye through an act or a journey that begins with a quest and demands practice and engagement. The object of study becomes luminous and excited to the state of illumination and then becomes knowable to them through experience and imagination (Ziai, 1990). In other words, vision is 'seeing through praxis' (Ziai, 1990, p. 218). Henry Corbin, the first translator of Suhrawardi into a Latin language, calls this realm *mundus imaginalis* (Corbin, 1964).

Suhrawardi's world of lights and illumination should not be read as the Platonic theory of forms and ideas (although he has borrowed some components from Plato). The difference lies in the plasticity of Suhrawardi's world of lights. Suhrawardi maintains that creators and artists, through rigorous practice, attain illumination and reach a condition that he calls *the state of Be* (مقام کون). This could be considered close to Sela-Smith's (2002) concept of inward reach. Suhrawardi suggests that, by their luminosity, they can shape the celestial forms and bring them to the terrestrial domain where they turn into works of art or abstracted concepts (Shafi & Bolkhari, 2012). Accordingly, for Suhrawardi, there is a dynamic dialogue between the realm of imagination (*mundus imaginalis*) and the realm of earthly self.

The foundations of illuminationism were outlined in the first chapters of Suhrawardi's book, *The Philosophy of Illumination*. However, reading his writings is not an easy task for a researcher. His narrative stories can feel like psychedelic reflections of a mystic dreamer, full of references to myths and symbols. Compared to the scholastic structured writings of peripatetic philosophers such as Avicenna, Suhrawardi's works may seem chaotic, tangled, enigmatic, and scattered. One reason may be because he had no time to organise his writings because following an accusation of heresy by Islamic jurists of Hallab he was executed at the age of 37, and he wrote his most important book, *The Philosophy of Illumination*, in about a month while in prison awaiting his execution.

Heuristic inquiry

In artistic research, heuristic inquiry can be framed as a form of discovery achieved and elevated through practical experience. Through the process of the practice, the researcher works without a predefined formula, using astute observation and questioning to explore and develop potentials within the work incrementally. Accordingly, the direction of the inquiry may change or be adjusted, and new questions may arise (Ings, 2011; Kleining & Witt, 2000; Moustakas, 1990). The protean nature of creative inquiry demands an adaptive strategy because not only the process but also the questions and problems that arise need to be reflectively adjusted (Ings, 2011). Heuristic inquiry characteristically employs both explicit and tacit knowledge and draws heavily on self-search, phenomenologically reincarnated reminiscences, and internalised wisdom that can result in new approaches (Douglass & Moustakas, 1985). In a heuristic inquiry the dynamic sphere needs to be iteratively updated to portray the active evolving quest of the researcher, and so the approach requires a concatenation of integrated re-adjustments and re-definitions (Scrivener, 2000).

Moustakas (1990) suggests that because heuristic research is concerned with interrelated and integrated elements it restores derived knowledge as a form of creative discovery that accompanies intuition and tacit knowing. The research process begins within the practitioner and their interior dialogue. Accordingly, one cannot expect the predictability factors and casual relations that we encounter in empirical inquiries. Thus, Moustakas (2001) notes that heuristic inquiry is illuminated through careful descriptions, illustrations, metaphors, poetry, dialogue, and other creative renderings rather than by measurements, ratings, or scores.

Illuminative heuristic inquiry

Having discussed the nature of illuminationist thinking, it is useful to consider how it might impact on a research methodology designed for artistic inquiry. Chilisa and Kawulich suggest that 'methodology is where assumptions about the nature of reality and knowledge, values, theory and practice on a given topic come together' (2012, p. 51). In my research I employ heuristic inquiry, but I look into it through the lens of Suhrawardi's Persian illuminationism. In exercising this connection between Western and Persian methodological thinking, I draw upon the metaphors of another Persian illuminationist, the poet Attar of Nishapur, whose famous poem *The Conference of the Birds* describes the journey of the self through an allegorical narrative.

Seven concepts/processes of a heuristic inquiry

In his book *Heuristic Research*, Moustakas (1990) suggests that research begins with a question that requires illumination and he notes seven concepts or processes that underpin the researcher's pursuit of a deeper understanding of the phenomenon being explored, i.e., identifying with the focus of inquiry, self-dialogue, tacit knowing, intuition, indwelling, focusing, and the use of the internal frame of reference.

Identifying with the focus of inquiry

In this process Moustakas describes a state similar to Suhrawardi's concept of the internal unification of the researcher with the question. Both scholars propose what Moustakas refers to as 'immersion in active experience' (1990, p. 2), which is achieved by delving freely into one's self. In this sense, both suggest that through this process the inquiry becomes identifiable.

Self-dialogue

Self-dialogue involves researchers immersing themselves in the phenomenon. This approach necessitates openness, receptiveness, and attunement to all facets of their experience with the question under consideration. Self-dialogue integrates intellect, emotion, and spirit in a disciplined manner (Bronowski, 1965; Craig, 1978). It also elevates the importance of being open to one's experiences, trusting in self-awareness, and maintaining an internal locus of evaluation throughout the research process (Rogers, 1969). This self-directed approach defies pre-imagined formulae but, rather, draws upon perceptual powers afforded by direct experience (Douglass & Moustakas, 1985).

Tacit knowing

Polanyi (1964, 1983) emphasises tacit knowledge as a foundational element of comprehension. He suggests that the tacit dimension permeates the research process, guiding the researcher into new directions and sources of meaning because he maintains, 'We can know more than we can tell' (Polanyi, 1983, p. 4). This concept suggests that there are things we understand intuitively and can apply or recognise, without being able to explicitly state or explain them.

Intuition

Intuition operates as a bridge between tacit, implicit knowledge, and a journey towards explicit, definable knowledge. Intuitively, the researcher drives knowledge immediately and directly, crosscutting logical reasoning.

Indwelling

This process involves immersing and living within the depth of the inquiry so that the researcher is able to reflect on details. Moustakas describes this as 'a painstaking, deliberate process. Patience and incremental understanding are the guidelines. Through indwelling the heuristic instigator finally turns the corner and moves toward the ultimate creative synthesis that portrays the essential qualities and meanings of an experience' (1990, p. 10).

Focusing

This refers to a process where the researcher clears away disparate qualities to concentrate on core meanings that define an experience. Douglass and Moustakas suggest that this process is concerned with the 'refinement of meaning and perception that registers as internal shifts and alterations of behaviour' (1985, p. 51).

The internal frame of reference

The heuristic process is grounded in the researcher's internal frame of reference, which is vital for understanding the nature, meanings, and essences of any human experience. Rogers (1951) maintains that empathic understanding and open, trustworthy communication are crucial for comprehending another's experience from this internal viewpoint.

Attar's illuminationist journey of the self

Having considered Moustakas' seven concepts underpinning heuristic inquiry, I turn to the thinking of Attar of Nishapur (1145–1221), the prominent Persian poet and mystic whose works shaped the landscape of Persian literature during the 12th century. Attar pursued a form of illuminationist self-discovery (Zwanzig, 2009). Although Attar lived at the same time as Suhrawardi, there is no historical record indicating that these thinkers met or maintained any form of correspondence (Mojtahedi, 2015), although Bahonar (2010) notes that the language, mythology, references, symbolism, and especially the illuminationism in his works, particularly in Attar's (1984) *The Conference of The Birds*, are akin to Suhrawardi's.

In contrast to the philosophical approach of Suhrawardi, Attar approached illuminationism from the position of a practitioner, although like Suhrawardi, Attar believes that wisdom is 'moving' and the path to wisdom is not predetermined but, instead, shaped by 'going' (Afshari-Mofrad et al., 2016). In a structured, poetically explained expedition, Attar elaborately documents the gradual progression of an internal exploration. Although Attar was not the first person to talk about processes of a mystic journey, he is one of the earliest to construct a framework and clarify a system through an allegorical narrative, providing examples to elucidate each process which, in effect, form stages of the mystic – and, by analogy, research – journey.

Attar offers similar ideas regarding phases in a journey to Moustakas (1990) regarding certain processes that underpin heuristic inquiry. For these reasons, I have come to adopt Attar's concepts (over Suhrawardi's) in shaping my Persian approach to heuristic inquiry.

Although many intellectuals during the Islamic Golden Age wrote stories using bird metaphors, Bahonar (2010) suggests that Attar's *The Conference of the Birds* is the finest example, both in terms of literature and conceptual cohesion.

Attar's *The Conference of the Birds* begins with a question posed among the birds of the earth: 'Who is our king?' The Hoopoe, the wisest of all, informs them of Simurgh, a divine bird who is the source of all the life and diversity in the universe. He claims the magnificence of China, the splendour of Persia, and all varieties of beauty around the world exist because the Simurgh has flown over those lands on each of which one of her glorious feathers has fallen. Her nest, he says, is on the Tree of Knowledge located on Mount Qaf, the peak of the world.[1] To reach Mount Qaf, the birds have to travel on an arduous journey through seven valleys. Most of them give up, return, or die. Eventually, out of thousands, only 30 birds[2] arrive at the magnificent throne of the Simurgh… but she is not there. Towards the dawn, when the sun illuminates, these birds see their shadows on the throne, and they realise that each of them contributes to a composite that is Simurgh.

The seven valleys

In this section I discuss the seven valleys which comprise the seven processes of a mystic journey, selecting a few lines from Attar's poem to illustrate the core meanings of each concept.

First, I compare Attar's stages of the journey of self-discovery with certain concepts of heuristic inquiry as described by Moustakas (1990) (Figure 3.2). As may be seen, the first three stages and concepts as well as the fifth in Attar's scheme have a surprising resonance with Moustakas' heuristic concepts. The concept – and stage – of knowledge in Attar's journey has qualities of both tacit knowing and intuition in Moustakas' model. I found the detachment process in Attar's story a pure Eastern gnostic perspective with no parallel in Moustakas' model, though has some resonance with his concept of incubation, which forms one of the phases of heuristic enquiry. I suggest that the last two processes of both models are vastly different (see p. 55). I don't find any resonance between Attar's concepts of wonderment and selflessness and Moustakas' concepts of heuristic inquiry, although there is some echo of selflessness in Sela-Smith's (2002) concept and encouragement of surrender.

The valley of quest

When the birds, motivated by Hoopoe's speech, embark on their journey to find Simurgh, the first encounter that challenges them is the valley of quest. This may be aligned with the first process in Moustakas' (1990) heuristic journey which involves the researcher identifying – and, I suggest, unifying – with the subject of inquiry. Similarly, Attar urges the birds to free their *hands* and *minds* from all distractions and internalise their quest and let their longing

Attar's seven stages of self-discovery journey   Moustakas' seven concepts of heuristic process

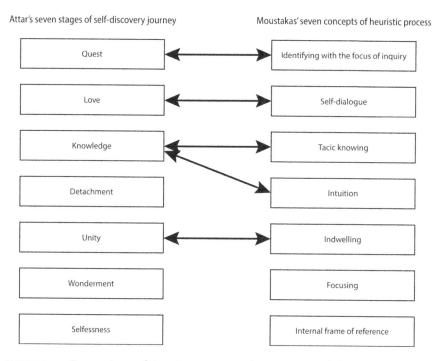

FIGURE 3.2 Comparison of Attar's stages – and concepts – of the journey of self with Moustakas' concepts of heuristic inquiry.

heart be illuminated by the splendour of their passion. This concept in Attar's journey is similar to that of Moustakas 'identifying with the focus of inquiry' (1990, p. 15).

ملک اینجا بایدت انداختن
ملک اینجا بایدت در باختن
در میان خونت باید آمدن
وز همه بیرونت باید آمدن
چون نماند هیچ معلومت به دست
دل بباید پاک کرد از هرچ هست
چون دل تو پاک گردد از صفات
تافتن گیرد ز حضرت نور ذات
چون شود آن نور بر دل آشکار
در دل تو یک طلب گردد هزار

Renounce the world, your power and all you own,
And in your heart's blood journey on alone.
When once your hands are empty, then your heart
Must purify itself and move apart,

From everything that is.
When this is done,
The divine light blazes brighter than the sun,
Your heart is bathed in splendour and the quest
Expands a thousandfold within your breast.

(Attar et al., 1984, p. 238)

The valley of love

The second encounter is the valley of love. For Attar, love here is more intro-spective and contemplative than physical attraction. In the valley of love, those birds who couldn't connect with the love within, quit the journey. This has the quality of Moustakas' (1990) concept of self-dialogue. The state of self-exploratory love that Attar is talking about here ascends the lover to a state beyond morality, where good and evil seem the same. Moustakas (1990) refers to the fact that because the researcher has already identified with the subject of study both enter into an intense, internal dialogue where the 'self' engages in a questioning conversation with the subject of inquiry. In Attar's valley of love, the wayfarer becomes attuned with their own presence and constituents. This concept can be interpreted as Moustakas' 'self-dialogue' (1990, p. 16).

بعد ازین وادی عشق آید پدید
غرق آتش شد کسی کانجا رسید
کس درین وادی به جز آتش مباد
وانک آتش نیست عیشش خوش مباد
لحظه‌ای نه کافری داند نه دین
ذره‌ای نه شک شناسد نه یقین
نیک و بد در راه او یکسان بود
خود چو عشق آمد نه این نه آن بود
گر ز غیبت دیده‌ای بخشند راست
اصل عشق اینجا ببینی کز کجاست
گر ترا آن چشم غیبی باز شد
با تو ذرات جهان هم راز شد
ور به چشم عقل بگشایی نظر
عشق را هرگز نبینی پا و سر

Love's valley is the next, and here desire
Will plunge the pilgrim into seas of fire,
Until his very being is enflamed
And those whom fire rejects turn back ashamed.
Who knows of neither faith nor blasphemy,
Who has no time for doubt or certainty,

To whom both good and evil are the same,
And who is neither, but a living flame.
If you could seek the unseen you would find
Love's home, which is not reason or the mind
And see the world's wild atoms, you would know
That reason's eyes will never glimpse one spark
Of shining love to mitigate the dark.
Love leads whoever starts along our Way

(Attar et al., 1984, p. 241)

The valley of knowledge

Attar describes this form of knowledge as intuitive, and one that enables a (re)
searcher making a journey to realise their unique personal qualities. This is
similar to Polanyi's (1966) idea of tacit knowing, which Moustakas (1990)
adopts, as well as the concept of 'intuition'. In this phase of their quest each
bird must come to an innate knowledge of its own road, i.e., a path that is
different for each of them. These routes are very elastic and are shaped by
each individual. No bird is able to comprehend or understand another bird's
trajectory.

هیچ کس نبود که او این جایگاه
مختلف گردد ز بسیاری راه
هیچ ره دروی نه هم آن دیگرست
سالک تن، سالک جان، دیگرست
باز جان و تن ز نقصان و کمال
هست دایم در ترقی و زوال
لاجرم بس ره که پیش آمد پدید
هر یکی بر حد خویش آمد پدید
کی تواند شد درین راه خلیل
عنکبوت مبتلا هم سیر پیل
سیر هر کس تا کمال وی بود
قرب هر کس حسب حال وی بود
لاجرم چون مختلف افتاد سیر
هم روش هرگز نیفتد هیچ طیر

Here every pilgrim takes a different way,
And different spirits different rules obey
Each soul and body has its level here
And climbs or falls within its proper sphere
There are so many roads, and each is fit
For that one pilgrim who must follow it.
How could a spider or a tiny ant,

Tread the same path as some huge elephant?
Each pilgrim's progress is commensurate
With his specific qualities and state
Our pathways differ, no bird ever knows
The secret route by which another goes

(Attar et al., 1984, p. 252)

Later, in this part of the book, Attar explains that when a wayfarer becomes aware of their unique quality they become illuminated and aware of all their atoms and the terrestrial furnace of living becomes a celestial heaven for them.

The valley of detachment

After intuitively coming to know their unique qualities, Attar suggests that the wayfarer recognises the insignificance of man in the cosmos. This is a state where one feels detached from the extraneous, and the individual is able to put aside distractions that might impede them from progressing into deeper discovery. This concept in an illuminationist journey has no equivalent in Moustakas' defined concepts; it can, however, be linked to his incubation phase of heuristic inquiry (Moustakas, 1990). In Attar's narrative, numerous birds find themselves hindered by their adherence to personal ideologies, material possessions, and attachment to their homeland, leading them to cease their pursuit along the path to discover Simorgh.

گر بریخت افلاک و انجم لخت لخت

در جهان کم گیر برگی از درخت

گر ز ماهی در عدم شد تا به ماه

پای مور لنگ شد در قعر چاه

گر دو عالم شد همه یک بارنیست

در زمین ریگی همان انگار نیست

گر نماند از دیو وز مردم اثر

از سر یک قطره باران در گذر

If all the stars and heavens came to grief,
They'd be the shedding of one withered leaf;
If all the worlds were swept away to hell,
They'd be a crawling ant trapped down a well;
If earth and heaven were to pass away,
One grain of gravel would have gone astray;
If men and friends never seen again,
They'd vanish like a tiny splash of rain

(Attar et al., 1984, p. 261)

The valley of unity

For many previous mystic teachers, the valley of unity marked the end of the wayfarer's journey. In this realm, by indwelling in the state of detachment, the inquirer attains eventual illumination, veils fade, and the hidden, interior sun shines through. Here the self is united with its hidden essence, i.e., the celestial state of one's existence, a state in which the birds indwell for a long time. However, although it appears to be a point of convergence, Attar doesn't consider that this is the end of the journey. The first signs of illumination emerge in this valley to the birds. Unity is very similar to Moustakas' concept of 'indwelling' (1990, p. 24).

هرک در دریای وحدت گم نشد
گر همه آدم بود مردم نشد
هر یک از اهل هنر وز اهل عیب
آفتابی دارد اندر غیب غیب
عاقبت روزی بود کان آفتاب
با خودش گیرد، براندازد نقاب
هرک او در آفتاب خود رسید
تو یقین می‌دان که نیک و بد رسید
تا تو باشی، نیک و بد اینجا بود
چون تو گم گشتی همه سودا بود

Be lost in Unity's inclusive span,
Or you are human but not yet a man.
Whoever lives, the wicked and the blessed,
Contains a hidden sun within his breast
Its light must dawn through dogged by long delay;
The clouds that veil it must be torn away
Whoever reaches to his hidden sun
Surpasses good and bad and knows One.
This good and bad are here while You are here;
Surpass yourself and they will disappear

(Attar et al., 1984, p. 271)

The valley of wonderment

Attar believes that, after unification and the elevation of the state of the self, the wayfarer faces the – or a – crisis of identity. The person is not their previous self, and this is confusing. The person loses their previous sense of a coherent self-identity. In his story, many birds perish in this valley because they cannot recognise who they are anymore. Attar argues that what saves some of the birds in this crisis of identity is the overwhelming, introspective, and contemplative love that is the essence of the illuminationist.

مرد حیران چون رسد این جایگاه
در تحیر مانده و گم کرده راه
هرچ زد توحید بر جانش رقم
جمله گم گردد از و گم نیز هم
گر بدو گویند مستی یا نه‌ای
نیستی گویی که هستی یا نه‌ای
در میانی یا برونی از میان
بر کناری یا نهانی یا عیان
فانیی یا باقیی یا هر دوی
یا نهٔ هر دو توی یا نه توی
گوید اصلا می‌ندانم چیز من
وان ندانم هم ندانم نیز من
عاشقم اما ندانم بر کیم
نه مسلمانم نه کافر، پس چیم
لیکن از عشقم ندارم آگهی
هم دلی پرعشق دارم هم تهی

He is lost, with indecisive steps you stray
the Unity you knew has gone; your soul
is scattered and knows nothing of the Whole.
If someone asks: 'what is your present state?
is drunkenness or sober, sense your fate,
and do you flourish now or fade away?
'the pilgrim will confess: 'I cannot say;
I have no certain knowledge anymore;
I doubt my doubt, doubt itself is unsure;
I love, but who is it for whom I sigh?
Not Muslim, yet not heathen; who am I?
My heart is empty, yet with love is full;
my own love is to me incredible.

(Attar et al., 1984, p. 278)

The valley of selflessness

Attar's final stage exists for those who survive the realm of the valley of identity crisis. Leaving the valley of wonderment, the searcher reaches the state of *Fana* (انف). This word is difficult to translate. Some writers have interpreted it as annihilation or even death, but this interpretation is too literal and fails to reflect the subtle ethos of the word. None of the birds who eventually arrive to the court of Simurgh dies or disappears. Instead, their egos fade away, and their inner excellence illuminates their surroundings to such an extent that their former self (now a realm of shadows) cannot be seen anymore, even though it still exists. I would suggest that the 'annihilation', therefore, is not death but the emergence of a different state of being, a resolution where the self disappears (self-loss). The searcher is subsumed within beauty, they are no longer what existed, but rather something dissipated but present. This state has been interpreted across generations in many masterpieces of Iranian-Islamic art and the reason these works are not signed is because the 'self' of the creator is understood to be absorbed into the excellence of their artwork. In terms of heuristic inquiry, this is similar to Sela-Smith's (2002) concept of surrender.

صد هزاران سایهٔ جاوید تو
گم شده بینی ز یک خورشید تو
بحرکلی چون بجنبش کرد رای
نقشها بر بحر کی ماند بجای
هر دو عالم نقش آن دریاست بس
هرک گوید نیست این سوداست بس
هرک در دریای کل گم بوده شد
دایما گم بودهٔ آسوده شد
گر پلیدی گم شود در بحر کل
در صفات خود فروماند بذل
لیک اگر پاکی درین دریا بود
او چون بود در میان زیبا بود
نبود او و او بود، چون باشد این
از خیال عقل بیرون باشد این

When sunlight penetrates the atmosphere,
A hundred thousand shadows disappear
And when the sea arises what can save
The patterns on the surface of each wave?
Whoever sinks within this sea is blest
All in self-loss obtains eternal rest
The heart that would be lost in this wide sea
Disperses in profound tranquillity,
And if it should emerge again it knows,
The secret ways in which the ways in which the world arose.
And evil souls sunk in this mighty sea
Retain unchanged their base identity;
But if a pure soul sinks the waves surround
His fading form, in beauty he is drowned
He is not, yet he is; what could this mean?
It is a state the mind has never seen

(Attaret et al., 1984, p. 288)

The journey in reflection

If we summarise the search journey through the valleys (Figure 3.3), we observe a move from a state in which (re)searchers free themselves from

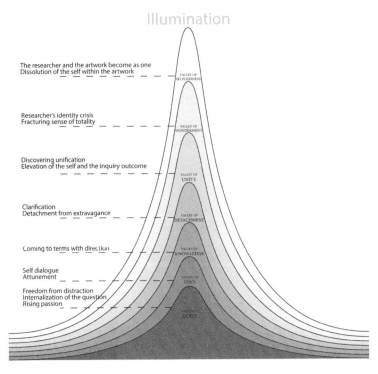

Illumination

The researcher and the artwork become as one
Dissolution of the self within the artwork — — — VALLEY OF
SELFLESSNESS

Researcher's identity crisis
Fracturing sense of totality — — — — VALLEY OF
WONDERMENT

Discovering unification
Elevation of the self and the inquiry outcome — — — — VALLEY OF
UNITY

Clarification
Detachment from extravagance — — — VALLEY OF
DETACHMENT

Coming to terms with direction — — VALLEY OF
KNOWLEDGE

Self dialogue
Attunement — — — VALLEY OF
LOVE

Freedom from distraction
Internalization of the question
Rising passion — VALLEY OF
QUEST

FIGURE 3.3   Diagram showing an inquiry as the researcher progresses through the seven valleys.

distraction and internalise their quest, to one in which they are subsumed within the work (dissipated but present). Unlike certain Western conceptualisations of a research journey that might end at the fifth stage of realisation resulting from unification (the valley of unity or discussion of findings), Attar's view of this journey includes two additional phases. The first (the valley of wonderment) may be framed as an identity crisis wherein the (re)searcher experiences a fractured sense of totality. If the (re)searcher progresses beyond this stage, and progresses to the valley of selflessness, they are transformed by the inquiry's journey and experience a state of 'oneness' with their artwork.

Bridging heuristic inquiry and Persian illuminationism

In this exploration of resonances between heuristic inquiry and Persian Illuminative thinking, we have journeyed through a rich landscape of comparative analysis. The comparison between Moustakas' heuristics and Attar's illuminationist journey of the self reveals remarkable parallels and intersections. In this concluding section, I propose that heuristic inquiry is flexible enough to find functioning resonances in non-Western ways of understanding research processes. As academia increasingly embraces diverse knowledge systems, this analysis might offer a more holistic and nuanced framework for research practices that operate in interdisciplinary, transcultural, and/or global environments.

Comparing Moustakas' heuristics inquiry and Attar's illuminationist journey of the self

Although Moustakas' heuristic inquiry represents a human scientific search based on seven concepts his methodology is designed to help a heuristic researcher discover the 'nature and meaning of experiences' (1990, p. 9). Thus, heuristic *inquiry* is a means to an end, rather than a process that is integral to, and inseparable from its outcomes.

While I accept that Moustakas' heuristic inquiry is essentially an academic discourse (Oram, 2019) and Attar's poem is an artwork that metaphorically illustrates the pursuit of self-realisation, I find Attar's thinking useful in constructing a framework for my research, and despite certain stylistic differences, the approaches of both thinkers have features in common.

Both acknowledge the importance of tacit knowing (or intuition) that enables subjective and creative connections between the (re)searcher and phenomena. Both propose self-dialogue as integral to development, and both emphasise reflection. In both bodies of thought, the (re)searcher chooses to become deeply engaged in the pursuit of knowing and to utilise self-experience in the process. Like Attar's illuminationist journey of the self, Moustakas' (1990) heuristic inquiry also encourages the researcher to explore with an open mind and to pursue a path of inquiry that originates inside themselves (Djuraskovic & Arthur, 2010). It is within this internal realm that research discovers its direction and meaning.

However, significant differences lie in Attar's last two stages and concepts: wonderment and selflessness and what Moustakas proposes. This may be because these 'valleys' emanate from an Eastern gnostic perspective that has little equivalence in Western thought. Accordingly, these stages and concepts contain ideas that fall outside of Moustakas' considerations. While Moustakas' concepts raise an awareness of intuitive self-reflection in the realm of the social sciences and artistic research, the valleys of wonderment and selflessness in Attar's journey are more metaphysical stances.

The valley of wonderment in which the searcher dispels identities is related to the mystic belief that humans are distanced from their divinity. This concept may be described as *Fana* (selflessness). This is an illuminationist idea that attributes material bodies to the world of shadows. When the self of the searcher is symbolically annihilated, divine light is able to shine within the self and also pass through the (re)searcher. Consequently, the entirety of the (re)searcher turns into an allegorically illuminating being that brightens their surroundings.

Synthesising the thinking of Moustakas and Attar: An illuminationist heuristic methodology

Heuristic inquiry offers a unique method 'in which the lived experience of the researcher becomes the main focus of the study, and it is used as an instrument in the process of understanding a given phenomenon' (Brisola & Cury, 2016, p. 95). The primacy of intuition doesn't predicate a rejection of reasoning in either illuminationism or heuristic inquiry because rational thinking resources knowledge by presence (Ziai, 1990), and by explication and creative synthesis (Moustakas, 1990).

According to 'knowledge by presence', when the essence of a phenomenon becomes present to the (re)searcher, they will experience it as an immediate and unmediated knowledge of themselves. To an illuminationist, to know something, the (re)searcher must elevate themselves through praxis. Therefore, 'knowing' is more than simply being informed; it must constitute an active engagement with the object of inquiry.

The knowing being and the known thing are different gradations of allegorical light. To be able to know a thing, both the (re)searcher and the object of inquiry have to be uplifted from darkness. The (re)searcher will be illuminated by journeying. Such a journey takes the form of a vigorous, dynamic engagement with the context and content of the research in such a way that the self of the (re)searcher becomes increasingly conscious of the self and the subject. In other words, they become illuminated. In Suhrawardi's (1186/2000) illuminationist thinking, the dedicated work of the (re)searcher throughout a journey not only illuminates the self but also excites the object of inquiry to the state of illumination. In this process, the self is internalised into the unmediated, immediate subject of inquiry. Here, there is a partial correlation with heuristic inquiry's emphasis on the internal self as a subject of inquiry. In heuristic inquiry, self-search, exploration, and discovery enable the researcher to pursue a 'creative journey that begins inside one's being and ultimately uncovers its direction and meaning through internal discovery' (Djuraskovic & Arthur, 2010, p. 1569). However, in heuristic inquiry, the self as the subject of inquiry can be differentiated from Attar's illuminationism, because the journey is neither predicated on illumination of the darker self nor the self's eventual symbolic annihilation.

Although the subject of inquiry might have been previously illuminated through the praxis of others, the darker self of the (re)searcher will, up until the journey of the inquiry, have been able to see the illumination. Once the (re) searcher becomes illuminated, the light of the self is able to unite with the light of the subject of the inquiry and the two merge. The knowledge that surfaces out of this unified state is innate, intuitive, immediate knowledge that is recognisably present, and the (re)searcher instantaneously comes to the state of knowing it. This knowledge by presence can be so direct that the (re)searcher often needs to pause and look back on their journey to understand it.

Sometimes the (re)searcher is so immersed that this reflective understanding becomes impossible, so an external critic is required to observe the process from an objective standpoint. From an illuminationist perspective, the external critic functions as a mirror that reflects the irradiated light of the (re)searcher back to themselves so they can recognise their own light. Thus, supervisors, critical collaborators, and reviewers may be understood as essentially illuminating beings who intensify and catalyse the process of becoming illuminated. They, in effect, 'climb inside' the subject of inquiry and cast light into dark corners of the pathway.

Conclusion

This chapter navigates the complex relationship between heuristic inquiry and Persian Illuminative thought, proposing a novel approach to research methodology. It highlights how the philosophical underpinnings of Persian thought, with its focus on inner experiences and intuitive understanding, can embrace and enrich heuristic methodologies. This synthesis of methodological processes and philosophical introspection proposes a cross-cultural shift in research paradigms, advocating for a more inclusive and reflective approach to knowledge creation. By drawing on the metaphorical journey in Attar's narratives to illustrate the (re)searcher's quest, the chapter has argued that the birds' (and the researchers') journey, although seemingly external, is also an internal journey of understanding. This integration of diverse epistemological perspectives offers a reimagined approach to research, encouraging a more nuanced, reflective, and comprehensive engagement with academic inquiry.

Notes

1 The letter Q (ق) is a sacred letter in the Quran and by itself it can contain a dense meaning. In some sentences it may mean to 'reclaim your abstinence'.
2 If simurgh is read in a separated form, i.e., si + murgh, the word means 30 birds.

References

Afshari-Mofrad, M., Ghazinoory, S., Montazer, G. A., & Rashidirad, M. (2016). Groping toward the next stages of technology development and human society: A metaphor from an Iranian poet. *Technological Forecasting and Social Change, 109,* 87–95. https://doi.org/10.1016/j.techfore.2016.04.029

Aminrazavi, M., & Nasr, S. H. (2013). *The Islamic intellectual tradition in Persia.* Routledge.

Attar, F. ud-Din. (1984). *The conference of the birds* (A. Darbandi & D. Davis, Trans.; re-issue edition). Penguin Classics.

Bahonar, M. (2010). روند تاریخی رساله الطیرها ؛ رازنامه های پرواز [Historical trajectory of treatise on birds] *221* مجله کیهان فرهنگی [Keyhan Farhangi Magazine, 221].

Barrett, E., & Bolt, B. (2007). *Practice as research: Approaches to creative arts enquiry.* I. B. Tauris.

Beheshti, M. (2015). معرفت شناسی از منظر شیخ اشراق [Epistemology according to Suhrawardi].۸۱ روش شناسی علوم انسانی [Humanities Methodologies, 81]. http://ensani. ir/fa/article/357171

Beheshti, M. (2016). روش شناخت حقیقت در حکمت اشراق [Methods to understand truth in illuminationism]. ۸۴ روش شناسی علوم انسانی [Humanities Methodologies, 84]. http://ensani.ir/fa/article/357190

Berenjkar, R. (2019). آشنایی با علوم انسانی [Introduction to Islamic philosophies]. سازمان مطالعه و تدوین کتب علوم انسانی دانشگاهها [Institution for Editing Islamic Books for Universities].

Brisola, E. B. V., & Cury, V. E. (2016). Researcher experience as an instrument of investigation of a phenomenon: An example of heuristic research. *Estudos de Psicologia (Campinas)*, *33*(1), 95–105.

Bronowski, J. (1965). *Science and human values*. Perennial Library.

Carroll, K. L. (1997). Researching paradigms in art education. *Research Methods and Methodologies for Art Education*, 171–192.

Chen, C. (2018). *Bright on the grey sea: Utilizing the Xiang system to creatively consider the potentials of menglong in film poetry* [Doctoral thesis, Auckland University of Technology]. Tuwhera Open Access Theses & Dissertations. https://hdl.handle.net/10292/11737

Chilisa, B., & Kawulich, B. B. (2012). Selecting a research approach: Paradigm, methodology and methods. In C. Wagner, B. Kawulich, & M. Garner (Eds.), *Doing social research: A global context* (pp. 51–61). McGraw Hill.

Corbin, H. (1964). *Mundus imaginalis ou l'imaginaire et l'imaginal*. Cahiers internationaux de symbolisme.

Craig, P. E. (1978). The heart of the teacher: A heuristic study of the inner world of teaching. *Dissertation Abstracts International Section A: Humanities and Social Sciences*, *38*(12-A), 7222.

Dabbagh, H. (2009). عشق مولانا و خیال سهروردی [Rumi's love and Suhrawardi's dream]. ۲۳ کتاب ماه فلسفه [The Philosophy Book of the Month, 23]. https://ensani.ir/fa/article/208622

Djuraskovic, I., & Arthur, N. (2010). Heuristic inquiry: A personal journey of acculturation and identity reconstruction. *The Qualitative Report*, *15*(6), 1569–1593.

Douglass, B. G., & Moustakas, C. (1985). Heuristic inquiry: The internal search to know. *Journal of Humanistic Psychology*, *25*(3), 39–55. https://doi.org/10.1177/0022167885253004

Gray, C. (1996). Inquiry through practice: Developing appropriate research strategies. *No Guru, No Method*, 1–28.

Hamilton, J. (2011). The voices of the exegesis. In L. Justice & K. Friedman (Eds.), *Preconference proceedings of Practice, Knowledge, Vision: Doctoral Education in Design Conference* (pp. 340–343). The Hong Kong Polytechnic University. https://eprints.qut.edu.au/41832/

Haseman, B. (2006). A manifesto for performative research. *Media International Australia Incorporating Culture and Policy*, *118*(1), 98–106. https://doi.org/10.1177/1329878X0611800113

Ings, W. (2011). Managing heuristics as a method of inquiry in autobiographical graphic design theses. *International Journal of Art & Design Education*, *30*(2), 226–241. https://doi.org/10.1111/j.1476-8070.2011.01699.x

Ings, W. (2015). The authored voice: Emerging approaches to exegesis design in creative practice PhDs. *Educational Philosophy and Theory*, *47*(12), 1277–1290. https://doi.org/10.1080/00131857.2014.974017

Ings, W. (2018). Heuristic inquiry, land and the artistic researcher. In M. Sierra & K. Wise (Eds.), *Transformative pedagogies and the environment: Creative agency through contemporary art and design* (pp. 55–80). Common Ground Research Networks.

Klein, J. (2010). What is artistic research? *Research Catalogue*, 1–6. https://www.researchcatalogue.net/view/15292/15293

Kleining, G., & Witt, H. (2000). The qualitative heuristic approach: A methodology for discovery in psychology and the social sciences. Rediscovering the method of introspection as an example. *Forum Qualitative Sozialforschung/Forum: Qualitative Social Research*, *1*. https://doi.org/10.17169/fqs-1.1.1123

Marcotte, R. (2019). Suhrawardi. In E. N. Zalta (Ed.), *The Stanford Encyclopedia of Philosophy* (Summer 2019). Metaphysics Research Lab, Stanford University. https://plato.stanford.edu/archives/sum2019/entries/suhrawardi/

Mockler, N. (2011). Being me: In search of authenticity. In J. Higgs, A. Titchen, D. Horsfall, & D. Bridges (Eds.), *Creative spaces for qualitative researching: Living research* (pp. 159–168). Springer.

Mojtahedi, K. (2015). سهروردی و افکار او [Suhrawardi and his ideas]. علوم انسانی و پژوهشگاه مطالعات فرهنگی [Institute of Humanities and Cultural Studies].

Moustakas, C. (1990). *Heuristic research: Design, methodology, and applications*. Sage.

Moustakas, C. (2001). Heuristic research: Design and methodology. In K. J. Schneider, J. F. Pierson, & J. F. T. Bugental (Eds.), *The handbook of humanistic psychology: Leading edges in theory, research, and practice* (2nd ed., pp. 263–274). Sage.

Nasr, S. H. (1964). *Three Muslim sages*. Caravan Books.

Oram, D. (2019). De-colonizing listening: Toward an equitable approach to speech training for the actor. *Voice and Speech Review*, *13*(3), 279–297. https://doi.org/10.1080/23268263.2019.1627745

Polanyi, M. (1964). *Personal knowledge: Towards a post-critical philosophy*. Harper & Row.

Polanyi, M. (1966). *The tacit dimension*. University of Chicago Press.

Polanyi, M. (1983). *The tacit dimension*. Peter Smith.

Pouwhare, R. (2020). *Ngā Pūrākau mō Māui: Mai te patuero, te pakokitanga me te whakapēpē ki te kōrero pono, ki te whaihua whaitake, mē ngā honotanga. The Māui narratives: From Bowdlerisation, dislocation and infantilisation, to veracity, relevance and connection* [Doctoral thesis, Auckland University of Technology]. Tuwhera Open Access Theses & Dissertations. https://hdl.handle.net/10292/13307

Rahbarnia, Z., & Rouzbahani, R. (2014). Manifestation of Khorrah Light [the Divine Light] Illumination in the Iranian-Islamic architecture from artistic and mystic aspects with an emphasis on the ideas of Sheykh Shahab ad-Din Suhrawardi. *Naqshejahan-Basic Studies and New Technologies of Architecture and Planning*, *4*(1), 65–74.

Rogers, C. R. (1951). *Client-centered therapy: Its current practice, implications, and theory*. Houghton Mifflin.

Rogers, C. R. (1969). *Freedom to learn: A view of what education might become*. C. E. Merrill.

Scrivener, S. (2000). *Reflection in and on action and practice in creative-production doctoral projects in art and design.* Working Papers in Art and Design 1. https://www.herts.ac.uk/__data/assets/pdf_file/0014/12281/WPIAAD_vol1_scrivener.pdf

Sela-Smith, S. (2002). Heuristic research: A review and critique of Moustakas's method. *Journal of Humanistic Psychology, 42*(3), 53–88. https://doi.org/10.1177/00267802042003004

Shafi, F., & Bolkhari, H. (2012). تخیل هنری در حکمت اشراق سهروردی [Creativity in Suhrawardi's illuminationism]. دانشگاه تربیت مدرس تهران [Tarbiat Modares University]. https://www.sid.ir/fa/Journal/ViewPaper.aspx?ID=194243

al-Din Suhrawardi, S. (1186/2000). *The philosophy of illumination* (J. Walbridge & H. Ziai, Trans.). Brigham Young University.

Wagner, C., Kawulich, B., & Garner, M. (2012). *Doing social research: A global context.* McGraw-Hill.

Walbridge, J. (2001). *The wisdom of the mystic East: Suhrawardi and platonic orientalism.* SUNY Press.

Walbridge, J. (2011). The devotional and occult works of Suhrawardī the illuminationist. *Ishrāq: Islamic Philosophy Yearbook, 2,* 80–97.

Yazdi, M. H. I. (1992). *The principles of epistemology in Islamic philosophy: Knowledge by presence.* SUNY Press.

Ziai, H. (1990). Beyond philosophy: Suhrawardī's illuminationist path to wisdom. *Myth and Philosophy,* 215–243.

Zwanzig, R. (2009). Why must God show himself in disguise? An exploration of Sufism within Farid Attar's The Conference of the Birds. *Disguise, Deception, Trompe-l'oeil: Interdisciplinary Perspectives, 99,* 273.

4

HEURISTICS IN VISUAL ARTS ENQUIRY

F. Derek Ventling

Introduction

This chapter discusses the nature and merit of heuristics as a working methodology of visual arts in practice-led artistic enquiry. Along with an example of scholarly research, a case study of a practicing artist is presented, both of which serve to illustrate how artistic exploration may be rooted in what could be called *heuristic consciousness*.

First, my own research is described as a practice-led, creative-production exploration into *inspiration as a phenomenological experience*. Working through orchestrated sensate experiences, heuristic principles allowed the questions and the work to evolve with the continuing iterations of introspective expression. Next, I introduce contemporary artist Debbie Mackinnon, a painter whose own principles are similarly aligned with heuristic dimensions in her ongoing artistic practice. The artist continually challenges herself, disrupting her processes in order to find fresh approaches, and to discover and explore new ways of seeing the world (Schön, 1983). Investigating aspects of her artistic pursuit, we recognise an application of heuristic enquiry comparable to the scholarly realm of practice. Studying such a similarity is the focus of this chapter, and I conclude with a discussion that views heuristics in a broader, more fundamental light: as an effective approach to deepening consciousness across visual art practice.

DOI: 10.4324/9781003507758-7

Aspects of heuristics in practice-led artistic research

In this part of the chapter, I wish to explain practice-led artistic research, and then isolate and define the distinct aspects of what constitutes a heuristic framework.

During my doctorate research, I adopted heuristics as the methodology that appeared most suitable for my practice-led exploration (Ventling, 2017). The terminology *practice-led research* describes a dynamic relationship whereby research and art practices advance and develop in partnership (Mäkelä et al., 2011). Making and sensing precede thinking or theory in an iterative creative and rationalising process that fuses mode and substance in perceptive experience (Klein, 2010, para. 10). Questions are often unstructured and vague at the outset, open for the unknown to emerge. Navigating this temporal unfolding requires a methodology that remains flexible to the researcher's questions, to the shifting practice, and to the relational dynamics between these two.

Influenced by its contribution to qualitative research in the field of psychology (Douglass & Moustakas, 1985; Moustakas, 1961, 1975, 1990), a number of artistic researchers have applied a heuristic methodology as a useful framework to enable navigating complex practice-led enquiries, e.g., Ings (2011), Nimkulrat (2012), and Mäkelä and Löytönen (2015). This type of research has become a growing field of study where diverse artistic processes, artefacts, and experiences are probed to generate meaning (Arnold, 2012; Brabazon & Dagli, 2010; Candy, 2006; Frayling, 1993; Mäkelä, 2009; Scrivener, 2000). Heuristic enquiry aligns with practice-led research because it allows an iterative creative and rationalising exploratory process (Klein, 2010) to unfold, as a protean question is pursued. The research is often an immersive experiential process that arises from the practitioner's personal issue or concern.

Summarising the distinct aspects of a heuristic framework within practice-led artistic research gives this fresh meaning and a clearer definition (Ventling, 2018), thus serving as a useful guide for such practitioners. The following aspects stand as defining criteria for an artistic practice-led heuristic enquiry.

The research question

The question or concern at the outset is personally significant and existential. A heuristic enquiry represents 'an effort to know the essence of some aspect of life through the internal pathways of the self' (Douglass & Moustakas, 1985, p. 39). As such, the enquiry does not pursue a solution to a problem, but explores an issue that calls out for immersive contemplation and reflective probing. It may be something that the researcher feels is incomplete, unclear, or disassociated, and demands to be clarified. It may be an experiential realm that summons investigative curiosity. Often, the concern is not only compelling to the artistic researcher, but also holds a universal significance or deep social meaning (Hiles, 2001; Sela-Smith, 2002).

The exploratory process

A distinctly defining feature of heuristic enquiry is that it offers opportunities for variable approaches. Discoveries can be unpredictable, and these may reveal new directions. Heuristics deals with this motif, not by pre-determining a path, but by allowing one to unfold progressively. The evolving research question itself helps to orchestrate the route of exploration, and its direction is determined only by what is most effectively revelatory. As Sela-Smith asserts: '"What works" becomes the focus, and anything that makes sense can be tested. What succeeds becomes "the right thing"' (2002, p. 58).

The tacit dimension

The researcher's tacit capacity is vital to the explorative artistic process. Intuition, pre-concepts, and imagination are legitimate resources from which to draw. These actively inform the quest by giving it momentum, and they are called upon to give rise to new insights. As Polanyi declares: 'we can know more than we can tell' (1966, p. 4), and it is this form of knowing that the practitioner utilises in the research.

Experiential learning

Heuristic research 'invites the conscious, investigating self to surrender to the feelings in an experience' (Sela-Smith, 2002, p. 59). In a practice-led enquiry, the artist may dwell in experiences as part of the ongoing exploratory activity. As the practice unfolds, experiences with materials, processes, dynamics, and spaces are generated. The artist is 'concerned with providing ways of seeing and ways of being in relation to what is, was, or might be' (Scrivener, 2002, para. 44). Through deliberation and intuitive sensing, the researcher attempts to find combinations, resonances, and insights, which, in turn, edge the practice into further experiences. This experiential learning leads to growing self-awareness and self-discovery and a deeper comprehension of the enquiry (Moustakas, 1990; Schön, 1983).

Reflection and the self

The artistic researcher cannot be anything but personally involved and deeply invested in the research (Bullough & Pinnegar, 2001). Griffiths suggests that the self is inescapable, 'because the person creating, responding to, and working on, developing or evaluating performances, artefacts and practices is central to those activities' (2010, p. 185). The discoveries are therefore as much internal as they are external. Thus, the investigative pursuit becomes a reflective discourse between some form of action in practice and the research-er's reaction(s) to this. The world and the self are in constant engagement as the researcher probes their responses to experiences with immersive, intro-spective questioning. This negotiation between the practitioner and the issue or theme that is being experienced is one of the defining aspects of heuristic enquiry.

Questioning as stimulation

In heuristic enquiry, persistent questioning is habitual. This involves a dynamic and intricate engagement between the practice and the self, the creative pro-cess, and the reflective thinking, with each stimulating the other as the work and the discoveries unfold (Hiles, 2001; Kleining & Witt, 2000). Schön's term 'reflection-in-action' describes this stimulation: 'Doing extends thinking in the tests, moves and probes of experimental action, and reflection feeds on doing and its results. Each feeds the other, and each sets boundaries for the other' (1983, p. 280). As the enquiry unfolds, the research question may morph into various iterations. Accordingly, the dynamic pursuit, rather than a pre-determined objective, becomes the driver of the enquiry.

Deepening consciousness

Heuristic research is an approach that requires high levels of self-reflection to drive the questioning deeper (Douglass & Moustakas, 1985; Ings, 2011). The researcher needs to be prepared to carry 'the urgency needed to reveal and explore shadings and subtleties of meaning' (Douglass & Moustakas, 1985, p. 41). This type of exploration demands considerable personal engagement because it can challenge the extremes of perception and blur existential boundaries, setting forth what is often an emotive and exhaustive self-search (Douglass & Moustakas, 1985; Pallasmaa, 2009). Submitting fully to such an immersive and consuming investigation may destabilise the researcher emo-tionally, and this intensity needs to be considered at the outset.

Recurring external exchange

Heuristic self-reflection may limit critical thinking if it becomes isolated in and to the artist's self and their own frame and terms of reference. At distinct stages the researcher should therefore turn outward and seek external exchanges, in order to discuss and analyse the surfacing meanings. Engaging with, and being stimulated by, multiple and differing opinions in the form of critical feedback or questioning, not least through supervision and peer-review, can reveal fresh perspectives. This exposure is valuable both academically and personally because it leads to increased awareness, recognition, and elaboration of relating connections, contextual themes, overarching principles, procedural knowledge, and differing approaches (Ings, 2011; Lawson, 1980/2005; Moustakas, 1990). This, however, requires the researcher to have an acute sensitivity to timing, recognising when to shift focus and when not to do so. An external exchange carries risks because it can bring confusion and be detrimental to the flourishing of nascent research ideas that are still fragile and nebulous. The concepts may become diluted, and the researcher may become increasingly disoriented or objective (Ings, 2011; Sela-Smith, 2002).

Perspective shift

While the researcher's background and repertoire underpin the investigative enquiry, heuristics offers the opportunity to imbue this foundation with new understanding. What begins as a series of subjective musings can develop into a 'systematic and definitive exposition' (Douglass & Moustakas, 1985, p. 40). As new meanings are discovered through the research, these lead to a shift in perspective, revised beliefs, and a new sense of self. This may not only influence the future research, but also have larger social and transpersonal implications (Sela-Smith, 2002). Although each heuristic enquiry is unique and individualised, uncovered meanings can nevertheless be exchanged, compared, and generalised.

I now turn to two examples of heuristic enquiry in visual arts: the first within academic research, the second in everyday artistic practice.

An example of practice-led artistic research

In this part of the chapter, I demonstrate how a heuristic framework can affirm and enable artistic enquiry, by giving a brief description of my own doctoral research. This summary comprises three parts: the philosophical background, the practical work, and how the heuristic framework enabled this journey.

Philosophical context

My practice-led thesis dealt with the concept of inspiration as metaphysical light, and its potential influence on myself and my creative endeavour (Ventling, 2017). Eight hundred years ago, the medieval scholar Bonaventure described a path of human cognitive development along a nexus of *making, sensing, and thinking* towards *wisdom* (Hayes, 1996; Miccoli, 2001; Schumacher, 2009). From the foundation of *making*, our consciousness starts working higher up into successive realms, and inspiration is the key to this advancement. Bonaventure reasoned that this process is illuminated by metaphysical light – in modern terms this might be defined as a connective agent and a life force, providing stimulus and purpose to cognitive potential (McAdams, 1991; Noone & Houser, 2014). I could see distinct parallels between Bonaventure's concept of experientially generating higher insights, and the modes of contemporary artistic research. Addressing making and sensing *before* thinking and theory is effectively another way of describing a practice-led research process (Mäkelä et al., 2011). Additionally, Bonaventure describes how light works downwards, from the metaphorical/spiritual to the literal/corporeal, inducing transformational activity. Following Bonaventure's ideas, visible light may perhaps be understood as perceptible evidence of the unseen permeating spiritual force.

These considerations became the genesis of my investigation. My enquiry took the form of a creative-production research project, whereby the artistic practice is realised through and in artefacts (Scrivener, 2000). Making and sensing were the places from which I sought to explore Bonaventure's ideas on light experientially. I was hoping to make meaning by bringing his proposition into a contemporary studio context, creating material spaces as experiences through which to probe a phenomenological resonance.

Practice-led exploration

As the research found its momentum, I set about building large environments with an array of materials, which I then lit with a variety of light sources. I then immersed myself in these assemblages (Figure 4.1), generating situations where I could be physically embodied within them, simply dwelling in light's catalytic capacity, and discovering meanings by 'focusing on the feeling dimension of personal experience' (Sela-Smith, 2002, p. 63).

Over a number of experiments, I kept changing, re-orchestrating, and combining materials (such as silver leaf, sheet metal, glass, fabric, sequins, water, wax, paint, cardboard, etc). These mediators harboured capacities and vitalities of their own (Bennett, 2010; Mäkelä & Löytönen, 2015), and I let them teach me how their reflection, radiance, opacity, and luminosity was influenced by light. Increasingly, I was able to develop my sensitivity to their emotive qualities and consider what they might contribute to the theme of the research and the new visual language I was trying to develop.

I tried to capture intimate moments of resonance spontaneously with the camera, attempting to find a form of visual expression beyond literal substance and shape. As the experimental conjunctions evolved, I collected a large number of photographs of what I called *Momentaufnahmen* (images of distinct spatio-temporal moments, Figure 4.2). Each of these images represented an ephemeral constellation, a distinct existential encounter – that brief

FIGURE 4.1 Immersive environment.

Source: © F. Derek Ventling, 2014.

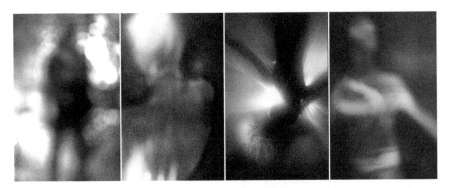

FIGURE 4.2 A series of self-portrait *Momentaufnahmen.*

Source: © F. Derek Ventling, 2015–2016.

glimpse of understanding whereby my rapport with permeating light made intuitive sense.

My self-portraits were drawn from my interaction with light as a fluid process of continuous unfolding. Through the physical immersion in the combination of material forces and the energy of light, I became aware how this transient relationship altered my perception and, seemingly, my corporeity. Atmospheric changes began to affect the way I perceived and experienced my self and being. Details of my appearance became more indistinct or prominent, my body constantly transforming its boundaries as I moved within the immersive assemblages. From this sensate embodiment I developed my thinking about Bonaventure's light as a distinct force, a permeating material, or an omnipresent influencing quality.

To communicate my research findings and generate reflective feedback from peers, I felt it was important to show the ephemeral qualities of light in a similar manner to my own exploration: that is, as an *experience*. I was not content with only organising paper presentations, or curated exhibitions of printed photographs. From this realisation the idea was born to bring the sense of deliquescent transformation to the presentation, and design experiential spaces for peers. Because of its flexible nature, heuristic enquiry enabled this approach, and allowed me to shift the focus (Griffiths, 2010). Although I continued with probing immersive encounters in assemblages, I added to this the design and modelling of experiential installation spaces, and devising ways to give my images an ephemeral presence.

The three designed installations that were built at distinct intervals along the research trajectory became a part of the research where I considered how to translate my captured encounters to an emotive spatial composition. I wanted to create unique atmospheric spaces that would be large enough for the viewers to dwell inside, thereby inviting their own immersive and emotive experience of light as an influential agency. Feedback could then become an exchange of experiential observations – and, even richer, a discussion around interpretations and feelings. I knew I was trying to 'make visible an invisible, metaphysical concept' (Klee, quoted in Read, 1974, p. 182), and therefore the emotive aspects of apprehension and the sensing itself were of particular relevance.

The first installation featured large fabric banners hung in a stark and darkened room. A projected selection of my images played across these banners, fading in and out while the audience moved within the space and interacted with the oversized images and their own shadow play. The second installation took the concept of immersion further. The space was designed and built as its own room, allowing only a singular viewer entry at a time. The floor and all side walls were covered in silver leaf, its subtle reflection seemingly dissolving physical boundaries, and heightening tactile and visual levels of enigmatic engagement. A slowly evolving sequence of my images was projected on to the front wall from the outside, so the space remained uncluttered. Viewers were enveloped by the images permeating into the space.

This final installation was again built as an immersive space for a singular viewer, more architecturally designed, with its angled walls and ceiling also clad in silver leaf. A sequence of images was projected from outside the space onto the entire front fabric panel, in order to permeate and be experienced from the inside. This space was higher and shorter than the second installation space, producing larger images at a closer distance to the viewer, enhancing the embodied sensation.

As the thesis, the articulation, and the imagery developed through enquiry and feedback, so did the conceptual planning of the final, cumulative installation. The images were the only source of light, so, as one photograph dissolved into the next, light ebbed and pooled, shifting boundaries and shapes within the space (Figure 4.3). Earlier feedback suggested preserving a meditative atmosphere without resorting to didactic content; this allowed every viewer to contemplate their own phenomenological relationship to light, and to consider its mysterious influence from their personal perspective.

Heuristic enquiry

This practice-led research represented a personal journey of experiential discovery that combined my situated artistic knowledge, philosophy, and sensate, embodied impressions.

It was aligned to a heuristic enquiry in several ways. The research question was in essence a deep-seated, existentialist one. It was not a problem seeking a solution, but rather a call to negotiate my inner feelings towards experienced spirituality. The question was broad at the outset of the work, and the creative output oscillated over a wide area with fluctuating quality until it gradually gained more focus.

I knew that, due to the iterative nature of the experiments, the exploratory process needed to be flexible. The practice of making and documenting material experiences was unpredictable. Favourably resonant outcomes drove the reflective thinking and generated new insights. These subjective responses in turn stimulated further questions and determined further directions and experiments. The heuristic framework allowed for this shifting as an integral part of the momentum.

Furthermore, the nature of this investigation called upon my tacit comprehension to help guide the exploration. Working towards an aspect of spiritual awareness through an embodied state required a constant dialogue between the intuitive and the physical, and the heuristic methodology provided the basis to foster this engagement. As the feeling dimension drew from my subjective self, my repertoire, history, and values, I was able to reflect on these surfacing questions and my consciousness deepened. As my thoughts permeated the artefactual constructs, the discoveries were as much internal as they were external.

Although the research developed through pathways of the self, eventually its externalisation into artefacts and manifest spaces allowed me to share my thinking with viewers. At certain stages along the trajectory my personal perceptions, meanings, and interpretations were communicated to viewers in the form of designed installations. The viewers were invited to experience and respond – and through this process, provide valuable

FIGURE 4.3 Interior of the third installation.

Source: © Derek Ventling, 2017.

feedback by adding their perspectives. This kept the enquiry resolute, as the opinions of others were evaluated, and either added to the thinking, or helped to refine parts of it.

Artistic pursuit – A case study of Debbie Mackinnon

In this part of the chapter, I discuss how a practising artist works and how many aspects of her practice are relatable to a heuristic system of enquiry. This overview contains two parts: an introduction to the artist, and an introduction to her methods of working.

Contemporary Australian landscape artist Debbie Mackinnon is a painter who rose through a foundation of illustration and book design in her formative years. She resides in Sydney where she runs a collective studio space 'ME Artspace' with other artists and is a member of several (physical and online) communities of painters with common interests. As an educator, Mackinnon is in high demand to run workshops for several specialist international art travel agencies, and it was in this capacity that I was able to organise and participate in a five-day workshop that she led (Figure 4.4).

FIGURE 4.4 Debbie Mackinnon, at her 'Fast and Loose' workshop in Leigh, New Zealand.

Source: © Derek Ventling, 2023.

At 70 years of age, and with a wealth of experience in pedagogy, colour, and painting, Mackinnon sustains a restless, energetic curiosity. She aligns her artistic ethos with that of Richard Diebenkorn, the late American painter. Diebenkorn wrote a list of points for beginning a painting, one of which is: 'Attempt what is not certain. Certainty may or may not come later. It may then be a valuable delusion' (quoted in Cohen & Baker, 2015). Mackinnon maintains that the search for new expression must overrule a yearning for constant success, and she consequently seeks to disrupt her practice through as many means as possible. She will purposefully forego a routine for risky techniques. Curiosity is the stimulant, she says, and the constant joy of *learning through play* keeps her motivation and momentum high. Opening herself to new possibilities and avenues, the artistic outcomes become dynamic and surprising, and generate further creative opportunities. This, in her view, is the paradigm for sustaining a robust and invigorating artistic practice. As a commercial artist, Mackinnon's work is constantly changing because she is more interested in advancing her unique form of practice than in selling similar paintings. A finished form finds itself on the journey of exploration, and it is not fixed at the outset. This allows an attitude of fluidity or risk-taking in practice.

Processes

Mackinnon's workshops are a distinct expression of how she works in practice. Apart from the pedagogical aspect, her modes of enquiry are the same. Thus, the days spent with her constituted an intimate sharing of making, sensing, and reflection, as an extension of Mackinnon's personality. Participants were urged to abandon old habits and approach art making as a discourse with circumstance rather than a pursuit of a fixed outcome, as she led them through a variety of her own experimental processes. In warm-up sketches, the charcoal sticks were moved from one hand to the other. Contour drawings were done blind, without looking at the paper. Papers were turned upside down to continue working on them. Sheets were torn into pieces to be reassembled differently. Driftwood, dried seaweed, and other objects were collected on walks to the beach, and these were used as brushes for large scale paintings. Landscapes were painted outdoors with a restricted colour palette of acrylics, then torn apart, with some pieces collaged together as a basis for further painting. Paintings were done off earlier paintings, creating a succession of adapted interpretations. Teams worked together on large A1 paper sheets across the floor, using brushes tied to sticks to paint a gestural series of intersecting lines intuitively. These sheets were then cut and folded to make concertina booklets as visual diaries, and these in turn were worked back into with paint, pastel, and markers. One- and two-colour gel plate monoprints were produced from natural objects such as shells, cones, bark, and leaves, and torn shreds of these textures were applied to augment the colours of other paintings. Mackinnon's workshop served as a reminder that visual art is a rich field for exploration, and art making should remain a continuous inquisitive endeavour.

Applying a heuristic lens

There are remarkable similarities between Mackinnon's processes and the processes and underlying concepts of heuristic enquiry within an academic context. Considering her processes through the lens of heuristic enquiry, the following aspects are of interest.

The question

For Mackinnon, the inherent question, or quest, is how to continue seeing the world in a new light, and in her way. This existential desire underpins her practice every day, encouraging landscape and still life paintings to emerge as personal responses to her experiences (Merleau-Ponty, 1948/2004). Mackinnon knows that this question remains indefinite, yet although it has no answer, it engenders a lifetime of harbouring an adventurous attitude and listening for meanings (Douglass & Moustakas, 1985).

The exploratory process

Artworks are constructed and deconstructed, layered, collaged, and repainted – Mackinnon utilises these experimental techniques purposefully in order to work beyond the confines of traditional processes, and in order to discover new avenues of expression. True to the heuristic nature of her processes, she welcomes serendipitous findings into her experiments as the reflection-in-action progresses (Schön, 1983).

Experiential learning

In her workshop, participants found working in such a variety of mediums and techniques with experimental abandon was exciting, grounding… and frustrating. Suspending linearity was a provocation that generated an internal conflict within participants. Mackinnon understands this conflict, because participants are generally more familiar with modes of work focused on outcomes. Committing to Mackinnon's disruptions required, as Sela-Smith puts it, a 'leap into the unknown' (2002, p. 54). Once the anxiety of the unknown (Carabine, 2013) was removed, spaces were discovered that allowed further ideas and actions to flourish. This effectively constitutes a reprogramming to heuristic process, allowing the unknown to reveal itself along an experiential journey, rather than pre-determining an outcome.

The tacit dimension

For Mackinnon, a finished piece reveals itself through the feeling dimension, a knowledge gained through a myriad of life, cultural, and artistic experiences. She slows down the mark making, adding only a few deliberate strokes as she reflects on a piece of work and lets it speak to her. She will repeatedly engage with this piece over a number of days or weeks, utilising her tacit sense as the underlying decisive agency – much the same as the heuristic research practitioner. The tacit dimension is what gives Mackinnon's process what Douglass and Moustakas refer to as 'energy, distinctiveness, form and direction' (1985, p. 49).

Reflective questioning

As a practising artist, immersed in her own work, Mackinnon's output calls on her to continually reflect on what she makes manifest. With her experience in materials, media, colours and processes, Mackinnon is constantly asking 'What if...?'. This iterative dynamic process of questioning, testing, and learning is what drives her work forward. As Klein points out: 'Artistic experience is a form of reflection' (2010, para. 15), and it is this sensory and emotional perception that assists with navigating the explorative journey.

Deepening consciousness

Negotiating an ongoing dialogue between her internal self and her emerging work, Mackinnon cultivates her subjective stance. As emotive responses resonate throughout the experience of making each artwork, Mackinnon's deeper understanding of her self is developed, and with it her visual and evaluative articulation.

Conclusion

Although Mackinnon's practice is a singular case, I believe that it is not dissimilar to the explorative practice of other visual artists. Many parallels can be found between her working methods and those of a heuristic research enquiry. As Schön says, 'When someone reflects in action, they become a researcher in the practice context' (1983, p. 68). Thus, if we remove the academic implications of the term 'researcher' to include all practice-led artistic exploration, the heuristic thinking remains just as robust. Even without the scholarly terminology, we might find many artistic enquiries that apply a similar heuristic frame of working. Mackinnon, for example, had not heard of the term heuristics before I mentioned it to her, yet she had already understood and embraced its application.

If heuristic enquiry is recognised as an agency of artistic exploration within and beyond research, we might ask if this is because of its inherently human qualities. This would seem sensible, since it is a methodology and method that enables and facilitates the human-centric experiential pursuit of discovery. Heuristics understands creative processes that deal with our imperfect yet typical human features: emotional involvement, experienced immersion, uncertainty, impulsivity, dissatisfaction, and confusion within contingent and provisional situations – and can help to put these to productive use. Throughout this chapter I have used words such as 'help', 'assist', 'enable', and 'allow' when describing a heuristic enquiry. These denote an inherently supportive openness that embraces and works with human curiosity.

Arguably then, heuristic thinking might represent a framework that appears to sit at the core of artistic endeavour. We could ask if the heuristic process might thus be acknowledged as an active form of creative consciousness, inasmuch as our explorative quest for understanding is a characteristically human way of existing. After all, we live a life of questioning, exploring, learning, imagining, and pursuing evolving ideas in the face of unpredictability.

Within this consciousness, artistic practitioners may be familiar with some of the heuristic aspects already present in their own modes of seeking meaning through experience. Recognising these aspects, their qualities, and their relationship to each other and to us as invested practitioners, gives us a valuable paradigm to intensify our creative journeys. The heuristic framework makes our tacit understanding more explicit because it draws it into our awareness, validating the reflective endeavour, making our processes more rigorous, and enabling us to drive our artistic practice to deeper levels.

References

Arnold, J. (2012). Practice-led research: Creative activity, academic debate and intellectual rigour. *Higher Education Studies*, *2*(2), 9–23. https://doi.org/10.5539/hes.v2n2p9

Bennett, J. (2010). *Vibrant matter: A political ecology of things*. Duke University Press.

Brabazon, T., & Dagli, Z. (2010). Putting the doctorate into practice, and the practice into doctorates: Creating a new space for quality scholarship through creativity. *Nebula: A Journal of Multidisciplinary Scholarship*, *7*(1), 23–43.

Bullough, R., & Pinnegar, S. (2001). Guidelines for quality in autobiographical forms of self-study research. *Educational Researcher*, *30*(3), 13–21. https://doi.org/10.3102/0013189X030003013

Candy, L. (2006). *Practice based research: A guide*. Creativity and Cognition Studios, UTS Sydney. https://www.creativityandcognition.com/wp-content/uploads/2011/04/PBR-Guide-1.1-2006.pdf

Carabine, J. (2013). *Creativity, art and learning – A psycho-social exploration of uncertainty*. Blackwell Publishing.

Cohen, L., & Baker, H. (2015, March 13). *Notes to myself: Diebenkorn's 10 rules for painting*. Royal Academy. https://www.royalacademy.org.uk/article/diebenkorn-ten-rules

Douglass, B. G., & Moustakas, C. (1985). Heuristic inquiry – The internal search to know. *Journal of Humanistic Psychology, 25*(3), 39–55. https://doi.org/10.1177/0022167885253004

Frayling, C. (1993). Research in art and design. *Royal College of Art Research Papers, 1*(1), 1–5.

Griffiths, M. (2010). Research and the self. In M. Biggs & H. Karlsson (Eds.), *The Routledge companion to research in the arts* (pp. 167–185). Routledge.

Hayes, Z. (1996). *On the reduction of the arts to theology: Works of Saint Bonaventure* (Vol. 1). Franciscan Institute Publications.

Hiles, D. (2001, October). *Heuristic inquiry and transpersonal research* [Paper presentation]. CPPE, London. https://psy.dmu.ac.uk/drhiles/HIpaper.htm

Ings, W. (2011). Managing heuristics as a method of inquiry in autobiographical graphic design theses. *International Journal of Art & Design Education, 30*(2), 226–241. https://doi.org/10.1111/j.1476-8070.2011.01699.x

Klein, J. (2010). What is artistic research? https://www.researchcatalogue.net/view/15292/15293

Kleining, G., & Witt, H. (2000). The qualitative heuristic approach: A methodology for discovery in psychology and the social sciences. Rediscovering the method of introspection as an example. *Forum Qualitative Sozialforschung/Forum: Qualitative Social Research, 1*. https://doi.org/10.17169/fqs-1.1.1123

Lawson, B. (1980/2005). *How designers think*. Architectural Press.

Mäkelä, M. (2009). The place and the product(s) of making in practice-led research. In N. Nimkulrat & T. O'Riley (Eds.), *Reflections and connections: On the relationship between creative practices, knowledge and academic research* (pp. 29–38). University of Art and Design Helsinki.

Mäkelä, M., & Löytönen, T. (2015). Enhancing material experimentation in design education. In R. Vande Zande, E. Bohemia, & I. Digranes (Eds.), *Proceedings of the 3rd International Conference for Design Education Researchers* (pp. 168–183). Aalto University.

Mäkelä, M., Nimkulrat, N., Dash, D., & Nsenga, F. (2011). On reflecting and making in artistic research practice. *Journal of Research Practice, 7*(1). https://jrp.icaap.org/index.php/jrp/article/view/280

McAdams, S. (1991). *The aesthetics of light: A critical examination of St. Bonaventure's doctrine of light in view of his aesthetics* [Unpublished doctoral dissertation]. Pontificia Universita Gregoriana.

Merleau-Ponty, M. (1948/2004). *The world of perception* (O. Davis, Trans.). Routledge.

Miccoli, L. (2001). Two thirteenth-century theories of light: Robert Grosseteste and Saint Bonaventure. *Semiotica, 2001*(136), 69–84. https://doi.org/10.1515/semi.2001.099

Moustakas, C. (1961). *Loneliness*. Prentice-Hall.

Moustakas, C. (1975). *The touch of loneliness*. Prentice-Hall.

Moustakas, C. (1990). *Heuristics research: Design, methodology and applications*. Sage. https://doi.org/10.4135/9781412995641

Nimkulrat, N. (2012). Hands-on intellect: Integrating craft practice into design research. *International Journal of Design, 6*(3), 1–14. https://www.ijdesign.org/index.php/IJDesign/article/viewFile/1228/520

Noone, T., & Houser, R. E. (2014). Saint Bonaventure. In E. Zalta (Ed.), *The Stanford encyclopedia of philosophy* (Winter ed.). https://plato.stanford.edu/archives/win2014/entries/bonaventure/

Pallasmaa, J. (2009). *The thinking hand: Existential and embodied wisdom in architecture.* J. Wiley & Sons.

Polanyi, M. (1966). *The tacit dimension.* Doubleday.

Read, H. (1974). *A concise history of modern painting.* Thames and Hudson.

Schön, D. (1983). *The reflective practitioner: How professionals think in action.* Ashgate.

Schumacher, L. (2009). *Divine illumination in Augustinian and Franciscan thought* [Doctoral dissertation, University of Edinburgh]. Edinburgh Research Archive. https://hdl.handle.net/1842/5816

Scrivener, S. (2000). Reflection in and on action and practice in creative-production doctoral projects in art and design. Working Papers in Art and Design 1. https://www.herts.ac.uk/__data/assets/pdf_file/0014/12281/WPIAAD_vol1_scrivener.pdf

Scrivener, S. (2002). The art object does not embody a form of knowledge. Working Papers in Art and Design 2. https://www.herts.ac.uk/__data/assets/pdf_file/0008/12311/WPIAAD_vol2_scrivener.pdf

Sela-Smith, S. (2002). Heuristic research: A review and critique of Moustakas's method. *Journal of Humanistic Psychology, 42*(3), 53–88. https://doi.org/10.1177/00267802042003004

Ventling, F. D. (2017). *Illuminativa – The resonance of the unseen* [Doctoral thesis, Auckland University of Technology]. Tuwhera Open Access Theses & Dissertations. https://hdl.handle.net/10292/10414

Ventling, F. D. (2018), Heuristics – A framework to clarify practice-led research. *DAT Journal, 3*(2), 122–156. https://doi.org/10.29147/dat.v3i2.88

5

DOCUMENTING GRIEF

A heuristic inquiry

Elizabeth Hoyle

Introduction

This chapter considers the role and nature of heuristic inquiry in the development of a documentary *Untitled Grief* (Hoyle, 2023), in which I explored ways of translating grief states into a visual and sonic narrative (Figure 5.1). Positioning myself as an 'inside researcher' (Kirpitchenko & Voloder, 2014) who examines a question that was both personally significant and existential, I unpack how a heuristic inquiry enabled me to navigate internal pathways of the self, in advance of my interpreting other people's shared, reflective narratives of grief later in the inquiry. Specifically, I discuss how methodologically a heuristic approach enabled me to move beyond many traditional, industry-based practices (with their emphasis on the strategic use of time and resources), towards an engagement in which emphasis was placed on activating flexible forms of exploration and heightening potentials for discovery. The chapter considers heuristic inquiry as a conceptual framework (Douglass & Moustakas, 1985; Moustakas, 1990; Ventling, 2018) that engages intuitive questioning which enables similarities, analogies, or homologies to surface while the researcher is processing and generating artistic data (Kleining & Witt, 2000). In applying this framework, I discuss four principles: embracing uncertainty and serendipity; extending periods of indwelling; pursuing a poetic sensibility; and developing a research orientation predicated on the Māori concept of *aroha* (showing consideration, love, and respect).

DOI: 10.4324/9781003507758-8

FIGURE 5.1   Title plate from the short, animated, autobiographical documentary *Untitled Grief.*

Source: Hoyle (2023).

Note: The full six-minute film can be accessed at: https://vimeo.com/847658432 [Password: untitled].

Forerunners

In 1991, I made my first documentary, *A Drop in the Ocean* (Hoyle, 1991). It was produced while I was a student at Film and Television School in Australia. At that time, I was a carer for a group of young people with cerebral palsy. While working with them I had observed high levels of thoughtlessness and discrimination they experienced. I wanted to find a way of making an empathic film about, for, *and with* them. I collected multiple photographs and, over a period of eight months, I began filming with whatever camera equipment I could access. The completed documentary employed video, 16mm film, and still images integrated with observational footage, performance, and interviews. I avoided interviewing health experts, instead positioning the young people as experts on their own world. This work was my earliest attempt to hold a mirror up to a complex human condition by illustrating individuals' realities.

The following year I approached a centre for homelessness in inner city Melbourne. They resided at a place called The Gill. This was a facility made up of clinker brick buildings that were tucked away near Victoria Market, close to the centre of town. A cobbled laneway separated the day centre from the hostel and administration buildings. Daily, men of all ages and walks of life gathered outside, smoking, sitting, talking. Today the building has been converted into luxury apartments, but when I was working there, it was a realm of extraordinary, marginalised stories. Before making the documentary I volunteered at the facility, and I came to see the difference between a 'social issue' and the complex humanity behind it. As I gained the trust of the men and the organisers of the community, they allowed me to begin filming their world. *Down at the Gill* (Hoyle, 1992) took approximately seven months to make. I worked at the centre most days, just sitting with the men, chatting and drinking coffee. I told everyone I encountered about wanting to make a film. Being in the world of these men for extended periods of time, sharing something of myself whilst being honest about my intentions, became a way of working that consumed time but also linked filmmaking with compassion and care beyond the commercial production of a story. The approach involved a kind of immersion, not in an issue but in the beauty and vulnerability of people's lives. As a consequence, we collaborated on story content and representation, and my production process became a form of embodiment where time was marked by need rather than a budget. Storytelling moved from observational recording to a form of untemplated development where anxious formulae were dissolved and space was made for listening, watching, dwelling, reflection, revisiting, and experimentation. The finished documentary was constructed from recorded conversations between the men at the centre. Occasionally I formed part of these discussions, so my presence and relationships with the men were visible in the final work.

Set against this world was a realm of commercial practice where I formed part of crews who produced dramatic work inside the constraints of time, schedules, and the pressure of perfection. Here, the needs of production exerted control over the story. In this world responsibilities to and for larger crews and prescribed resources shaped what could be envisaged. I found this way of working difficult, and as a consequence the film projects I directed privately progressed into two, longer form documentary research projects, *Waiting for Wood* (Hoyle, 2000) and *Night Workers* (Hoyle, 2001). While *Waiting for Wood* centred on the production of X-rated films in Australia, *Night Workers* involved interwoven portraits of night nurses, tugboat and dock workers (whose job was to retrieve suicides from the Westgate bridge), 'stringers' (night journalists), traffic controllers, and 24-hour café operators. While the second project attracted development funding, a conflict arose between my desire for depth and production constraints. The story required time to understand the layers and nuances of what I was discovering. I was also occupied with considerations about the safety of the participants, their feelings, their trust, and my desire to enable them to veto the inclusion of anything in the film about which they felt uncomfortable. Such considerations do not work well in commercial documentary production. I realised that, constrained by schedules, budgets, executive producers, and the expectations of broadcasters and distributors, my approaches to documentary storytelling required rethinking. The more I dwelt inside complex human stories, the less at ease I felt with established approaches.

Accidentally heuristic

Returning to the academy, I enrolled in a master's degree in documentary making. I was searching for a different environment in which to explore ways of depicting the human experience. During this time, I made a film called *16mm Maxwell* (Hoyle, 2006). This documentary was a first-person account about returning home. Inside a road movie, my father and I explored the rural heartland of New Zealand, discovering an amateur filmmaking community in my local town and, specifically, a local cinephile called Maxwell. Positioning myself as the narrator, I guided the story, comprising interviews interspersed with personal impressions. Although at the time I did not know the term, I approached the film heuristically, examining my desire to be a filmmaker, the difficulties of our family dynamics, and the history of filmmaking in a rural province. The work was exploratory, open, and flexible. It was driven by a strong desire for discovery. I would assemble multiple edits, watch the cut then re-edit material, adding or subtracting footage and narration. I rewrote and recorded the voiceover several times until I had found a structure for the story. The process required a state of focused immersion in the evolving archi-tecture of story, where editing and recording became a dialogue with poten-tial. My work improved because I was able to bring to the story deep levels of consideration inside flexible timelines that facilitated reflection, questioning, and iterative experimentation.

After the completion of my master's degree, I remained hungry for approaches that might afford greater flexibility and depth of discovery. At this time, I had begun teaching screen production at a university and I found myself advising students to explore stories that were personally significant. In this environment, I was surrounded by scholar-filmmakers and crews who asked deep questions about process. During this period, I began directing a longitudinal documentary about my transgender friend Geena. This was a work without a template, but it relied on elevated levels of reflection to draw out a story that was protean in nature. Unrestrained by time schedules or fixed budgets I was able to work in a fluid manner that meant I could journey into the subtlety and nuances of my friend's narrative.

It was at this time that I was introduced to heuristic inquiry. In 2015, work-ing as a sound recordist on a colleague's doctoral documentary, I witnessed how she articulated her process. For her, heuristic inquiry functioned as a foundation for excavating deep insight into the lived experience of raising a child with schizophrenia. Her work was seen from the perspective of a film-maker listening to the stories of other people who were facing similar chal-lenges. Witnessing a methodology applied to the practice of documentary making caused me to think more deeply about systems of inquiry. As I began reading research that had adopted heuristic inquiry, I became aware of several heuristic studies that had used this approach to understanding the nature of human trauma. Significant among these were Clark Moustakas' inquiry into loneliness (1961), and Sandy Sela-Smith's self-study of sexual abuse (1998).

The system of inquiry was one of recognition that may be aligned to Osborne's recollection that:

> Much of what I discovered was somewhat known to me in a tacit, raw, unformed, pre-conscious level. However, the... heuristic process, birthing from pre-conscious to conscious explication, allowed the raw material of experience and tacit knowing to transform into something processable, and I could apprehend these dynamics with increased wholeness and clarity.
>
> (Osborne, 2023, p. i)

The action of heuristics in documentary practice

In 2021 I began a doctoral study that explored ways in which a documentary filmmaker might interpret narratives of grief through animated images and sound. In adopting this approach, I was trying to find ways of developing heightened levels of resonance in storytelling. In the study, I wanted to draw together my professional experience, my thinking about my heuristic inquiry, and the experienced nature of loss. Here, I briefly consider this in terms of the heuristic concepts of identifying with the focus of inquiry and immersion.

Identifying with the focus of inquiry

I had always been curious about death. As a small child when weekends arrived, I would ask to be driven to the cemetery. At the age of 12, a close school friend was killed in an accident. This became my first encounter with grief. Towards the end of 2020, COVID-19 took the mothers of two of my closest friends. I had known these women for over 30 years. The death of my aunt, who had been my carer during my childhood, occurred in May 2022. Now, grief is something that I anticipate. It has many guises, and it is experienced in different ways by different people, yet it is something that we all have in common.

When embarking on the project I began asking questions like: what does my grief look like? What is its aural texture? How do I feel when I lose someone I love? Is it possible to visualise such a thing beyond simply holding a camera up to a person's face and filming them answering questions?

Immersion

I had seen in colleagues' work how they had used immersion in various ways to gain deeper insights into an issue or topic. Hiles (2002) proposes that the heuristic researcher begins with an immersive process in which they yield to an inquiry. Researchers such as Sela-Smith (1998, 2002), Kleining and Witt (2000), Ings (2011, 2018), Ventling (2018), and Najafi (2023a) all suggest that in a state of immersion and surrender the heuristic researcher engages with sensitive and continual questioning, seeking diverse perspectives that might enhance chances of enrich discovery.

The production of my first film, *Untitled Grief* (Hoyle, 2023), began with a series of autobiographic interviews through which I explored the memories and emotions surrounding the loss of loved ones. The central focus of these became the death of my grandmother 45 years ago. For these recordings I used a very simple set and lighting rig, and worked with a colleague who was a cinematographer. My colleague asked me a series of focused questions and prompted me to expand on my responses. Because the first recording had poor sound, we shot a second body of work for which I had redesigned a set of new questions that were a response to hearing how distinctively my responses had utilised metaphors and visual description (of which I had not been aware of until I listened to myself giving accounts of past experiences).

My experience of being interviewed heightened how vulnerable future participants in the project might be. The encounter underscored the importance of ensuring that they could opt out of questions and take time out whenever needed. During this period, I also realised how useful it was for me to work with a grief counsellor, and in this relationship I witnessed my grief again and again as I worked through the structure of the storytelling. When it became difficult, I wandered away and looked at images or went walking, returning only when I felt that I was ready.

The process of gathering filmed footage involved four shoots. Rather than simply edit this material, I tried transcribing the data and rewriting the documentary in the form of a script. I drafted scenes for each part of the narration and created visual storyboards. As I progressed with this experiment I collected copyright-free illustrations, sound, and family archives from various online websites. These eventually became a palette that allowed me to translate my words into animated, collaged sequences. Thus, while the monologue comprised direct recordings from interviews, the iconography was a step removed from autobiographical depiction. In the liminal space between the aural account and orchestrated fragments of anonymous imagery, I began to construct a documentary voice for something vulnerable.

Working with these two threads in an immersive state, I engaged in reflective dialogue with the research question and the emerging hypotheses (Ings, 2011; Moustakas, 1990), by engaging in a process that Kleining and Witt describe as seeking 'similarities, accordance, analogies or homologies with the most diverse and varied data' (2000, para. 5).

The emergence of principles

I began the project by working with Kleining and Witt's four rules for optimising the chances of discovery in a heuristic inquiry, because I noted their influential use in other doctoral projects in which storytellers had worked with

TABLE 5.1 Four rules for optimising chances for discovery in a heuristic inquiry (Kleining & Witt, 2000) compared with four principles developed for *Untitled Grief* (Hoyle, 2023)

Rules for heightening discovery in heuristic inquiry (Kleining & Witt, 2000)	Principles developed while creating Untitled Grief (Hoyle, 2023)
Maintaining openness to the fluidity of the topic	Consciously engaging uncertainty and serendipity
Preparedness to embrace change	
Willingness to adopt a variation of perspectives	Extending indwelling and flexibility as a way of expanding perspectives
Unearthing parallels, patterns, and similarities in data	Emboldening poetic sensibility
	Actioning *aroha* (care, respect, and love and reserving judgement)

visualising narratives (Brannigan, 2019; Ings, 2006; Najafi, 2023a; Sinfield, 2020; Tavares, 2019). Although each rule (see Table 5.1) is designed to operate in relation to the others, the first and second rules connect the researcher and the research in a mutual relationship, while the third and fourth rules connect them (the researcher) to the methods of data collection and analysis. However, as I progressed with the study and Kleining and Witt's rules as I reshaped the creative work, a unique relationship emerged between myself as the artistic researcher, and the specific nature of the research. Because one of the qualities of a heuristic inquiry is its ability to responsively adapt to the evolving nature of a research question (Douglass & Moustakas, 1985; Ings, 2011; Kenny, 2012), the context of the inquiry resulted in distinctive shifts in emphasis.

As the documentary developed, I recognised that I was being guided by four principles (Table 5.1): consciously engaging with uncertainty and serendipity; extending periods of indwelling; emboldening poetic sensibility; and actioning *aroha*.

I now turn to a discussion of how these three principles shaped the inquiry.

Consciously engaging uncertainty and serendipity

Given that throughout a heuristic inquiry, multiple factors will cause the study to be destabilised and change, I needed to find ways of utilising uncertainty. In this regard, Kleining and Witt's first rule for optimising the chances of discovery in heuristic inquiry proposes that the researcher must maintain openness and embrace the mutability of the topic.

Beghetto and Jaeger suggest that uncertainty is 'an undeniable and indelible feature of learning and life' (2022, p. 1). They observe that this can be disquieting, thereby activating both apprehension and insecurity. In a similar vein, Carabine (2013) observes that feelings associated with unfamiliar territories and constant change may also trigger artistic immobility. Although such anxieties can generate uncertainty, Beghetto (2021) suggests that if inculcated into practice, they can expand exploration and novelty so long as the researcher is prepared to embrace the discomfort. As an extension of this observation, both Beghetto (2021, 2022) and Runco (2022) propose that uncertainty is actually a requisite for creativity, and integral to nourishing thinking and prompting exploration.

At the beginning of my project, uncertainty surfaced in multiple ways because I was examining distressing memories and emotions, learning new technologies, and working in an academic as distinct from a professional environment.

The emotional experience of grief has neither a script nor a use-by date; Parkes (2016), Lloyd (2017), Holinger (2020), and Bonanno and Kaltman (2001) all note that grief can be a traumatic journey. Unlike many of my past professional projects, I chose to enter the production phase without a script or outline. In so doing, I was embracing the risk of exploring difficult emotions without a roadmap. Being simultaneously a director and interview subject was also a new experience, and it required that I come to terms with my self-consciousness. I felt uncertain about answering my questions in the interviews and I was anxious about my ability to integrate sound design and collaged imagery into an articulate account of what I was feeling. As a consequence, I had to 'engage in a new form of reasoning' (Beghetto, 2021, p. 2), where uncertainty was treated as a positive attribute because, as Beghetto (2021) suggests, if reframed, it can be 'marked by multiple characteristics [including] openness, nonlinearity, perspectivism and future orientation' (p. 76). Accordingly, I began to trust in the potential of experimentation and questioning, rather than relying on a previsioned outcome.

As I began synthesising segments of the interviews I explored the potential of new technologies, trialling animation templates, rotoscoping, and motion graphics. In this state of uncertainty, I also gathered a collection of digital materials, amassing hundreds of copyright-free images, video, and sound segments that resonated with my experiences of loss. From these, I began composing combinations of disparate elements, and inside their surface disparities, I explored harmony through uncertain associations (Figure 5.2).

When working on the documentary, this preparedness to change took a distinctive form. Early in the creative process, I noticed that many of my most productive decisions resulted from letting go of formulaic responses and opening myself up to the potentials of the serendipitous. When I did this, my tacit knowledge emerged, providing opportunities to 'find' answers to difficult creative problems. Although discoveries appeared to be accidental, on closer consideration I realised that they occurred because I was consciously holding myself open to variation, unexpected connection, and an accrued sense of potential that had many of its roots in posteriori knowledge.

Kleining and Witt's second rule for optimising discovery is also related to the productive management of uncertainty. They proposed that a heuristic researcher must be prepared to consciously embrace change throughout a project and increasingly this occurred because I altered my attitude towards the serendipitous.

The word serendipity was coined by Horace Walpole in reference to the Persian parable of the Three Princesses of Serendip who made discoveries through sagacity and wit (Walpole, 1754/1937–1983).

Although De Rond notes that serendipity has been conventionally framed as 'chance coincidence, luck or providence' (2014, p. 342), when viewed as a capability in research, it has also been acknowledged as an agent of discovery (Andel, 1994; Fine & Deegan, 1996; Kennedy et al., 2022; Merton & Barber, 2011; Pearce, 1912; Ross & Copeland, 2022). Thus, serendipity can be viewed as an aptitude that heightens the capacity to see connections that others might not perceive. De Rond (2014) proposes that this facility melds the researcher's depth of knowledge with their perceptiveness. Glăveanu (2022) suggests that serendipity is likely to emerge if the researcher taps consciously into a state of inquisitiveness and wonderment. This approach, he argues, activates the material under consideration in addition to the researcher's social and cultural domains, and what surfaces is not an accident, but rather an unforeseen perception that springs from the flow of events and enables the researcher to uncover novelty and the unexpected.

FIGURE 5.2 Screen grab from *Untitled Grief* showing fragments taken from existing imagery that were reassembled and graded.

Note: Elements in this image were then subtly animated to express the sensation of the physicality of loss.

Source: Hoyle (2023).

Serendipitous discovery surfaced multiple times while I was creating *Untitled Grief*. For example, while looking through material that had been shot I could feel the tension in my body as I felt myself re-experiencing situations I was recounting. I am not sure quite why I did this, but I asked the cinematographer to film me listening to a recording of my storytelling. Perhaps I was imagining that I might be able to use a cut away of a filmic detail like my hands moving. However, what I encountered was sudden, unexpected, interior insight. When I played the footage alongside the collages I was assembling, it felt like an emotional door was opened, where the illustrated surface was peeled back and we saw the rawness of grief connected to the storyteller.

The decision to document my loss in this way suddenly opened a range of possibilities, including the potential of making a whole documentary where we just observed a storyteller listening to her interview talking about grief. However, in the end I felt that a few seconds of this footage might function more profoundly as a momentary punctuation; a fleeting witness to the vulnerability of the self (Figure 5.3).

My fossicking for online images, archives, and sound also functioned as a serendipitous engagement because I opened up my searches to unexpected expansion. I came to think of this searching as 'serendipitous grazing'. I did not limit my considerations to what was pictorially referred to in the interview. Instead, I embraced the potential of the unexpected. I accepted the uncertainty of using disparate imagery for expression and I was driven by tenuous (seemingly irrational) connections between feelings and iconography. The results were unexpected and fruitful, and slowly I began to develop a visual language for the documentary. Before serendipitous grazing, I had not considered that cartography might suggest that grief was a journey, nor that chromolithographs of flowers might allude to nostalgia and fragility. These things became considerations because I meandered through uncharted algorithmic alleyways, enlisting the serendipitous to maintain an open mind that would entertain possibility inside seemingly illogical connections.

FIGURE 5.3 Screen grabs from the preceding and following animated sequences interspersed with the single moment from the footage of me listening to my account of grief.

Source: Hoyle (2023).

Extending indwelling

The second principle that surfaced during the production of *Untitled Grief* was 'indwelling'. Indwelling is a period that some heuristic researchers describe as an initial immersion (Douglass & Moustakas, 1985; Ings, 2011; Ventling, 2018). Moustakas sees it as an interior environment where one experiences an internalising of a question and 'immersion in active experience' (1990, p. 15). He suggests that this contemplative space compels deep reflection and determined effort, 'until fundamental insight is achieved' (1990, p. 25).

Researchers such as Sela-Smith (2002) employ indwelling as the primary stage in a heuristic inquiry. However, in my practice indwelling functioned as an embracing state that ran parallel to external considerations of artistic iterations of my work. In this state, what existed and what was being created became part of an integrated whole.

In his discussion of Polanyi's (1965) state of indwelling, Brownhill writes:

We 'indwell', or we immerse ourselves, in the clues of perception to gain a knowledge of the whole. This does not mean we concentrate on the particulars and that this gives us a knowledge of the whole, but it means we assimilate the particulars, we make them part of ourselves, and only then can we gain a knowledge of the whole.

(Brownhill, 1968, p. 118)

Thus, by indwelling I do not refer to a demarcated state of atomised attention but a wholeness where the self, the research question, and emerging creative responses coexist. In my approach to heuristic inquiry I 'bridged the gap between the sensible world and the super-sensible world by the process of "indwelling" and by the gradual movement of the knower to a knowledge of a mainly hidden reality' (Brownhill, 1968, p. 120). In this pursuit I was attentive to the potential of what is not explicit. I returned to indwelling especially when I was examining or expressing sensations of loss. Inside this state I engaged in a form of self-dialogue.

The animator Hossein Najafi (2023a) also discusses heuristic indwelling in filmmaking as 'dialogic'. In describing how his animated work *Stella* (Najafi, 2023b) was developed, he says,

Here, I spoke to the world that began to take form on the screen in front of me and it talked back to me. In this process, the story and I intensified the intimacy of our journey (both physically and esoterically), as we transcended into realms of greater knowing.

(Najafi, 2023a, p. 68)

In my project, the need to shift between indwelling and external review became an intuitive oscillation. It was necessary because at times the work was emotionally exhausting. In these extended periods of indwelling, I was able to consider the expression of grief in relation to imagery and sound because I was able to feel the resonance in the work I was making and respond emotionally while I was making connections. This meant that I journeyed into many cul-de-sacs but I eventually came to understand that these were not 'wrong turnings'; instead, they represented the way heuristic inquiry encourages the researcher to push at parameters to see what might be found.

One illustration of a cul-de-sac was a series of images I composed that featured a 1950s television moving through a rural landscape. While the image theme was visually arresting, when I compared the work to my experiences in the immersive space, I was unable to feel the sensations of grief. The images looked distinctive but there was little connection with the emotional revelations surfacing from my inner search to know. As a consequence, I moved on to experiments in which I began connecting my sense of melancholia and nostalgia with multiple floral backgrounds, fabrics, paper frames, and archival film. These combinations felt more intimate and familiar because they carried with them tinges of the bittersweet. The inclusion of family archive material and the crafting of a muted colour scheme served to reinforce a melodic sense of loss, and from this theme I was able to design background soundscapes that sang to the imagery and interview in harmonious ways.

Emboldening poetic sensibility

During the creation of the documentary, I experimented with visual leitmotif to locate interactions and rhythms that might suggest unusual coherency. Inside these experiments, I sought to elevate high levels of poetic sensibility. Released from the idea of an expository account (Nichols, 2017) of autobiographical grief, I was able to counterpoint the immediacy of the interview material with symbolic poetic animations that unfolded in a working environment that was very different to the professional contexts and culture of commercial documentary making.

Imagery, music, sound effects, and interview recordings provided the source material for poetic affinities and relationships. Broadly, this may be related to Kleining and Witt's fourth rule for heightening the chances of discovery in heuristic inquiries that is concerned with identifying parallels, patterns and similarities in data.

Although difficult to define, poetic sensibility operates as an interior state that Fuchs-Holzer suggests is intuitive and aesthetic. She proposes that poetic sensibility 'requires a keen multisensory experience of the surrounding world; an ability to ask questions of, and see patterns in, that world; and an ability to make both logical and intuitive connections' (2017, para. 1).

I used my poetic sensibility to seek out uncommon relationships between sound and visual metaphors, editing rhythms, delicate imagery, and the pain

FIGURE 5.4 Screen grab from *Untitled Grief* showing a paradoxical landscape combining a dreamlike sky, parched earth, and tropical vegetation. In this part of the documentary the narration discusses the despair of navigating the concurrent absence and presence of one who has departed.

Source: Hoyle (2023).

of grief. This sensibility rejected the rational, allowing combinations of imagination and tacit knowledge to mix and materialise. When employing a poetic sensibility I found beauty in the darkest of places, harmony in paradoxes, and continuities in the disparate (Figure 5.4). Here, I slowed my pace, and exchanged the literal and obvious for the enigmatic and metaphoric. Within this sensibility, I continually applied a sense of rightness or seeking after inherent harmony, which resulted in patterns and connections being identified and brought forward in the work. This process may be aligned to Simmel's discussion of method, where he observes that 'out of complex phenomena, the homogeneous will be extracted… and the dissimilar paralyzed' (1908, p. 1).

As the documentary progressed, the vintage illustrations and photographs were treated with sepia tones and softened colour palettes. These decisions alluded to the period of my grandparents' lives. The application of subtle, animated movement provided the documentary with a sense of inevitable timelessness.

Actioning aroha

As the inquiry progressed, a fourth principle became increasingly significant (especially when the project moved into its second phase where I began working with the stories of other participants). To describe this principle, we might turn to the indigenous language of New Zealand Māori, for the word *aroha*. Simply translated, *aroha* means to show love, compassion, and respect, but it is more nuanced than this. Barlow (1996) notes that *aroha* also renounces judgement and is expressed as genuine concern and care.

In a project where one is researching autobiographically, Ellis and Bochner suggest that a researcher engages 'multiple layers of consciousness, connecting the personal to the cultural' (2000, p. 739). This means that considerable thought needs to be given to how a researcher actions a 'duty of care' towards others, including, in autobiographic work, towards themselves. Although Behar (2022), Ryang (2000), and Eriksson (2010) each propose that vulnerability can lend a degree of authority to autobiographic inquiries, this vulnerability can also be emotionally costly (Doloriert & Sambrook, 2009; Ings, 2014; Tolich, 2010). Clandinin and Connelly remind us that 'the researcher is always speaking partially naked' (1994, p. 423), and Ings cautions that with insufficient care and forethought, an autobiographical research project 'can cost a researcher emotionally and professionally' (2014, p. 168).

Consequently, as the study progressed, I began to consciously monitor my emotional and mental health. I took breaks from intense immersion and alternated between technical research (into software applications and contextual reading), and deeper levels of self-search and creation. I also aligned a personal therapist with the project and took care to build strong, honest relationships within the study. For example, I chose to work with a cinematographer with whom I already shared years of professional experience. This is because I knew his work ethic and attitude to documentary making, and I could trust in his practice, and be open about my feelings. I also knew that he would be sensitive and comfortable asking deep, personal, metaphorically orientated questions about how I experienced grief. He would also treat what he recorded in confidence, be honest in his opinions, and allow time for me to think about how I responded to questioning.

In preparation for the second phase of the study I also began adopting strategies for extending *aroha* to new people who I intended to interview. Working effectively as a documentary practitioner requires mutual trust between participants and the maker, and such a relationship becomes important when one is asking people to share intense or painful experiences. Pryluck (1976), Nash, (2011), Nichols (2017), and Sanders (2013) all argue that ethical responsibilities lie at the heart of documentary production processes, and these responsibilities permeate all periods of production (Sanders, 2010; Thomas, 2012).

Although the study was afforded university ethics approval, I found it necessary to reach beyond these provisions. I took time to talk with people who considered sharing their stories. We ate together, spent time in each other's worlds, shared our creative work, and clarified parameters they might have, so my questions could afford them opportunities for deep reflection, without intruding on issues about which they felt uncomfortable.

My previous production work had demonstrated the importance of caring for people whose lives and experiences I document. Like Thomas (2012), when I am working with intimate accounts that are distressing (both for the participant to share, and for me to record), I value the establishment of deep connection and reflexivity that supports compassion and empathy. While working heuristically in such environments, because I am navigating discovery without a roadmap, I know that potentially I will be engaging with vulnerability. Accordingly, I have found that *aroha* is not a luxury but a necessity that enables the researcher to heighten integrity and care.

Conclusion

This chapter has considered four principles which surfaced during the production of a short, animated documentary. Three of these grew out of Kleining and Witt's (2000) rules for heightening chances of discovery in heuristic inquiry, i.e., embracing uncertainty and serendipity, extending periods of indwelling, and pursuing a poetic sensibility. In addition, as the inquiry deepened, I became aware of a fourth principle, that of actioning *aroha*, which guided how I might embody a duty of care for participants inside the inquiry, including both the researcher and crew.

The production of the documentary *Untitled Grief* spanned 12 months, and it constituted an intimate and sometimes melancholic examination. Adopting a heuristic inquiry enabled me to adjust my production processes so I was able to exhume and disclose insights into autobiographical grief while artistically exploring the illustrative and sonic potentials of interview material. While navigating the project, I critically examined existing phases and rules related to heuristic methods. This led to a contextualised rethinking of Kleining and Witt's rules for increasing discovery in a heuristic inquiry, and the development of four alternative principles that enabled me to work in greater depth and with increased levels of confidence.

Moving away from professional methods, sustained by the luxury of time and a revised attitude to flexibility, I experienced heuristic inquiry as an evolving potential inside creative documentary filmmaking. I found that when fully embraced, I was able to turn what is tacitly actioned into a conscious consideration of how I might heighten chances for discovery when giving an artistic voice to autobiographical experience.

In support of this, the chapter has offered insight into a research journey that navigated such territory.

References

Andel, P. V. (1994). Anatomy of the unsought finding. Serendipity: Origin, history, domains, traditions, appearances, patterns and programmability. *The British Journal for the Philosophy of Science*, *45*(2), 631–648. https://www.jstor.org/stable/687687

Barlow, C. (1996). *Tikanga whakaaro: Key concepts in Māori culture*. Oxford University Press.

Beghetto, R. A. (2021). There is no creativity without uncertainty: Dubito Ergo Creo. *Journal of Creativity*, *31*, 100005. https://doi.org/10.1016/j.yjoc.2021.100005

Beghetto, R. A., & Jaeger, G. J. (Eds.). (2022). *Uncertainty: A catalyst for creativity, learning and development*. Springer.

Behar, R. (2022). *The vulnerable observer: Anthropology that breaks your heart*. Beacon Press.

Bonanno, G. A., & Kaltman, S. (2001). The varieties of grief experience. *Clinical Psychology Review*, *21*(5), 705–734. https://doi.org/10.1016/S0272-7358(00)00062-3

Brannigan, R. (2019). *How then to act? A performance as research investigation into the potentials of expanding an actor's agency* [Doctoral thesis, Auckland University of Technology]. Tuwhera Open Access Theses & Dissertations. https://hdl.handle.net/10292/12298

Brownhill, R. J. (1968). Michael Polanyi and the problem of personal knowledge. *The Journal of Religion*, *48*(2), 115–123. https://doi.org/10.1086/486119

Carabine, J. (2013). Creativity, art and learning: A psycho-social exploration of uncertainty. *International Journal of Art & Design Education*, *32*(1), 33–43. https://doi.org/10.1111/j.1476-8070.2013.01745.x

Clandinin, D., & Connelly, F. (1994). Personal experience methods. In N. K. Denzin & Y. Lincoln (Eds.), *The SAGE handbook of qualitative research* (3rd ed., pp. 413–427). Sage.

De Rond, M. (2014). The structure of serendipity. *Culture and Organization*, *20*(5), 342–358. https://doi.org/10.1080/14759551.2014.967451

Doloriert, C., & Sambrook, S. (2009). Ethical confessions of the 'I' of autoethnography: A student's dilemma. *Qualitative Research in Organizations and Management: An International Journal*, *4*(1), 27–45.

Douglass, B. G., & Moustakas, C. (1985). Heuristic inquiry: The internal search to know. *Journal of Humanistic Psychology*, *25*(3), 39–55. https://doi.org/10.1177/0022167885253004

Ellis, C., & Bochner, A. (2000). Autoethnography, personal narrative, reflexivity: Researcher as subject. In N. K. Denzin & Y. S. Lincoln (Eds.), *Handbook of qualitative research* (pp. 733–768; 2nd ed.). Sage.

Eriksson, T. (2010). *Being native – Distance, closeness and doing auto/self-ethnography*. https://gupea.ub.gu.se/handle/2077/24689

Fine, G. A., & Deegan, J. G. (1996). Three principles of serendip: Insight, chance, and discovery in qualitative research. *International Journal of Qualitative Studies in Education*, *9*(4), 434–447. https://doi.org/10.1080/0951839960090405

Fuchs-Holzer, M. (2017). Poetic sensibility: What it is and why we need it in 21st century education. Poets.org. https://poets.org/text/poetic-sensibility-what-it-and-why-we-need-it-21st-century-education

Glăveanu, V. P. (2022). What's 'inside' the prepared mind? Not things, but relations. In W. Ross, & S. Copeland (Eds.), *The art of serendipity* (pp. 23–39). Springer.

Hiles, D. (2002). Narrative and heuristic approaches to transpersonal research and practice [Paper presentation]. CCPE, London. https://psy.dmu.ac.uk/drhiles/N&Hpaper.htm

Holinger, D. P. (2020). *The anatomy of grief*. Yale University Press.

Hoyle, E. (Director). (1991). *A drop in the ocean* [Film]. Swinburne Film and Television School.

Hoyle, E. (Director). (1992). *Down at the Gill* [Film]. Victorian College of the Arts, Film and Television School.

Hoyle, E. (Director). (2000). *Waiting for wood* [Unpublished documentary proposal]. Kath Shelper.

Hoyle, E. (Director). (2001). *Night workers* [Documentary proposal]. Film Victoria.

Hoyle, E. (2023). *Untitled grief* [Digital file]. https://vimeo.com/847658432 [Password: untitled].

Hoyle, E. (Director). (2006). *16mm Maxwell* [Film]. Victorian College of the Arts, Film and Television School. https://www.screenaustralia.gov.au/the-screen-guide/t/16mmmaxwell-2006/24754

Ings, W. (2006). *Talking pictures: A creative utilization of structural and aesthetic profiles from narrative music videos and television commercials in a non-spoken film text* [Doctoral thesis, Auckland University of Technology]. Tuwhera Open Access Theses & Dissertations. https://hdl.handle.net/10292/346

Ings, W. (2011). Managing heuristics as a method of inquiry in autobiographical graphic design theses. *International Journal of Art & Design Education, 30*(2), 226–241. https://doi.org/10.1111/j.1476-8070.2011.01699.x

Ings, W. (2014). Narcissus and the muse: Supervisory implications of autobiographical, practice-led PhD design theses. *Qualitative Research, 14*(6), 675–693. https://doi.org/10.1177/1468794113488128

Ings, W. (2018). Heuristic inquiry, land and the artistic researcher. In M. Sierra & K. Wise (Eds.), *Transformative pedagogies and the environment: Creative agency through contemporary art and design* (pp. 55–80). Common Ground Research Networks.

Kennedy, I. G., Whitehead, D., & Ferdinand-James, D. (2022). Serendipity: A way of stimulating researchers' creativity. *Journal of Creativity, 32*(1), 100014. https://doi.org/10.1016/j.yjoc.2021.100014

Kenny, G. (2012). An introduction to Moustakas's heuristic method. *Nurse Researcher, 19*(3), 6–11. https://doi.org/10.7748/nr2012.04.19.3.6.c9052

Kirpitchenko, L., & Voloder, L. (2014). Insider research method: The significance of identities in the field. In *Sage research methods cases. Part 1*. Sage. https://doi.org/10.4135/978144627305014533940

Kleining, G., & Witt, H. (2000). The qualitative heuristic approach: A methodology for discovery in psychology and the social sciences. Rediscovering the method of introspection as an example. *Forum Qualitative Sozialforschung/Forum: Qualitative Social Research, 1*(1). https://doi.org/10.17169/fqs-1.1.1123

Lloyd, C. (2017). *Grief demystified: An introduction*. Jessica Kingsley Publishers.

Merton, R. K., & Barber, E. (2011). *The travels and adventures of serendipity: A study in sociological semantics and the sociology of science*. Princeton University Press.

Moustakas, C. (1990). *Heuristic research: Design, methodology, and applications*. Sage.

Najafi, H. (2023a). *Displacement of self-continuity: An illuminative heuristic inquiry into identity transition in an allegorical animation* [Doctoral thesis, Auckland University of Technology]. Tuwhera Open Access Theses & Dissertations. https://hdl.handle.net/10292/15784

Najafi, H. (2023b). *Stella post-visualisation document* [Video]. Tuwhera Open Access Theses & Dissertations. https://openrepository.aut.ac.nz/bitstreams/2fad26b6-2d46-4340-9519-dedfaea7e4dd/download

Nash, K. (2011). Documentary-for-the-other: Relationships, ethics and (observational) documentary. *Journal of Mass Media Ethics*, *26*(3), 224–239. https://doi.org/10.1080/08900523.2011.581971

Nichols, B. (2017). *Introduction to documentary* (3rd ed.). Indiana University Press.

Osborne, C. (2023). *What is the client experience of online video-calling equine-facilitated therapy? A heuristic study* [Master's thesis, Auckland University of Technology]. Tuwhera Open Access Theses & Dissertations. http://hdl.handle.net/10292/17016

Parkes, C. M. (2016). The price of love. *Grief Matters*, *19*(1), 4–9. https://search.informit.org/doi/10.3316/informit.104194019501451

Pearce, R. M. (1912). Chance and the prepared mind. *Science*, *35*(912), 941–956. https://www.jstor.org/stable/1638153

Polanyi, M. (1965). On the modern mind. *Encounter*, *24*(5), 12–20.

Pryluck, C. (1976). Ultimately we are all outsiders: The ethics of documentary filming. *Journal of the University Film Association*, *28*(1), 21–29. https://www.jstor.org/stable/20687309

Ross, W., & Copeland, S. (2022). On creativity and serendipity. In W. Ross & S. Copeland (Eds.), *The art of serendipity* (pp. 1–21). Springer.

Runco, M. A. (2022). Uncertainty makes creativity possible. In R. A. Beghetto & G. J. Jaeger (Eds.), *Uncertainty: A catalyst for creativity, learning and development* (pp. 23–36). Springer. https://doi.org/10.1007/978-3-030-98729-9

Ryang, S. (2000). Ethnography or self-cultural anthropology?: Reflections on writing about ourselves. *Dialectical Anthropology*, *25*, 297–320. https://doi.org/10.1023/A:1011626917988

Sanders, W. (2010). Documentary filmmaking and ethics: Concepts, responsibilities, and the need for empirical research. *Mass Communication and Society*, *13*(5), 528–553. https://doi.org/10.1080/15205431003703319

Sanders, W. (2013). Documentary ethics in contemporary practices. Alternative participation, alternative ethics? In J. C. Suarez Villegas, A. Zurbano Berenguer, & O. Saadi Haddach (Eds.), *II International Conference on Media Ethics* (pp. 223–234). https://idus.us.es/handle/11441/41602

Sela-Smith, S. (1999). *Regaining wholeness: A heuristic inquiry into childhood sexual abuse* [Unpublished master's thesis]. Saybrook University.

Sela-Smith, S. (2002). Heuristic research: A review and critique of Moustakas's method. *Journal of Humanistic Psychology*, *42*(3), 53–88. https://doi.org/10.1177/00267802042003004

Simmel, G. (1908). *Soziologie*. Duncker & Humblot.

Sinfield, D. (2020). *Typographical voices: Poetic reflections on the Pātea Freezing Works* [Doctoral thesis, Auckland University of Technology]. Tuwhera Open Access Theses & Dissertations. https://hdl.handle.net/10292/13601

Tavares, T. (2019). *Paradoxical realities: A creative consideration of realismo maravilhoso in an interactive digital narrative* [Doctoral thesis, Auckland University of Technology]. Tuwhera Open Access Theses & Dissertations. https://hdl.handle.net/10292/12958

Thomas, S. (2012). Collaboration and ethics in documentary filmmaking–a case study. *New Review of Film and Television Studies, 10*(3), 332–343. https://doi.org/10.1080/17400309.2012.695979

Tolich, M. (2010). A critique of current practice: Ten foundational guidelines for autoethnographers. *Qualitative Health Research, 20*(12), 1599–1610. https://doi.org/10.1177/1049732310376076

Ventling, D. (2018). Heuristics: A framework to clarify practice-led research. *Journal of Design, Art and Technology, 3*(2), 122–156. https://doi.org/10.29147/dat.v3i2.88

Walpole, H. (1754/1937–1983). Letter to Horace Mann. In W. S. Lewis (Ed.), *The Yale Edition of Horace Walpole's Correspondence* (Vol. 20, pp. 241–244). New Haven Yale University Press.

6

A HEURISTIC FOR THE HABITS OF IMPROVING CARE

Maurice Hamington

In the 1990s, Ohio elementary school teacher Laurie Anthony and her spouse decided to leave their jobs and move to New York City for one year so that their theatrically inclined teenager could attend a performing arts high school in Manhattan. Anthony resisted at first, but then she embraced the adventure of the pending experience. An aspect of living in New York City became regular encounters with people experiencing homelessness on the streets. When her son innocently asked how she could walk past homeless people daily, Anthony reflected on her casual detachment. Thereafter, she gave an elderly black man sitting on the street some change (Anthony is white). The brief exchange was friendly, so when she went out the next day and saw him again, Anthony approached him with an offering of some breakfast. They started a conversation, and Anthony learned the man's name was J.C. Despite her fears and biases, Anthony returned daily to see J.C. and bring him breakfast. They would have long conversations. As she later wrote:

> J.C. talked on and on while I tried to envision his life as he explained it to me... I felt like we were two friends just talking, and I could tell he enjoyed telling his story. He cracked jokes and laughed and kidded me about being so persistent. My heart went out to him.
>
> (Anthony, 1999, p. 46)

Eventually, she discovered that he had grown up in the segregated South, was college-educated, had been a teacher, and had managed a restaurant. Their relationship allowed Anthony to understand J.C. better: Anthony demonstrated respect for J.C., learned more about him, connected with him, and acted for his benefit. Yet, he still perplexed her. For example, J.C. had adult

DOI: 10.4324/9781003507758-9

children who lived nearby, but never saw them. She discovered that he was not consistently homeless but felt more comfortable on the streets and not dealing with the complexities of housing and paid labour.

Anthony discovered that J.C. found it challenging to deal with bureaucratic processes that those with more privilege in society might find merely annoying. For instance, J.C. had lost his identification and birth certificate. He also did not have a bank account, which complicated his receiving of social security checks. Over the year, Anthony helped him obtain his birth certificate and passport and assisted his move into a new apartment (Anthony, 1999). After their year in New York City, and as planned, Anthony and her family moved back to Ohio.

Anthony subsequently corresponded with J.C. and visited occasionally.[1] Connecting her experience with the more significant social problem of the unhoused, Anthony wrote *Have A Great Day! A Homeless Man's Story* (Anthony, 1999). The book includes multiple practical appendices for engaging with the housing crisis, one of which provides data to spark discussions on this crisis, while the others suggest actions that an individual can take to help the homeless. Also offered is an extensive list of resources for assisting the homeless and advocating on their behalf.

This tale is remarkable. Few people give money to those living on the streets (Charities Aid Foundation, 2022). Finding someone who will take the time to form a relationship with a homeless person is rare. Anthony goes further than many by writing a book to leverage her particular experience with one man into a catalyst for broader social action. This story is an example of care for a stranger. It is easy to care for familiar others who are like us and live in proximity to us, and more difficult to do so for others who aren't and don't.

Many people are described as caring, as witnessed by their actions and disposition. We all know outstanding caregivers. Yet it is clear from news reports of violence, neglect, and suffering that the world needs more and better care. This chapter explores whether a provocative relational heuristic for improving care – a set of open-ended habits – might facilitate a care ethos or spirit of care by helping us to focus our bodies and minds on this moral imperative. Specifically, the heuristic suggested is a method or process for improving care consisting of the habits of humble enquiry, inclusive connection, and responsive action.

A heuristic for improving care is intended to open up rather than narrow our thinking and actions regarding care by providing touchstones for reflection. The scope of this chapter is ambitious. Firstly, I define feminist care theory and acknowledge why clarifying 'good care' is tricky. I then discuss a heuristic approach and argue that the elements of a care heuristic resonate with John Dewey's open-ended definition of habit, following which I explain the three-part heuristic of care improvement habits. I conclude by briefly addressing the power of such a heuristic for fomenting a more caring society.

The world needs more and better care. Numerous writers and scholars have characterised the modern context as perpetuating a 'crisis of care' (Bunting, 2020; Dowling, 2021; Phillips & Benner, 1994). A heuristic for improving care can focus attention on the habits one can adopt to elevate care.

Care theory

'Care' is a ubiquitous word. It is part of our everyday language in phrases like: 'I don't care', 'We should care about the environment', and 'They don't have a care in the world'. Furthermore, advertisers recognise that 'care' has positive connotations; therefore, it appears in slogans for selling various products and services. Care entered the lexicon of Western moral thought in the 1980s through the work of feminist theorists in many disciplines. Some early care theorists included philosopher Sara Ruddick (1980), developmental psychologist Carol Gilligan (1982), and philosopher Nel Noddings (1984). These scholars, working independently, voiced similar dissatisfaction with dominant ethical theories that presumed an individualistic approach to moral thinking, and which sought universalisable rubrics for decision-making, such as rule-based and consequence-based theories. Feminist theorists recognised that 'care' was coded feminine and thus did not have the moral gravitas of traditional male formulations of ethics. They endeavoured to rectify the flaws in conventional ethical theory by developing a care-based approach to ethics that emphasises relationality and context to suggest morality should respond to the needs of particular others rather than abstract generalities. For care theorists, humans were assumed to be fundamentally relational, and so that which is moral must account for our web of relationships, interdependencies, and interactions.

Although a robust understanding of care is relatively new to Western moral philosophers, many non-Western and indigenous cultures have rich traditions of thinking about care in nuanced ways. For example, some African communities employ the concept of *ubuntu*, and the Cree of Canada has a concept of *wahkohtowin* (Wildcat & Voth, 2023). Also, there are a number of Chinese philosophers who suggest that the ancient notions of *ren* are akin to care (Yuan, 2019). The point is that the West is late to take care seriously as a philosophical subject.

Gilligan defines the ideal of care as 'an activity of relationship, of seeing and responding to need, taking care of the world by sustaining the web of connection so that no one is left alone' (1982, p. 62). Noddings explains that through care, 'we are attentive to expressed needs and wants, and we are committed to respond to them' (2010, p. 5). The most frequently quoted definition of care comes from political philosophers Joan Tronto and Berenice Fisher, who describe it as 'a species of activity that includes everything we do to maintain, contain, and repair our "world" so that we can live in it as well as possible. That world includes our bodies, ourselves, and our environment' (1990, p. 40). These feminist theorists re-centre the central concern of morality as caring for one another.

Today, the field of care ethics is enjoying widespread recognition across various disciplines in the humanities, social sciences, and the health and social care professions. Theorists have provided insightful efforts at explicating the components of care. For example, Tronto (1993) offers the four ethical elements of an ethic of care: attentiveness, responsibility, competence, and responsiveness. The heuristic proposed in this chapter does not contradict such descriptions. Instead, it emphasises care as a *process morality* whereby people work toward better care or skill building, intending to provide good care.

One final note about care theory is relevant to describing a heuristic for better care. When discussing care, it is sometimes addressed as a binary: care/ no care or good care/bad care. More often than not, the care experience ranges from damaging or harmful care to helpful, reassuring, and revitalising, as well as multiple possibilities in between. Furthermore, 'perfect care' is likely unobtainable. Care is a practice (Held, 2006) and an experience that can continually be improved upon but typically not perfected. Thus, care ethics is a non-ideal theory (Mills, 2005). Accordingly, care is an activity of mind and body that we develop through reflective and iterative exercise. If someone wants to improve at cooking, they apply their intellect, imagination, and body in practicing culinary skills. The same is true of care. Thus, even someone who provides exemplary care is capable of bettering their care. Furthermore, if someone aspires to improve their care, they should be motivated to reflect on their practices and seek feedback from those receiving their care. A heuristic for better care attends to vital habits for enriching our care for others and is not predicated on an ideal form of care.

Although a heuristic for better care addresses the skills of the care giver, care is a relational activity. Accordingly, no one provides care in a vacuum. Care receivers are active participants in the relationship. Not only do care receivers respond to the experience of care practices, they have responsibilities within the relationship (Tronto, 2013).

The challenges of characterising good care

As mentioned above, care is a common and frequently used word. However, it is often employed in imprecise or euphemistic ways. In some contexts, to 'take care' of someone means to kill them. In other contexts, to take care of someone is slang for giving them sexual pleasure. In this chapter, we will ignore the euphemistic utterances of care. Nevertheless, imprecision remains. In non-euphemistic articulations, if someone indicates that they will take care of someone, they usually mean to take *good* care. There is a presumption of positive behaviour. Noddings writes, 'To care, we feel, requires some action in behalf of the cared-for' (1984, p. 10). She assumes the actions will be helpful, meet needs, or benefit the one receiving them. However, the word 'care' without context or accompanying modifiers can be a neutral term (i.e., good, bad, or in between) and thus can be associated with either harm or benefit. The situation and action matter.

Care theorists are focused on the results of actions rather than intentions. Caring is a phenomenon that occurs in the world as an experience; it is not merely a disposition of the mind or heart. When care is harmful, unwanted, oppressive, or abusive, it matters little if the intention is positive or negative. The efficacy of caring must centre on the assessment of the one cared for rather than the person giving care. Just because a person or entity invokes the word 'care' to characterise their actions does not make them positive or moral. For example, colonial powers often take oppressive measures in the name of care. Philosopher Eva Boodman describes how care can be entangled in the exercise of power:

> There are certainly good reasons not to construe as care the assimilationist programs for Cree and Salteaux youth in Saskatchewan, including racist over- or under-medication in Winnipeg emergency rooms, broad relocation policies that remove people from their ancestral lands for the sake of 'better access' to education and health institutions, or foster-care programs that remove Indigenous children from their parents to place them with settler families.
>
> (Boodman, 2023, p. 332)

Boodman warns the reader that modern societies exist within a settler-colonial paradigm; thus, any project, mission, or program of care that flows from a privileged position to marginalised people must be suspect and scrutinised: 'I question whether care theory should seek to expand the concept of care, rather than to refract, multiply, or disrupt it' (2023, p. 333). Boodman's analysis reminds us that the roots of care ethics are in feminism, so vigilance in attending to power and privilege is always required. Postcolonial scholars are not the only theorists cautious about care and its sometimes dark history. Disability studies thinkers and advocates are also wary of how care has been used to limit some people's autonomy (Davy, 2019).

This discussion of the forms of harmful care points to a fundamental tension in developing care theory. Although the notion of good care is vital, addressing how to achieve good care is fraught with potential pitfalls. The word care is insufficient to establish the actions taken as morally good. At a minimum, care must include respect for the dignity and autonomy of the one cared for and resist universalised prescriptive approaches that do not account for their intersectional context or power dynamics. Care is essential for human existence, and the world has witnessed how the lack of care creates harm. Thus, a heuristic for good care must avoid perpetuating imperial power and paternalism that can spur further injury.

Why a heuristic?

We all use heuristic thinking as a coping mechanism in our daily lives. Daily experience contains too many possibilities for action so there is not enough time to fully consider all that influences our decision-making.

For those who study feminist care ethics, heuristics, as they are understood in computer science or decision theory, are an unlikely subject for exploration. European and North American mainstream philosophers have emphasised ethics as a normative means for making difficult decisions; in other words, determining right and wrong action. Relatedly, heuristics sometimes serve as a satisficing model of choice that seeks an adequate resolution to a dilemma rather than an optimal one that considers all or most of the variables at play. When it comes to morality, similar to utilitarian approaches, heuristic reasoning seeks an optimal solution to a dilemma, given the information available.

However, for this project, the definition of heuristic employed is not a shortcut to a solution but a *method of interpersonal research and action*. Like research, care is a process heavily invested in knowledge production (Barnes & Henwood, 2015; Dalmiya, 2002; Puig de la Bellacasa, 2017). Psychologist Clark Moustakas (1990/2011) characterises the heuristic process as a way of knowing infused with self-discovery. He describes heuristic methodology this:

> Methods of heuristic research are open ended. They point to a process of accomplishing something in a thoughtful and orderly way, a manner of proceeding that guides the researcher. There is no exclusive list that would be appropriate for every heuristic investigation; instead, each research process unfolds in its own way.
>
> (Moustakas, 2014, p. 312)

Moustakas abandons the idea of social scientific research as impartial observation. For Moustakas, in a heuristic investigation, 'not only is knowledge extended but the self of the researcher is illuminated' (1990/2011, pp. 10–11). The emphasis on self-discovery is a bit individualistic for care theory, which centres on relationships, yet there is a sense that in caring for others, we learn about ourselves. A relational ontology suggests that a little of ourselves is in others and vice versa.

Although care theory has normative significance, its relational approach endeavours to do more than problem-solve moral quandaries. The form of heuristics employed here returns to the root understanding of the term.

Heuristics is derived from the Ancient Greek *heurískō*, meaning to find or discover (Moustakas, 1990/2011). Someone who values care is on a journey of discovery as to how to make a positive difference in the lives of others. A commitment to care entails a desire to improve one's caring abilities. Being a moral person means being a more caring person.

A care heuristic is not aimed at solving a problem but instead provides a means for valuing, reflecting upon, and practicing care skills. In light of this focus, John Dewey's notion of habit is particularly relevant. The elements of a heuristic of care can be described as valued habits to develop.

Deweyan habits as elements of a care heuristic

A heuristic for good care should open up diverse local abilities to improve caring. Instead of variables that assist in making a decision, the elements of a heuristic for good care can be touchstones for growth. In other words, the effort here is not to offer a fixed or narrowly defined prescription for good care. This heuristic is intended to be flexible and open-ended.

Dewey's robust notion of habit provides a liminal and supple conceptual foundation for a heuristic approach to care. For Dewey, habits are acquired and open-ended structures or ways of being. As he describes it, 'The essence of habit is an acquired predisposition to *ways* or modes of response, not to particular acts except, as under special conditions, these express a way of behaving' (1988, p. 32). Dewey addresses habits throughout his writings regarding ethics, enquiry, and aesthetics. Here, I suggest why these character-istics are significant to a heuristic of good care.

Habits as thought and action

Dewey's integration of thought and action is crucial to care theory, at least as I formulate it. He claims that 'habits deprived of thought and thought which is futile are two sides of the same fact' (1988, p. 49). We certainly can have rote habits, but developing more complex chains of habits and developing proficiency in habits requires attention and reflection. How does anyone improve at anything? Not simply by repeating the same mistakes but through enacting reflections on how to get better at something. Dewey (1988) con-fronts the Cartesian mind/body dualism with another liminal response, being clear that his conception of habit integrates the physical and the cognitive. For Dewey, a fully realised habit opens up reflective opportunities but is also an instance of potential attention and reflection.

Similarly, what I have described as embodied care represents individual acts of care and also serves as a means of thematising a broad range of activ-ities (Hamington, 2004). Ideally, and more often than not, our bodies have acquired habits of caring from others – particularly those who have cared for us. These habits manifest in various ways, including touch, voice inflection, eye contact, facial expressions, and bodily comportment. However, these habits are more than physical repetitions. They also describe habits of disposition, knowledge acquisition, and action planning. Why should morality be any different than any other set of habitual structures? Ethics is a negotiation between mind and body, between action and reflection. To leave out one or the other element is to truncate the concept. Noddings (2010) distinguishes between 'natural caring' and 'ethical' caring, and although this appears to be an essentialist distinction, she is addressing the perception of ease. Many habits of caring have an immediacy and physicality to them, such as tending to the hunger of one's child, that make them appear easier to acquire than other habits of care, such as helping to provide resources for the hungry in distant lands. However, here is where thought and action can help to create chains of interlocking care potential. Reflecting upon the significance of physically caring for a hungry child can provide the intellectual material that makes caring for a hungry unknown other more possible. When either the physical or cognitive aspect of habit is underdeveloped, the robust potential of habit is not fully realised or consummated. Accordingly, habit development requires reflective practice, but the implication of reflection in the process of habit development is that there is competency and, thus, the potential for discriminating habit proficiency. Therefore, care is not a purely relativistic or arbitrary activity. Some people are more capable than others of engaging in caring activities, but such capabilities are not fixed or determined but can be developed or exercised.

Habits as will and shaped by environment

Dewey's collapsing of means and ends represents a powerful challenge to modernist categories – including those of philosophy. In particular, we can see the liminality of habits as neither nature nor nurture and neither solely internally nor externally influenced. Dewey views humans as fundamentally social animals, for example, when he claims, 'Apart from the social medium the individual would never "know himself"; he would never become acquainted with his own needs and capacities' (1989, p. 388). Yet Dewey repeatedly claims that humans ultimately amalgamate wilful habits. For example, in *Human Nature and Conduct*, he claims: 'All habits are demands for certain kinds of activity; and they constitute the self. In any intelligible sense of the word will, they *are* will' (1988, p. 21). In this case, habit is both a means and an end. He claims that habits are will (means), and yet we can will to change habits and thus these habits can also become an object of the will (ends). Although Dewey states that habits represent a form of will, he does not mean it as an absolute or existentialist notion of free will. The will is constrained by, and in dialogue with, society regarding habit development. Steven Fesmire describes 'Habits [as] coordinated with environing conditions, so they cannot magically be changed simply by will or coercion' (2003,

p. 21). No, not magically changed, but habits can be negotiated, challenged, or shaped to resist sedimentation if there is will and motivation, for example, the habits of 'whiteness' which Terrance MacMullan (2009) explains are not internal developments, but rather racial behaviours learned from society through myriad avenues. However, they are not deterministic. As MacMullan relates, we can attend to and subsequently change these habits if we make them an object of the will.

Society dictates normal standards of care between individuals depending upon the context within a range of activities, from substandard care to supererogatory care. Most people develop habits of care within this range. However, given the motivation and will, these habits can extend to higher levels of the moral ideal – that of improving care.

Habits as frameworks for knowledge acquisition

Like all human activity, Dewey describes enquiry as consisting of habits, or more accurately, chains or interconnections of habits. Again, the concept is dynamic for Dewey as every experience serves to modify the framework of the habit: 'The basic characteristic of habit is that every experience enacted and undergone modifies the one who acts and undergoes, while this modification affects, whether we wish it or not, the quality of subsequent experiences' (1966, p. 35). Knowledge is an indispensable outgrowth of every experience; if not, our habits are sedimented and thus lack growth potential. Regarding caring habits, the habituation of activity can allow the other to be foregrounded in a way that the absence of habitual structure would make challenging. For example, the various acts of caring for another through putting them at ease – physically and emotionally – allow the form of enquiry to be more about the underlying essential needs of the other. Habits can accelerate and open up the enquiry process. Furthermore, habits of sympathy and empathy are mechanisms that can also facilitate knowledge creation as the one caring draws upon visceral and cognitive resources to understand the plight of another better. Here, Dewey, like many feminist theorists, is not afraid to validate the significance of emotions for enquiry. He claims, '*Emotional* reactions form the chief materials of our knowledge of ourselves and others' (Dewey, 1960, p. 129). While feelings can signal disruptive knowledge that foregrounds significance, social intelligence habits must be well-developed to use them best. Good care is more than emotion, yet emotions play a crucial role in connecting us with others.

Habits as structure for achieving moral ideals

Interlocking chains of habits support the pursuit of moral ideals like care. For example, habits of playfulness and openness spur imaginative thinking. Sympathy is one imaginative flight of fancy, and Dewey (1960) describes sympathy as animating moral thinking. For Dewey, imagination transforms the cold calculation of utilitarianism into a rich consideration of the future. He characterises an ideal as higher values that are not fixed and remote perfections but motivations for growth. Dewey chastises the individual who stands pat with their habits and does not endeavour to improve them. As such, habits should and can be a means to achieving moral ideals. Dewey describes deliberation as an imaginative or dramatic rehearsal of courses of conduct.

Mapping Dewey's structure on to care involves considering the role of imagination. One's ability to care – particularly for unfamiliar others – relies on well-developed habits of imagination. It is easy to imagine the impact and thus act accordingly to care for those in proximal relations to us, such as family and friends. It is much more challenging to care for those who are strangers or distant from us. The ability to imaginatively understand the consequences of actions makes caring possible. Therefore, if care is a moral ideal, habitual mechanisms can be developed or exercised to help achieve it. Dewey (1988) recognises that habits have a political dimension, and describes institutions as embodying habits. In this manner, the impact of care theory is both subtle and profound. Subtle gestures on the part of an individual can express a great deal of care in a simple conversation. Yet, collectively, habits of care have great potential to influence social practice and policy.

Habits and the self

How do we conclude that someone is a caring person? We recall the iterations of that person's actions and see a pattern of caring. One can thus say that identity and sense of the self are found in the trajectory of one's actions. Dewey makes a claim with ontological implications about habits in *Ethics*:

> Habit reaches even more significantly down into the very structure of the self... because of their common relation to an enduring and single condition – the self or character as the abiding unity in which different acts leave their lasting traces.
>
> (Dewey, 1989, p. 171)

This ontological understanding of habits can be very empowering. Habits are not fixed and static but rather are dynamic and subject to our desire for change and development. If I choose caring as a moral ideal that I aspire to, I can work to habituate caring actions and decisions, both in mind and in body. At first, the acts of caring may need more attention and practice, but as they become habituated frameworks for confronting or transacting with others, they seep into self-identity. A well-developed habit of caring can provide physical and cognitive structures that can be applied to various unique circumstances. A heuristic is one such structure.

In the next section, I employ the Deweyan notion of habit to help differentiate the heuristic elements used here from those of a decision-based heuristic. In particular, I describe the specific habits in the heuristic for care improvement.

A three-fold heuristic for improving care

Habits of humble enquiry

Good care requires a well-informed caregiver. I intentionally use the term 'enquiry' here to suggest that the care provider plays an active role in learning from the person cared for. Possible areas of information sought include but are not limited to: the nature of harm or need; the context and circumstances (such as cultural practices) of the person cared for; and options for caring actions. The knowledge required for good care can be characterised as general and specific. For example, professional generalised knowledge of medicine is crucial in healthcare settings. However, technical skill, experience, and information recall are insufficient conditions for good care. They certainly contribute to the patient's experience of the care provided, but particular knowledge of the individual is also crucial to the provision of care. Much of that specific knowledge can only come from the one cared for.

One must engage in social enquiry by employing social skills to gain that knowledge. Listening is one vital aspect of those social skills. This heuristic element for improving care has the adjective 'humble' attached to remind us that care is a relationship for which mutuality is essential. To glean important information from the other, the discussion should be entered into with humility rather than a quick jump to conclusions. The time pressures of a market-based society tend to favour snap judgments, but they do not always result in the most caring experience. Good listening skills yield a two-fold benefit. Active listening is a significant learning opportunity and, if engaged with humility, communicates care and respect to the other. Care theorist Fiona Robinson describes this thus: 'When we regard the activities of care as a primary form of moral and social activity, we begin to see the importance of listening attentively to others and making long-term commitments to those others and thereby gaining their trust' (2011, p. 851).

Furthermore, humble enquiry should be holistic, for which factual knowledge gained alongside the tacit and emotional understanding is most effective. The body's posture, positionality, tactile contact, facial expressions, vocal intonations, and gestures provide a wealth of information relevant to care if one is receptive to it. The spoken word is only one part of the vast amount of data one brings to a caring relationship.

As one element of this tripartite heuristic, humble enquiry reminds us of the value of understanding others without paternalistic or predetermined responses. Humble enquiry is a habit of body and mind that can be developed and adapted to whomever we encounter. One who cares well is a continuous learner who is open to discovery for the sake of understanding others. This understanding of humble enquiry is consistent with the work of anti-racism scholars who have developed the term 'cultural humility' which is understood as learning about others in 'a lifelong commitment to self-evaluation and self-critique' (Tervalon & Murray-Garcia, 1998, p. 117) rather than a fixed standard of cultural competence.

Inclusive connection

This heuristic element addresses an emotive aspect of caring. 'Making a connection' suggests finding a source for shared understanding, which can be challenging when encountering unfamiliar others. Furthermore, making a connection does not imply that one understands perfectly what another person is going through, nor does it suggest that one imposes one's experiences on others. We are discrete individuals yet joined by relationality in an embodied, temporal existence. Humans share a great deal, even if from different cultures and languages. Our connections are inklings, glimmers, or impressions that allow us a vague and partial sense of the other's plight.

Because humans more easily and comfortably connect with others who are like them or are close to them, the idea of connection is modified with the word 'inclusive'. Here, inclusive is not intended as a privileged gatekeeping whereby someone is allowed in or included but rather as a provocation that good care requires vigilance in being open to new experiences of others, even when they are not like us. Some connections will need more effort, yet they can yield affirming results.

This heuristic element of connection suggests empathy. A translation from the German *Einfühlung* means feeling oneself into another's emotions, experiences, or situation. One delineation of types of empathy divides it (and them) between the heart and mind. Affective empathy is an emotional resonance with another person that allows for perceiving and, to a lesser degree, experiencing the other's feelings, while cognitive empathy is an imaginative connection to someone's circumstances. Through empathy we can transcend ourselves to realise our relational concerns. The emotional pull of empathy can be a significant motivator for greater enquiry and, ultimately, action (Slote, 2007).

Care theorists have written extensively on empathy, most finding that it plays a role in caring (Hamington, 2017). Nevertheless, empathy is a contested term, as Jolanda van Dijke and her colleagues point out:

> According to its proponents, empathy is a unique way to connect with others, to understand what is at stake for them, and to help guide moral

deliberation. According to its critics, empathy is biased, inaccurate, or a form of projection that does not truly grasp and respect the otherness of the other, and that may be distorted by prejudices.

(van Dijke et al., 2019, p. 1292)

Inclusive connection is a skill that can be learned, exercised, and improved. Although some people are characterised as more or less empathetic, which some people interpret as an inherent trait, social scientific research indicates that empathy is a skill that can be learned and refined (Zaki, 2019). Human bodies and many nonhuman bodies have the cognitive and affective tools for empathy, but they must be developed. A heuristic in service of good care focuses attention on value, becoming proficient at inclusive connection.

Responsive action

The third touchstone of a heuristic for improving care is the habit of responsive action. Care, as care theorists understand it, is more than a disposition. It is not sufficient to declare that one cares for someone non-human – animals or the environment. That declaration of care must be transformed into action to be morally relevant. Care is a relational participation or enaction. Of course, sometimes caring requires inaction, but even then, it is an active choice of knowledge and empathy not to insert oneself into a circumstance. Citizen Potawatomi Nation Botanist Robin Wall Kimmerer describes the occasional need for inaction while honouring that care is about active, responsive action:

A lot of the time you hear people say that the best thing people can do for nature is to stay away from it and let it be. There are places where that's absolutely true and our people respected that. But we were also given the responsibility to care for land. What people forget is that that means participating – that the natural world relies on us to do good things. You don't show your love and care by putting what you love behind a fence. You have to be involved. You have to contribute to the well-being of the world.

(Kimmerer, 2013, p. 363)

Kimmerer's description resonates with the claim of care theorists that care is a practice. Marian Barnes views care as an essential activity of everyday life:

We need to think about care as a practice – we need to be able to recognise what is involved to 'do care' or, as Tronto has put it, we need not only to care about but also to care for.

(Barnes, 2014, p. 6)

The character of caring actions must be responsive. As Robert Stake and Merel Visse point out, 'Responding means answering when given an offering, a challenge, a situation needing attention. We address the persons or problems in this situation, taking aim, moving toward something, going somewhere, perhaps with hope or expectation' (2021, p. 16). That hope and expectation of caring action may involve risk, particularly when the responsive action is directed toward unfamiliar others. Anthony took a risk in caring for J.C. Much good resulted from her efforts. Still, her hopes and expectations were not entirely met when she became disillusioned about J.C.'s activities, yet she strove to respond to his needs.

Experientially, the heuristic elements of humble enquiry, inclusive connection, and responsive action – the habits of improving care – do not present themselves in any order and likely overlap. The responsiveness of care means that to be good carers, we should aspire to be nimble and respond to needs and circumstances at the moment. This care heuristic of humble enquiry, inclusive connection, and responsive action describes improvisation tools.

Tools for creating a care ethos

Every day, we are reminded that the world needs more and better care. Collectively, we cannot end all the world's suffering and strife, but a significant change is possible through improved care practices. Laurie Anthony is one example of a person who sought to care well. She was not employing a heuristic, but we can find the habits of care in her actions. Anthony approached J.C. with humility and respect in getting to know him and his situation. She connected with him in seeking to reunite him with his family. Anthony responded to his particular needs rather than paternalistically offering what would make her feel better. She took a risk and made mistakes. For Anthony, the practices were habituated in her care for others.

Care can seem like a vague amalgamation of activities and dispositions. A care heuristic for improving care habits can help us focus on care's essential role in human sustenance and flourishing. It gives us a tangible set of skills to develop personally, yet collectively, it can be leveraged to assist us in achieving a care ethos or social spirit of care.

Note

1 In the years following her departure from New York, Anthony discovered that J.C. had not always been forthright in information about his activities. He was involved in drugs and prostitution. Eventually, he found housing in a mental institution. Although disillusioned about J.C., Anthony appropriately concluded that his was just a single story and she continued to work on behalf of the homeless. She learned a great deal from her experience with J.C. about how to better care for people living on the street and how to better care for herself (L. Anthony, personal communication, 6 October 2023).

References

Anthony, L. (1999). *Have a great one! A homeless man's story*. Anthony Publishing.

Barnes, M. (2014). *Care in everyday life: An ethic of care in practice*. The Policy Press.

Barnes, M., & Henwood, F. (2015). Inform with care: Ethics and information in care for people with dementia. *Ethics and Social Welfare, 9*(2), 147–163. https://doi.org/10.1080/17496535.2014.969753

Boodman, E. (2023). Medical colonialism and the power to care: Unsettling participatory inclusion in the settler-state care paradigm. *Hypatia, 38*(2), 330–352. https://doi.org/10.1017/hyp.2023.24

Bunting, M. (2020). *Labours of love: The crisis of care*. Granta Publications.

Charities Aid Foundation. (2022). *Charities aid foundation: U.K. giving report 2022*. https://www.cafonline.org/about-us/publications/2023-publications/uk-giving-report

Dalmiya, V. (2002). Why should a knower care? *Hypatia, 17*(1), 4–52. https://doi.org/10.1111/j.1527-2001.2002.tb00678.x

Davy, L. (2019). Between an ethic of care and an ethic of autonomy. *Angelaki*, 24(3), 101–114. https://doi.org/10.1080/0969725X.2019.1620461

Dewey, J. (1960). *Theory of the moral life*. Irvington Publishers.

Dewey, J. (1966). *Democracy and education*. Free Press.

Dewey, J. (1988). *Human nature and conduct. The middle works of John Dewey, 1899–1924* (Vol. 14, J. A. Boydston, Ed.). Southern Illinois University Press.

Dewey, J. (1989). *Ethics. John Dewey: The later works, 1925–1953* (Vol. 7, J. A. Boydston, Ed.). Southern Illinois University Press.

Dowling, E. (2021). *The care crisis: What caused it and how can we end it*. Verso.

Fesmire, S. A. (2003). *Moral imagination: Pragmatism in ethics*. Indiana University Press.

Gilligan, C. (1982). *In a different voice: Psychological theory and women's development*. Harvard University Press.

Hamington, M. (2004). *Embodied care: Jane Addams, Maurice Merleau-Ponty, and feminist ethic*. Routledge.

Hamington, M. (2017). Care ethics and empathy. In H. L. Maibom (Ed.), *The Routledge handbook of philosophy of empathy* (pp. 264–272). Routledge.

Held, H. (2006). *The ethics of care: Personal, political, and global*. Oxford University Press.

Kimmerer, R. W. (2013). *Braiding sweetgrass: Indigenous wisdom, scientific knowledge, and the teachings of plants*. Milkweed Editions.

MacMullan, T. (2009). *Habits of whiteness: A pragmatist reconstruction*. Indiana University Press.

Mills, C. W. (2005). 'Ideal theory' as ideology. *Hypatia, 20*(3), 165–184. https://www.jstor.org/stable/3811121

Moustakas, C. (1990/2011). *Heuristic research: Design, methodology, and applications*. Sage.

Moustakas, C. (2014). Heuristic research: Design and methodology. In K. J. Schneider, J. F. Pierson, & J. F. T. Bugental (Eds.), *The handbook of humanistic psychology: Theory, research, and practice* (pp. 309–319). Sage.

Noddings, N. (1984). *Caring: A feminine approach to ethics and moral education*. University of California Press.

Noddings, N. (2010). *The maternal factor: Two paths to morality*. University of California Press.

Phillips, S. S., & Benner, P. (1994). *The crisis of care: Affirming and restoring caring practices in the helping professions*. Georgetown University Press.

Puig de la Bellacasa, M. (2017). *Matters of care: Speculative ethics in more than human worlds*. University of Minnesota Press.

Robinson, F. (2011). Stop talking and listen: Discourse ethics and feminist care ethics in international political theory. *Millennium: Journal of International Studies, 39*(3), 845–860. https://doi.org/10.1177/0305829811401176

Ruddick, S. (1980). Maternal thinking. *Feminist Studies, 6*(2), 342–367. https://doi.org/10.2307/3177749

Slote, M. (2007). *The ethics of care and empathy*. Routledge.

Stake, R., & Visse, M. (2021). *A paradigm of care*. Information Age Publishing.

Tervalon, M., & Murray-Garcia, J. (1998). Cultural humility versus cultural competence: A critical distinction in defining physician training outcomes in multicultural education. *Journal of Health Care for the Poor and Underserved, 9*(2), 117–125. https://doi.org/10.1353/hpu.2010.0233

Tronto, J. C. (1993). *Moral boundaries: A political argument for an ethic of care*. Routledge.

Tronto, J. C. (2013). *Caring democracy: Markets, equality, and justice*. New York University Press.

Tronto, J. C., & Fisher, B. (1990). Toward a feminist theory of caring. In E. K. Abel & M. Nelson (Eds.), *Circles of care* (pp. 36–54). SUNY Press.

van Dijke, J., van Nistelrooij, I., Bos, P., & Duyndam, J. (2019). Care ethics: An ethics of empathy? *Nursing Ethics, 26*(5), 1282–1291. https://doi.org/10.1177/0969733018761172

Wildcat, M., & Voth, D. (2023). Indigenous relationality: Definitions and methods. *AlterNative, 19*(2), 475–483. https://doi.org/10.1177/11771801231168380

Yuan, L. (2019). *Confucian ren and feminist ethics of care: Integrating relational self, power, and democracy*. Lexington Books.

Zaki, J. (2019). *The war for kindness*. Crown.

7

HEURISTIC INQUIRY AND NARRATIVE ANALYSIS IN PSYCHOTHERAPEUTIC RESEARCH

Elizabeth Nicholl

Introduction

In psychotherapeutic research, the topic under investigation can often be one that is of personal significance to the researcher; either something they are grappling with in their client work, or their own personal issues that remain unresolved or not fully worked through. This has been the case in the psychotherapeutic research that I have undertaken. When exploring subjects that are of personal significance, a difficulty is that the research process becomes a subjective exercise despite the researcher's efforts to remain objective while taking into consideration their lived experience and acknowledging their reflexivity. Willig writes that researcher reflexivity demands 'an awareness of the researcher's contribution to the construction of meanings throughout the research process' (2013, p. 10), and that the position the researcher takes will influence the study. Our own values and experiences shape the research process. Therefore, the difficulty to which I refer is that when the study is informed by the researcher's lived experience there is a possibility that it becomes a solipsistic exercise whereby the researcher places their self to the fore, giving themselves primacy at the cost of their co-participants.

In this chapter I show how my research combined an exploration into my lived experience with that of my co-participants and how, in doing so, I attempted to avoid a solipsistic subjective position. I also consider the implications of this for psychotherapeutic practice with clients with a diagnosis of psychosis or 'schizophrenia'. What follows is not a straightforward example of how to conduct heuristic research but a demonstration of how a specific form of heuristic inquiry, i.e., heuristic self-search inquiry (HSSI) (Sela-Smith,

DOI: 10.4324/9781003507758-10

2002), can be conducted in harmony with another research method, in this case narrative analysis.

There can be a tension between researching a story or issue of personal significance and having to conduct research that demands a particular method be followed when it is conducted within an institution or in the context of a higher degree, where time is limited. This was a factor in my first choice of method for my research, which resulted in me initially rejecting heuristic research. My belief was that it would be too lengthy a process to properly engage in heuristic inquiry, but what I could not admit to myself at that point was that I was resistant to exploring my own story, and engaging with it at the depth required by this method. I wanted to externalise my experience and listen to what other people had to tell me; in doing so, I was mirroring my work as a psychotherapist whereby I listen to others and facilitate their healing whilst revealing little of myself. However, psychotherapists work on themselves in order to be as present as possible for their clients and, although I had been in personal therapy for many years throughout my training, my study proved to be the final frontier in working through what I had hidden from myself and others for decades.

The context of the research

The question and title of my doctoral research project was *In what ways, if any, do people diagnosed with 'Schizophrenia' perceive their label as having affected their personal therapy?* (Nicholl, 2019). The diagnosis or label 'schizophrenia' is one that is particularly contentious. For this reason, it will be noted in scare quotes throughout this chapter as an acknowledgement that 'the scientific validity of the term is widely held in contention' (Cotton & Loewenthal, 2015, p. 90). For example, Slade and Cooper (1979) have written that the term 'schizophrenic' is problematic because it is used in two ways, both as a description of the disorder itself, and as a description of the person diagnosed with the disorder. As Moncrieff states, the diagnosis of 'schizophrenia' is a process which both identifies and designates a disease, and a 'diagnosis [of "schizophrenia"] is merely a formal sounding label given to behaviour that has already been identified as problematic' (2010, p. 374). My initial focus had been upon the experience of therapists working with people with a diagnosis of 'schizophrenia' because I was working with two clients with this diagnosis, and I was finding it interesting and challenging work. However, what I was not acknowledging was my own experience. I had been given a diagnosis of 'paranoid schizophrenia' at the age of 18, at a time when I was negotiating my way from a difficult childhood and adolescence into adulthood, and spectacularly failing to do so. I was certainly very unwell, but, after two hospital stays and a couple of years on anti-psychotic medication, I recovered from my psychotic episode outside the psychiatric system. I then spent the next decades self-silencing. I worked and raised a family all the while hiding my past, although this was not without an element of suffering; in particular, my experiences of recurring bouts of deep depression for which I never sought help, and that I survived free of medication. When I commenced my training as a psychotherapist, I began to reveal my past in my personal therapy. It was difficult but my therapist met the disclosure of my former diagnosis with care and started to help me work through my feelings of shame. However, after we had worked together for nearly two years, she suddenly became unwell, and I had to stop working with her. In order to meet the requirements of my course, I needed to find another therapist and so I had an assessment with someone to whom I disclosed my history, feeling safe to do so because the work with my first therapist had been so helpful. At the end of this initial assessment, she asked what medication I was on. Although I had already told her that I had not taken medication since the age of 19, I repeated this, but I was left feeling as though she had not listened to what I had told her about my recovery. My assumption was that she was fixated on the diagnosis I had been given and I felt my old shame flooding me, leaving me feeling unheard and violated. I was relieved when she phoned me a couple of days later to say that she felt she couldn't work with me. Despite having disclosed my former diagnosis previously in therapy and having been treated with compassion, what had happened in this assessment opened a deep well of shame within me that overshadowed the previous care I had received. I found another therapist with whom I worked for another five years but I had been damaged by this interaction, and I believe that it contributed to me making assumptions about how others experienced disclosure in their personal therapy.

It was only shortly before I had to submit my doctoral research proposal that I realised that I felt compelled to focus upon how clients diagnosed with 'schizophrenia' experience their personal therapy, rather than upon how psychotherapists experience working with clients with this diagnosis. I had been hiding from myself and others for too long, and to heal fully I needed to face what shamed me. In addition, because of my experience of feeling unheard by the psychotherapist I was hoping to work with, an overriding concern throughout the research process was how one might hear the other both in research and in psychotherapy.

'Schizophrenia' and first-person accounts

Once I had arrived at my research question, the next stage was to conduct a literature review. The initial focus of this review was on how the client voice can be heard in general in psychotherapy, through the lens of a variety of different therapeutic approaches. Psychotherapeutic ways of working with psychosis have been advocated as a way of understanding mental distress in a different way from those approaches that locate the origins of human distress within a disease-oriented biomedical model. It has been argued that talking therapies generally see mental distress as located within relational and/or cultural contexts (Johnstone, 2000). Therefore, when the prevailing Western social and cultural paradigm is one in which our dominant understanding of mental distress remains informed by biomedical approaches, it is important to ask what effect this might have on how therapists understand and respond to severe mental distress. Therapists' narratives can shape the response they give to their clients, which may then shape clients' responses both to the diagnosis/label and to therapy. Given that I was focusing on the client's perception of their diagnosis and the way in which their therapist might respond to it, I needed to include the client voice in the literature review. Not to do so would perpetuate the silencing of marginalised voices.

People who have been able to tell their stories have reported that this is an important process, particularly because it helps them make sense of their experience and allows them to share it with another. Rather than being told what their experience means, they are the ones doing the telling. Because a client's explanations of their experiences may be at odds with professional explanations, they can run the risk of feeling unheard and/or invalidated (as I felt I had been). Nevertheless, it is important for them to feel involved in a therapeutic process rather than simply being the recipient of the therapist's knowledge and authority. The general absence of the client voice in mainstream psychiatry and in the other 'psy' professions (other than when it is being used as a commodity), is an example of where a large body of knowledge and experience has been subjugated and marginalised, mainly because it may challenge the dominant medical discourse (Geekie, 2004).

A rich source of first-person experience was accessible in internet blogs. For example, on the *Mad in America* website, Douglas Bloch refers to his stigma as 'toxic feelings of blame, guilt or shame that I had internalized' (2014, para. 13). On the same website, the author who goes by the name 'Mad in Finland' (2024) says:

> I would never have recovered if I hadn't been able to talk through my childhood experiences in a safe caregiving relationship....The most important thing was to be able to tell what had happened and at the same time free myself from the thought that the events were my own fault.
>
> (para. 5)

The book *Our Encounters with Madness* contains a number of first-person accounts of experiences of mental illness, with the aim of allowing such narratives to demonstrate what it is like to experience mental health problems, and to move away from 'formal accounts [that] deal with human distress by proxy' (Grant et al., 2011, p. 3).

These accounts include:

- 'Having the opportunity to tell and retell the story of my journey through mental health services has enabled me to gain a rich personal under-standing of my own experiences' (Leigh-Phippard, 2011, p. 108).
- 'I hold that narrative is a powerful tool; it's helped me. It's helped me to leave behind the days of neglect and abuse in the old asylums, and to connect with those of a like mind' (Voyce, 2011, p. 14).
- 'Talking about my experiences and learning not to be ashamed of what had happened to me was of huge benefit'

(Nayler, 2011, p. 68)

My first research method

Reading these first-person accounts confirmed for me the need provide my co-participants with the means to tell their stories within the formal context of an academic study, so I chose Bruner's narrative analysis as my primary research method (1990, 1991, 2001, 2004). Polkinghorne describes narrative as the foremost means by which one can make sense of human existence, and proposes that the identity one constructs through narrative is created both through recollections of the past and through future stories which serve to provide hope. Narrative is seen as 'one of our fundamental structures of com-prehension [which] shapes the character of our existence in a particular way' (Polkinghorne, 1988, p. 15).

The central premise of narrative analysis is that the primary sources of research data are the stories told by co-participants, and that the main assumptions underpinning narrative research are: that both co-participant and researcher have personal agency in constructing a story for themselves; that as humans we desire meaning, so telling stories about our experiences is a way of creating meaning; and that narrative research is a co-constructed dialogue between the story teller and the listener. As humans we participate with others in the world around us in creating our identities through the sto-ries that others tell about us and that we tell about ourselves. Narratives can be used not only as a means of establishing a cultural identity, but also a self-identity. By amending those narratives, we can renegotiate and alter our iden-tity (Hiles & Čermák, 2008). Although it could be argued that this is what happens in qualitative research in general, it is how data are used that is key. For example, in what have become phenomenological methods, according to McLeod, the stories tend to be 'analysed in terms of constituent themes, meaning units or categories' (2011, p. 105), whereas narrative approaches are more concerned with 'the additional meanings conveyed by the story-as-a-whole' (2011, p. 105).

Therefore, when conducting my research, I needed to bear in mind how I interpreted the interviews with my co-participants and how my motivation to conduct the research might influence that interpretation, because our personal values and experiences shape the research process. However, a particular strength of narrative analysis is that researcher's reflexivity is understood to be the way in which they retain an awareness of their self throughout the process, and this allows for an examination and analysis of both the research and of the role that the researcher plays in engaging in and writing up the study. Narrative analysis perceives the research process as not only producing a description of what might be understood to be reality but also constructing some form of reality.

I presented the findings from the narrative analysis of my co-participants' interviews as a series of individual narratives that were brought together and related as a coherent story because 'narrative displays the extensive variety of ways in which life might be drawn together into a unified adventure' (Polkinghorne, 1988, p. 36). I used Braun and Clarke's (2006) approach to thematic analysis as a means of organising the research data into a series of common themes. These common themes were then presented as a narrative showing progress from one state (pre-diagnosis), through being diagnosed, and ending with the disclosure of the diagnosis. I also included sub-themes such as experiences with medication, stigma, and self-stigma and a consideration of how beliefs that may seem odd to others are pathologised.

Heuristic research

It can be seen that I perceived narrative analysis as a means of allowing my co-participants' voices to be heard through the narrative I constructed for them. I was, nevertheless, aware that whatever I presented would be in essence my own narrative which was borne of my assumptions about what others had experienced in their personal therapy. Through the process of conducting interviews with my co-participants and writing up the findings I had become more aware that I had been wanting my experience of feeling unheard to be validated by others. Therefore, I needed to find a way of excavating my shame and guilt so it wouldn't infect others' stories. Initially, I had dismissed heuristic inquiry as an appropriate method for this research, but I now realised that this rejection was rooted in a hitherto unconscious fear of what I was hiding from myself. It was only after having completed the interviews and conducted a narrative analysis of the interview data that I came to believe that heuristic research could further illuminate the research question. Given that my research project had its foundations in my lived experience, and with a heuristic method offering the possibility of using such experience, as well as investigating the experiences of others, I realised that it could be of significant benefit to my study. As Kenny notes, heuristic research, in common with narrative inquiry, 'values the process of gathering stories that can give voice to human experiences' (2012, p. 9).

Moustakas describes heuristics as a way of discovering and uncovering new understandings of the research topic, with both the researcher and co-participants gaining in self-knowledge at the same time. He also states that 'The heuristic process is autobiographic' (1990, p. 15) and so, with the research question being one of personal significance to me, this method was appropriate for my research. Moustakas writes that the heuristic process begins with something that has called to the researcher from their life experiences. This something may not be fully in the researcher's awareness and an element of mystery may remain around the phenomenon but, by engaging in heuristic research, there is the possibility of regaining a deeper understanding of what it is to be human. The data lie within the researcher and through both dialogue with others and oneself, a story can be created which, according to Moustakas, 'portrays the qualities, meanings and essences of universally unique experiences' (1990, p. 13).

I had been skirting around heuristics through the whole (narrative) project. However, once I had completed writing up my initial findings, I became stuck. Something more needed to be said, and I found that Sela-Smith's heuristic self-search inquiry (HSSI) seemed to offer me a way out of my stuckness. An HSSI may begin when the self-searcher comes to realise that they have a sense of internal uneasiness or disharmony. This sense of discomfort can be as a result of the researcher experiencing something that gives rise to painful feelings such as guilt, shame, and sadness (Sela-Smith, 2013).

Sela-Smith formulated HSSI as a response to what she viewed as the limitations of Moustakas' method, arguing that the final frontier of human knowledge is the internal world, or interiority, an area which had hitherto been resisted as a legitimate source of scientific knowledge. She asserts that there is a danger in heuristic research that the findings will be derived from co-participants rather than from within the researcher, and there had been a move to the observation of experience rather than immersion in self-search. The use of co-participants (à la Moustakas) means that their experience becomes part of the data and so, as Sela-Smith observes, the validity of the researcher's experience is 'established by the similar experiences of others' (2002, p. 76). Critiquing this position, she argues that 'coparticipants, if they are used in self-search, are valuable as reflectors of possible areas of resistance that may be out of conscious awareness' (2002, p. 78). Indeed, in her work, Sela-Smith highlights the importance of resistance, which, as Tweedie puts it, 'is addressed by Sela-Smith as difficulty staying with the "*I-who-feels*" and this acknowledgement is what separates heuristic self-search inquiry from Moustakas' heuristic inquiry' (2015, p. 49). Checking one's own experience against that of others does not make that experience more valid, but using the experience of others to illuminate one's own blind spots does add value. It also takes courage to do this as others will then experience the researcher's deepening self-awareness through the story the researcher tells. When telling this story, it is important for the researcher to speak from the 'I' and to remain connected to the feelings, both past and present, that the experience evokes rather than simply adopting a reporting style.

For Sela-Smith, heuristics is the process of the researcher's conscious self-surrendering to the actual feeling of an experience as a way of travelling to 'unknown aspects of self and internal organizational systems not normally known in waking-style consciousness' (2002, p. 59). She proposes that, whilst language can facilitate interpersonal communications as well as enhance self-awareness, it can also cause a split in the experience of the self. Experiences that cannot be verbalised are driven underground and are then 'disconnected from the verbal-thinking self' (2002, p. 62). She argues that, by accessing these felt experiences through a heuristic process, they can be reconstructed anew and a transformation in the meaning one makes of one's life can come about. The researcher must always remain present (Atkins & Loewenthal, 2004), but if the researcher avoids a full immersion in their self-search, there is the danger that there will be no story of self-transformation on the part of the researcher. However, should the researcher be able to immerse themselves in their interior world 'by moving through resistance and remaining focused until self-transformation occurs... long-hidden tacit knowledge, suppressed, repressed, rejected, and feared by the individual, by social systems, and by humankind, may finally emerge' (Sela-Smith, 2002, pp. 83–84).

However, if the research topic is one that is personally painful then the researcher may try to resist the heuristic process in an attempt to avoid re-experiencing pain. This is what I had done before I realised that I needed to re-experience my pain in order to understand my stories and those of others. As Ozertugrul has written, Sela-Smith saw Moustakas' heuristic method as offering the possibility of opening 'a radical shift from the medical model and [allowing] a view of a person who can engage himself or herself in life and make choices, even in the presence of severe personal problems (or diagnosis)' (Ozertugrul, 2017, p. 1). HSSI therefore offered me an opportunity to make a radical shift, to move beyond my internal uneasiness, and to engage in exploring my story. I immersed myself in the life experiences that influenced my doctoral research and attempted to stay connected to my feelings throughout. I told the story of my childhood and adolescence, describing my gradual implosion into psychosis. I described what it is like to be psychotic, trying to stay with the feelings this brought up in me through the process of writing about it. Then I wrote about my recovery and subsequent self-silencing (Nicholl, 2019). Because I allowed myself to stay connected with the emotions that this exploration of my story evoked, it became a transformative experience. I had spent years talking around it in my personal therapy but undertaking the self-search inquiry meant that I was facing my pain in a different way. I was travelling to my interior world alone in order to overcome my fear, shame, and guilt. This is where the transformation lay. I became more forgiving of myself, and I was able to put aside much of the shame that I had carried with me for decades.

Research findings

I have already indicated the content of the research findings but what was important to me in writing up these findings was how they might be presented in a way that would do justice to the co-participants' voices but also demonstrate how I had illuminated my blind spots. I asked, 'How might I show that my deepened self-awareness was of value to the research?' This felt particularly important once the interviews were underway and it was becoming clearer that the initial research question about therapy and disclosure (although still significant), played a smaller part than I had assumed.

Before I presented the narrative containing the co-participants' stories, I began by relating my story, describing who I was, who I am now, and detailing my psychotic breakdown and recovery (Nicholl et al., 2021). Despite the drive to tell this story, it was difficult and it took several months to do. However, it was an illuminating process. I had not realised the extent to which I had felt unheard by my family and mental health professionals and how this might have influenced concerns that my co-participants needed to be heard too. In addition, conversations with my Director of Studies helped me to articulate how I had suppressed my own story. He pointed out that conducting an HSSI appeared to have enabled me to hear myself more, with the effect that I could better hear the stories of others.

In the final write-up of the study, my story was followed by those of the ten co-participants. They all embodied different ways of experiencing, and were recovering, or attempting to recover, from a 'schizophrenia' diagnosis. They also held a variety of views about the medical model approach to psychological distress, with some having found it beneficial and others holding vehemently 'anti-psychiatry' views. Overall, my experiences and those of my co-participants were presented as a form of quest from relative 'normality' through a period of transformation after which there occurs a kind of battle to recover a sense of self.

I had found the disclosure in therapy of my diagnosis difficult and shameful, and I had assumed that this would be a universal experience. However, the disclosure of a diagnosis of 'schizophrenia' was only concerning for two of the co-participants. Indeed, although the co-participants reported that it might be difficult to disclose in general life, the overall finding was that it is believed to be important to disclose in therapy. For some, disclosure is a way of screening therapists who won't work with people diagnosed with 'schizo-phrenia' and for others it was because there is little point in working with someone who doesn't know about their diagnosis. What was more important was that when seeking therapy, the co-participants reported wanting to find a space in which to glean some kind of meaning from their experiences as well as to attempt to heal. It seems that this is largely dependent upon whether the therapist is willing to explore their client's world or whether they are fearful of doing so. The question of disclosure is more pertinent for some people than for others but what feels most pressing for everybody is the desire to be heard and taken seriously.

However, what emerged from the findings is that life post-diagnosis is about more than therapy. It is about finding helpful people within mental health services, or extricating oneself from those services in order to preserve a modicum of sanity. For some, it is expedient to stay with mental health ser-vices in order to survive materially and financially. Some people never really recover fully, but others do, and they live lives in which they fulfil their aca-demic and career aims despite having been told that as a 'schizophrenic' they can never expect to fulfil any potential they may have. Above all, it can be about finding the will to live one's life despite ongoing difficulties and to make that life one that has meaning and hope.

Conclusion and creative synthesis

The aim of my doctoral research was to explore the lived experience of peo-ple with a diagnosis of 'schizophrenia', with a focus upon the disclosure of this diagnosis in their personal therapy. I have shown how this question was formed from assumptions I had made that my difficult experience of disclo-sure was universal, but that, through interviewing my co-participants and conducting a narrative analysis of the research data, I found that, in fact, it was not a universal experience. I came to realise that my research topic was very much about my personal preoccupations, and so it was only through conducting an HSSI that I was able to understand these assumptions and why I had made them. My personal experience in therapy was influenced by a sense of shame and self-stigma, but through engaging in an HSSI I had a fur-ther personal epiphany. I recalled that my overriding thought after the assess-ment session with the therapist who rejected me was 'She just didn't listen to a word I said'. This linked to a theme of feeling unheard throughout my life by the people closest to me, and it resulted in me believing that I had to give my co-participants a voice, before my interior exploration helped me realise that I also had to permit myself to have a voice.

Narrative analysis played an important role in co-constructing a dialogue between me and my co-participants, and in creating a shared meaning from the stories they told me. However, I was aware that, in presenting the research findings as a story, I was using their words to construct a story of my own making. This is where the HSSI was useful, not only in helping me face old, buried emotions in order to move away from the shame and guilt I carried, but also in helping me become clearer about how my baggage stopped me from fully hearing the voices of my co-participants. Sela-Smith's (2002) critique of Moustakas was that the researcher would validate their own experiences through hearing about others' experiences, but I believe that, if one can stay with the *I-who-feels* alongside the stories of one's co-participants, then there is the possibility of offering both the researcher and their co-participants their voices. The nature of the knowledge uncovered in this way is both deeply personal and it has a broader social significance. As Sela-Smith (2002) argues, a heuristic self-search inquiry should be conducted with the desire to tell a story about one's personal transformation as a means of offering the possibility of transformation to those who hear or read it.

Whilst it may be something of which the researcher is (consciously or explicitly) aware, this process illuminates aspects of experiencing which were hitherto unknown, and which then become new realms of knowledge for both the researcher and a wider audience. For example, Bazzano suggests a way of bringing together Moustakas' and Sela-Smith's heuristic methods through neuro-phenomenology, which combines first-person reports and third-person descriptions and can thus 'take the enquiry beyond both mere subjectivity and the objectivism of hard science… it offers one possible way out of a defensive subjectivist position' (Bazzano, 2021, p. 112). For this reason, I believe that Sela-Smith's HSSI and Bruner's approach to narrative analysis can also work in harmony together. By using both methods I was able to move from the solipsism of projecting a personal experience on to others and assuming it was a universal experience, to presenting each individual's story as a discrete narrative that nevertheless has a wider significance.

One aspect of this wider social significance is the implication that the findings could have for psychotherapeutic practice and how one can hear the other. Aaltonen et al. (2002) have suggested that the development of psychotherapy with psychotic clients has been hindered by the view that it is a difficult area of practice, and that psychotherapy practice and trainings are restricted to the treatment of less disturbed clients than those diagnosed with psychotic disorders. The implication of this is that although there are therapists who will work with people with a diagnosis of 'schizophrenia', such as those seeing the co-participants, there are others who may be reluctant to do so. Donna Orange's (2012) work on clinical hospitality is therefore helpful to consider. Orange argues that there are specific ethical challenges in all types of psychotherapeutic work and that Emanuel Levinas, Jacques Derrida, and Paul Ricoeur's writings on hospitality can help us restore dignity to our clients. This is because these philosophers can act as 'reminders of the vocational aspects of a profession often mired in the pressures to diagnose and prescribe, to evade and murder, to totalize and finalize' (Orange, 2012, p. 165). This is not only relevant for psychotherapeutic work with people who have been given psychiatric diagnoses, but it is also useful for researchers when considering how to do justice to their co-participants' stories. In offering hospitality to the other, it is possible that we might restore their, and our own, humanity.

To conclude, there is always the risk that a heuristic project can be too self-focused and that it offers nothing more than an opportunity for the researcher to confirm their own beliefs. An advantage of Sela-Smith's (2002) approach is that it offers the opportunity to highlight the researcher's blind spots when compared to the experience of others. My experience is that it showed me that my experience is not universal and that not everyone feels the same shame that I did. At the same time, I didn't want to give myself primacy in the study, so I sought to juxtapose other voices with my own. Like my story, the co-participants' stories told of trauma, being drawn into psychiatric services, and being diagnosed. Most importantly, they talked about how they managed their lives and made personal meanings from these experiences. Above all, I found that my co-participants' stories prompted me to try to understand my own through heuristic inquiry, and together we co-created a collective narrative.

We are people who, despite having had a diagnosis at some point in our lives, have as much right to a fulfilling, meaningful, and hopeful life as anybody. An important aspect of heuristic research is the creative synthesis, which Moustakas (1990) describes as an encapsulation of the essence of the co-participants' experience alongside the personal illuminations that the researcher has uncovered as a result of the research process. In the poem *Creative synthesis* that concludes this chapter, I have woven together my own voice with that of my co-participants, creating a chorus of united yet individual voices, asking to be listened to.

Creative synthesis

This is terrifying:
The final sloughing off of my shame.
I have to confront what I have long known:
They are not 'other'. They are me.

I have been sitting in a dark room for most of my life,
Allowing a part of myself to flourish and hiding the rest.

My co-participants have illuminated me.
We are all aspects of each other.
In childhood, for some, there is no sanctuary.
Fear, blame, a turning away, expectations and recriminations.
The child creates their own world.
It is safe but it is lonely, and their voice is lost to all but themselves.
For others their voice is lost when they are older; stress, anger, control, and fear.

Initially we can speak but lose the ability to be heard.
Things stop making sense, they fall away,
The centre holds but the edges of the world crumble.
Dreams and waking life intermingle… become confused.
So, we surrender to the care of those who say they know best.
Retreat to bed.
Aimless wandering, the days measured out in pills and cigarettes.
Emerge into the world and what now?
More pills and cigarettes.

Friends drop away, nothing to do, can't read, can't think, can't be me.
I am the sum of the chemicals they say are keeping me 'well'.
If this is being 'well' I would rather be 'sick'.
I feel dead but haven't the will to live or die.
Zombie flesh and zombie mind.

So, how then do we find the desire to live?
We carry a mark that sets us apart.
We are mad.
The stain colours us.
Tongues form words, lips and teeth spit them out, but we still have no voice.
No-one listens and no-one believes us.
Who knows what is best for us? This is a lifelong illness.
Don't try too hard. Don't get stressed. Don't live. You're sick now.

There is a choice to be made between compliance and subversion.
In order to survive which way will we jump?
There is no easy answer to this, so we survive however we can.
Comply or lie.
We need meaning in order to keep living.
Faith, friendship, academia, work, we tether ourselves to life.
But we find it hard to be heard.

People don't listen:
'I was expecting help.
You know, somebody who listens to me,
But it ended up very different.
They won't listen to you, and they do things that harm you.
He was just trying to work out how to treat me but without listening to
me at all.
I just didn't feel that he was listening to me or validating any of it.
She didn't believe what I was saying,
And she just kept interrupting me.
Well, it wasn't listening, it wasn't hearing'.

And so why choose therapy?
Hope that it will help.
Someone to hear, to believe, and to bear witness to a life lived under the
mark of madness.
There is always hope.

References

Aaltonen, J., Alanen, Y. O., Keinänen, M., & Räkköläinen, V. (2002). An advanced specialist-level training programme in psychodynamic individual psychotherapy of psychotic and borderline patients: The Finnish approach. *European Journal of Psychotherapy and Counselling*, *15*(1), 13–30. https://doi.org/10.1080/13642530210159215

Atkins, D., & Loewenthal, D. (2004). The lived experience of psychotherapists working with older clients: An heuristic study. *British Journal of Guidance and Counselling*, *32*(4), 493–509. https://doi.org/10.1080/03069880412331303295

Bazzano, M. (2021). Maculate conceptions. In D. Loewenthal (Ed.), *Critical existential-analytic psychotherapy: Some implications for practices, theories and research* (pp. 103–116). Routledge.

Bloch, D. (2014, March 17). *Overcoming the stigma of depression*. Mad in America. https://www.madinamerica.com/2014/03/overcoming-stigma-of-depression/

Braun, V., & Clarke, V. (2006). Using thematic analysis in psychology. *Qualitative research in psychology*, *3*(2), 77–101. https://doi.org/10.1191/1478088706qp063oa

Bruner, J. (1990). *Acts of meaning*. Harvard University Press.

Bruner, J. (1991). The narrative construction of reality. *Critical Inquiry*, *18*(1), 1–21. https://www.jstor.org/stable/1343711

Bruner, J. (2001). Self-making and world-making. In J. Brockmeier & D. Carbaugh (Eds.), *Narrative and identity: Studies in autobiography, self and culture* (pp. 25–37). John Benjamin Publishing Company.

Bruner, J. (2004). Life as narrative. *Social Research*, *71*(3), 691–710. https://www.jstor.org/stable/40970444

Cotton, T., & Loewenthal, D. (2015). Personal versus medical meaning in breakdown, treatment and recovery from 'schizophrenia'. In D. Loewenthal (Ed.), *Critical psychotherapy, psychoanalysis and counselling: Implications for practice* (pp. 77–92). Palgrave MacMillan.

Geekie, J. (2004). Listening to the voices we hear. In J. Read, L. R. Mosher, & R. P. Bentall (Eds.), *Models of madness: Psychological, social and biological approaches to schizophrenia* (pp. 133–145). Routledge.

Grant, A., Biley, F., & Walker, H. (2011). *Our encounters with madness*. PCCS Books.

Hiles, D., & Čermák, I. (2008). Narrative psychology. In C. Willig & W. Stainton-Rogers (Eds.), *The SAGE handbook of qualitative research in psychology* (pp. 147–164). Sage.

Johnstone, L. (2000). *Users and abusers of psychiatry*. Routledge.

Kenny, G. (2012). An introduction to Moustakas's heuristic method. *Nurse Researcher, 19*(3), 6–11.

Leigh-Phippard, H. (2011). Surviving: From silence to speaking out. In A. Grant, F. Biley, & H. Walker (Eds.), *Our encounters with madness* (pp. 103–109). PCCS Books.

Mad In Finland. (2024, January 10). What helped – and what didn't help – my recovery. https://www.madinamerica.com/2024/01/what-helped-my-recovery/

McLeod, J. (2001). *Qualitative research in counselling and psychotherapy*. Sage.

Moncrieff, J. (2010). Psychiatric diagnosis as a political device. *Social Theory and Health, 8*(1), 370–382. https://doi.org/10.1057/sth.2009.11

Moustakas, C. (1990). *Heuristic research: Design, methodology and application*. Sage.

Nayler, S. (2011). Recovery and rediscovery. In A. Grant, F. Biley, & H. Walker (Eds.), *Our encounters with madness* (pp. 63–71). PCCS Books.

Nicholl, E. (2019). *In what ways, if any, do people diagnosed with 'schizophrenia' perceive their label as having affected their personal therapy?* [Unpublished doctoral thesis]. University of Roehampton.

Nicholl, E., Loewenthal, D., & Davies, J. (2021). Finding my voice: Telling stories with heuristic self-search inquiry. In D. Loewenthal (Ed.), *Critical existential-analytic psychotherapy: Some implications for practices, theories and research* (pp. 57–73). Routledge.

Orange, D. (2012). Clinical hospitality: Welcoming the face of the devastated other. *Ata: Journal of Psychotherapy Aotearoa New Zealand, 16*(2), 165–178. https://doi.org/10.9791/ajpanz.2012.17

Ozertugrul, E. (2017). A comparative analysis: Heuristic self-search inquiry as self-knowledge and knowledge of society. *Journal of Humanistic Psychology, 57*(3), 237–251. https://doi.org/10.1177/0022167815594966

Polkinghorne, D. E. (1988). *Narrative knowing and the human sciences*. State University of New York Press.

Sela-Smith, S. (2002). Heuristic research: A review and critique of Moustakas's method. *Journal of Humanistic Psychology, 42*(3), 53–88. https://doi.org/10.1177/00267802042003004

Sela-Smith, S. (2013). *Heuristic self-search inquiry*. https://web.archive.org/web/20201129102743/http://www.infiniteconnections.us/heuristic-self-search-inquiry-january-2003

Slade, P. D., & Cooper, R. (1979). Some conceptual difficulties with the term 'schizophrenia': An alternative model. *British Journal of Social and Clinical Psychology, 18*(3), 309–317. https://doi.org/10.1111/j.2044-8260.1979.tb00341.x

Tweedie, K. L. (2015). *Relinquishing knowing and reclaiming being: A heuristic self-search inquiry of becoming a counsellor through learning to tolerate uncertainty by reflecting on experience in life, counselling practice and research* [Doctoral thesis, University of Edinburgh]. Edinburgh Research Archive. https://hdl.handle.net/1842/15780

Voyce, A. (2011). On hearing my diagnosis. In A. Grant, F. Biley, & H. Walker (Eds.), *Our encounters with madness* (pp. 13–14). PCCS Books.

Willig, C. (2013). *Introducing qualitative research in psychology.* Open University Press.

Reaching Across

8

A COMPARATIVE STUDY OF HEURISTIC INQUIRY IN AI AND ARTISTIC RESEARCH

Akbar Ghobakhlou and Hossein Najafi

Introduction

This chapter is written by a computer scientist and an artistic practitioner who embarked on a discussion about the nature of heuristics in their respective fields of inquiry. Although seemingly distant, we recognised significant connections between heuristic inquiry in artificial intelligence and in artistic research. The application of heuristics is crucial in navigating the complexities of problem-solving, particularly in fields that demand creative and flexible thinking. To begin the discourse on the necessity of heuristic approaches to problem-solving, a simple yet illustrative example may serve as an effective starting point.

Imagine you are a salesperson with the task of visiting a number of cities, selling goods, and then returning home. To do this, you must find the most efficient route between the cities to save both time and fuel. Let's begin by assuming that there are only three cities to visit. In this scenario, determining the shortest route is relatively straightforward because there are only a few possible paths to compare. For cities A, B, and C, you could travel A-B-C-A or A-C-B-A, and it would be easy to determine which journey will be shorter. However, as you add more cities, the complexity of the problem increases dramatically. With each additional city, the number of potential routes grows exponentially, making it very challenging to find the shortest route. For example, with ten cities, you face over 3 million possible routes, and visiting 60 cities, the number of possible routes becomes more than the estimated number of atoms in the observable universe. This phenomenon is known as *combinatorial explosion* (Schuster, 2000).

DOI: 10.4324/9781003507758-12

This famous example is called the *Traveling Salesman Problem*, a conundrum which, in computational complexity theory falls within a class of nondeterministic polynomial (NP) time, and is considered NP-hard (Jünger et al., 1995). NP-hard, in computer science, refers to problems that are notoriously difficult to solve because the time required to solve them increases exponentially with the size of the problem. In essence, as the number of cities grows, finding the absolute shortest route becomes impractical. To tackle this, we utilise heuristics. Heuristics trades off completeness, accuracy, and precision for speed. For example, for the *Traveling Salesman Problem*, heuristic methods provide good enough solutions. These might not provide the absolute shortest route, but they come close in a fraction of the time it would take to calculate an exact solution. Techniques like the nearest neighbour, where you always visit the closest unvisited city next, or the genetic algorithm, which mimics natural selection to find progressively better routes, are examples of heuristic approaches (Jünger et al., 1995).

In a completely different kind of challenge, when an artist is navigating an immense number of unknown possibilities inside a complex project, they also employ heuristic methods (Ings, 2011). However, this application is more qualitative than quantitative. This said, both approaches elevate broad estimation or a sense of effectiveness over the pursuit of certainty or absolute accuracy.

Heuristics in artificial intelligence

Artificial intelligence (AI) is a generic term that encompasses a broad range of computational techniques designed to mimic or replicate human-like intelligence. In this chapter, AI is discussed on multiple levels, from that of a generic concept to artificial neural networks (Figure 8.1). AI systems are capable of performing tasks that typically require human intelligence, such as visual perception, speech recognition, decision-making, and language translation (Russell & Norvig, 2010). Within the domain of AI, machine learning (ML) emerges as a crucial subset. It focuses on the development of processes and statistical models that enable computers to learn and make predictions or decisions based on data, rather than being explicitly programmed (Alpaydin, 2020). ML encompasses different methods including a specialised approach known as deep learning (DL), which involves training artificial neural networks to work with large volumes of data. DL models can automatically discover the representations needed for feature detection or classification from raw data, so this makes it a powerful tool for many AI tasks (LeCun et al., 2015). A pivotal element of DL is artificial neural networks (ANNs), which are inspired by the biological neural networks of animal brains. ANNs are composed of interconnected groups of nodes, resembling the vast networks of neurons in the biological brain. These are used for pattern recognition and cognitive tasks (Goodfellow et al., 2016).

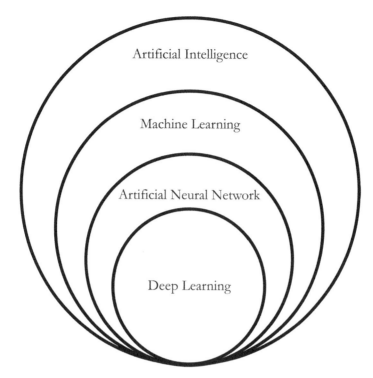

FIGURE 8.1   Mapping a scheme of artificial intelligence, machine learning, artificial neural networks, and deep learning.

Heuristics in AI refers to strategies or methods of problem-solving when encountering complex and difficult problems.[1] They operate quickly at the expense of accuracy, so they can potentially lead to errors or suboptimal solutions. Heuristics are essential to AI because if we put the need for optimality aside, they allow a system to make rapid progress when solving complex problems. They are essential tools for moving about the wide, frequently dark spaces that exist in many AI problems.

Given the distinctive nature and use of heuristics in AI, the next section provides an overview of evolutions in the field.

A brief history of artificial intelligence

The term 'artificial intelligence' was first coined by John McCarthy during a seminal workshop at Dartmouth College in 1955, and this use marked the formal birth of the field (Flasiński, 2016). Having convened leading researchers from diverse disciplines, McCarthy's workshop sought to create machines capable of mimicking human cognitive functions. However, despite their initial enthusiasm, early researchers in AI faced formidable challenges, such as the complexity of natural language and the constraints of computational resources available at the time (Flasiński, 2016).

Between the 1950s and the 1980s, AI research predominantly focused on symbolic AI (an approach in which systems manipulated symbols to perform tasks, akin to human reasoning). This era saw the rise of expert systems,[2] which operated based on predefined rules and knowledge bases, thereby enabling such systems to emulate the decision-making abilities of human experts in specific domains (Jackson, 1986). However, this approach was limited because of its reliance on extensive domain-specific knowledge and its inability to handle uncertainties and learn from data.

The late 20th century witnessed periods known as 'AI winters' (Harguess & Ward, 2022, p. 1) that were characterised by reduced funding and a decline in interest in AI research. These winters were largely a result of the limitations of symbolic AI, particularly its ineffectiveness in dealing with real-world uncertainties and learning challenges, which, in turn, led to a more sceptical public perception of AI (Crevier, 1993).

A resurgence of interest in AI emerged in the 1990s with the advent of machine learning (ML). Unlike its predecessors, ML algorithms empowered systems to recognise patterns from data, and they marked a significant shift from rule-based methodologies to data-driven approaches. Techniques such as decision trees, support vector machines, and clustering became instrumental in this new era, enabling machines to learn and make predictions or decisions based on data (Alpaydin, 2020).

The 2000s saw the rise of artificial neural networks (ANNs), inspired by the structure and function of the human brain. A notable subset of ML, known as deep learning, involved the use of neural networks with multiple layers. This approach achieved remarkable success, including image recognition and natural language processing (Goodfellow et al., 2016). The growth of deep learning may be attributed to several factors including the availability of large volumes of labelled data, significant advances in hardware and software, and the development of new architectures and algorithms, including heuristics (Schmidhuber, 2015).

Machine learning

As a subset of AI, machine learning has gained significant traction and application across various fields including computer vision, cybersecurity, health, and language processing. Driven by data, ML algorithms recognise patterns and statistical relationships, thereby enabling learning and adaptation, and encompass a variety of approaches such as regression, random forests, support vector machines, and artificial neural networks, each with unique capabilities to address diverse problems (Cioffi et al., 2020).

ML algorithms are commonly categorised into three main types:

1 Supervised learning, which is an approach that involves training algorithms and processes on labelled data, where the relationship between input and desired output is known. The algorithm learns to map input to output, identifying patterns within the data. It is further divided into two main categories: classification and prediction. Classification involves the process of categorising data into predefined groups or classes, while prediction involves forecasting continuous or discrete values (Dridi, 2021). Applications range from email filtering to medical diagnosis and price prediction.

2 Unsupervised learning, whereby algorithms learn from unlabelled data, discovering hidden patterns without guidance, which results in being able to cluster similar data points and reduce data dimensionality. Examples of unsupervised learning include business use of clustering for customer segmentation, and association rules in market analysis (Hruschka, 2021).

3 Reinforcement learning, in which using a trial-and-error approach an agent learns optimal actions through rewards or penalties. This type of learning is a growing area in autonomous systems such as self-driving cars, where the vehicle learns and improves decision-making over time.

(Moussaoui & Benslimane, 2023)

ML turns data into useful predictions and decisions. To do this well, ML follows six steps, which help us progress from collecting data to ensuring that the ML model works properly (Figure 8.2).

Each step plays a key role in making sure we obtain reliable results from models, while the process as a whole forms the backbone of a successful ML project.

Data gathering involves collecting relevant information from various sources to create a comprehensive dataset (Provost & Fawcett, 2013). Data preparation is used to clean and structure the data, for instance, addressing inaccuracies, and ensuring it's in the right format (Mansingh et al., 2016). Feature engineering focuses on selecting and modifying key data elements to enhance model learning. This requires domain expertise (Zheng & Casari, 2018). Model selection entails choosing the appropriate ML model based on

FIGURE 8.2   The six-step process in machine learning.

problem type and data characteristics, while model training involves adjusting parameters and avoiding overfitting or underfitting (James et al., 2021). Finally, model evaluation assesses the model's performance using appropriate metrics on a separate testing dataset (Kuhn & Johnson, 2013).

Kuhn and Johnson (2013) note that the iterative nature of this process often requires revisiting and refining steps based on model performance, and this underscores the dynamic and adaptive essence of ML. James et al. (2021) argue that this not only enhances the predictive accuracy of ML models but also reinforces their applicability across diverse domains.

Deep learning, an advanced subset of machine learning, involves computers learning from examples, not explicit instructions, allowing them to undertake complex tasks like speech recognition and object identification in images (Goodfellow et al., 2016; Schmidhuber, 2015). Central to this are artificial neural networks (ANNs), inspired by the human brain (Figure 8.3), which use interconnected artificial neurons to learn data patterns, enabling them to recognise intricate details like handwritten digits (LeCun et al., 2015).

Deep inside ANNs lies the latent space, an abstract, multidimensional arena where data patterns are simplified and compressed. This space, crucial for tasks like facial recognition, is often incomprehensible to humans, leading

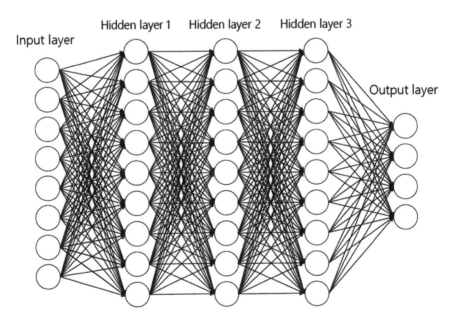

FIGURE 8.3 Schematic of an artificial neural network with multiple hidden layers.

Source: Merenda et al. (2020).

Note: Used under Creative Commons Attribution-NonCommercial-NoDerivatives 4.0 International.

to the *black box* problem, where AI decisions are not easily interpretable (Guidotti et al., 2020). Current research is addressing this by developing techniques to make AI more interpretable, ensuring its decisions are more aligned with human understanding (Doshi-Velez & Kim, 2017).

Examples

As noted earlier, the *Travelling Salesman Problem* is generally considered an NP-hard problem because producing an optimal solution even for a small or moderate-sized dataset is a challenging task (Jünger et al., 1995). This means that there is no known efficient algorithm that can solve the problem in polynomial time, and the time required to find the best solution grows exponentially with the number of cities. An example of a heuristic method used for the *Travelling Salesman Problem* is 'the greedy algorithm'. This works by choosing the closest city to the current location and repeating this process until all cities are visited. This method does not guarantee the optimal solution, but it is fast and easy to implement. The *Travelling Salesman Problem* is a combinatorial optimisation problem that has multiple applications in our daily lives. This includes airport networks, goods delivery, logistics (planning and scheduling), the maritime industry, public transportation networks in top-tier cities, vehicle routing, and so on (Matai et al., 2010).

In another example, in search optimisation problems, the A* (A-star) algorithm stands out for its effective use of heuristics to find the most efficient path between two points. A* combines the principles of breadth-first and greedy best-first searches. Breadth-first search examines the search space comprehensively by exploring all nodes at a certain depth before moving deeper, ensuring a thorough search but often at the cost of efficiency. Greedy best-first search, in contrast, focuses on paths that appear to lead directly to the target, guided by a heuristic that estimates the closest path. A* merges these strategies by using a heuristic that considers both the travelled distance (breadth-first aspect) and an estimated distance to the goal (greedy aspect). This integrated approach allows A* to prioritise paths based on the total estimated cost, effectively balancing thoroughness and efficiency. Widely used in fields like robotics and navigation, A* optimises routes to reach the destination, demonstrating its effectiveness in complex problem-solving scenarios (Wilt et al., 2010).

Heuristics are also crucial in practical applications like antivirus software. They enable these programs to effectively detect and isolate various forms of malware by identifying code or behaviour patterns indicative of viruses. Such heuristic approaches are particularly adept at identifying new or mutating threats, showcasing their adaptability and providing foresight in cybersecurity (Dube et al., 2012).

Another significant application of heuristics in AI is in decision-making processes where situations are marked by uncertainty and ambiguity. Fuzzy logic, proposed by Zadeh (1988), employs a heuristic approach to model the imprecision inherent in real-world scenarios. By allowing for gradations or degrees of truth rather than a strict binary approach, fuzzy logic facilitates more nuanced and human-like problem-solving in AI applications, ranging from control systems to natural language processing (Sarker, 2022).

Finally, we find heuristics involved in what is sometimes described as the *Knapsack problem*. Imagine a thief sneaking into a bank vault filled with treasures. The thief has only one knapsack and there are countless valuable items available. The thief must decide which items to take to maximise the heist without overloading the bag. In the *Knapsack problem* the objective is to select the most valuable combination of items without exceeding a weight limit. To tackle this, AI often employs a heuristic method that mirrors the thief's strategy (Cacchiani et al., 2022). An evaluation of each item will be based on its value-to-weight ratio and the thief will grab the most valuable items first, while ensuring that the knapsack is not too heavy to carry. This assessment allows the thief to make the most out of a risky venture. In real-world applications, such methods help in optimising resource allocation and decision-making across various industries, and are applied across the fields of logistics and asset management to network optimisation and energy efficiency (Cacchiani et al., 2022).

Having now considered the nature of heuristics in the development of AI, we turn to research in the field of artistic inquiry, by which we refer to research where artistic knowledge is pursued and embodied in products of art (Klein, 2010; Lesage, 2009).

Heuristics in artistic research

Heuristic inquiry is increasingly recognised and embraced by creative researchers working in practice-based and practice-led artistic studies (Hoyle, 2023; Peacock, 2023). Rooted in humanistic and phenomenological traditions, heuristic inquiry in such creative contexts emphasises the role of imagination, intuition, and subjective experience in the process of knowledge creation. It offers a framework that not only acknowledges but also actively incorporates the researcher's personal experience, emotional engagement, and creative intuition in the research process (Douglass & Moustakas, 1985). This methodology contrasts with more conventional research approaches that often prioritise objectivity and detachment. In practice-led artistic research, the self cannot be separated from the inquiry, because the creator is central to the creation, evaluation, and development of their practice (Griffiths, 2010). When developing an artistic inquiry, Klein states that research engages sensory and emotional perception 'through artistic experience, from which it cannot be separated' (2010, p. 6). He argues that, 'whether silent or verbal, declarative or procedural, implicit or explicit… artistic knowledge is sensual and physical, "embodied knowledge". The knowledge that artistic research strives for, is a felt knowledge' (2010, p. 6).

However, there is always a tension between the self within the arena of practice, and the self as an objective reviewer of context (Hamilton, 2011). The researcher must negotiate this balance without tipping too far towards the solipsistic (or confessional), or too far towards the objectified (Sela-Smith, 2002). This is because to function authentically as an artistic researcher, one must be positioned as a subjective, critical insider (Duncan, 2004).

Heuristic inquiry emphasises the role of the researcher as a whole person, integrating their cognitive, emotional, and creative capacities. This holistic view, suggested by scholars like Clark Moustakas, underscores the importance of creativity and artistry in research. Heuristic inquiry encourages researchers to embark on a personal creative journey. Such an approach is particularly effective where innovation and personal interpretation are key elements, allowing researchers to uncover new understandings (Scrivener, 2000) and new meanings (Ings, 2011). Ultimately, heuristic inquiry has practical implications in bridging the gap between research and real-world applications, especially in humanistic and artistic fields. By focusing on embodied experiences and fostering a profound understanding of the self and the surroundings, heuristic inquiry enhances the relevance and impact of research. As a system of inquiry, it is particularly beneficial in domains where human experience and personal narratives are central, because it provides a bridge between academic research and practical, humanistic applications (Snyder, 2012).

Phases of heuristic research

In 1990 Clark Moustakas posited a flexible framework for heuristic inquiry contained by (as he experienced it) six phases, each of which he saw as integral to facilitating a journey from initial curiosity to profound understanding and creative synthesis. The phases were: initial engagement, immersion, incubation, illumination, explication, and creative synthesis.

However, these phases rarely play out as a chronological sequence of engagements in artistic research. If we trace the earliest applications of heuristic inquiry in postgraduate theses in art and design, Moustakas' six-phase framework appears to have emerged in a dissertation in 2006 when Welby Ings employed it in his practice-led doctoral thesis *Talking Pictures*. In this study he drew on the thinking of John Wood who, in 2000, had suggested that because heuristics is more concerned with discovery than proof, it is a useful method for designers because it enables them to move away from the pursuit of linear, finite questioning.

Since Ings' thesis, heuristic inquiry has been employed in a range of research projects by candidates working in visual communication design, film, and photography. Among these, it has generally been adopted as a conceptual framework that avoids following a 'how to do' template that Douglass and Moustakas (1985) were so wary of proposing. In artistic research one normally encounters a broad heuristic approach, within which specific artistic methods are brought to data gathering and creative synthesis, with emphasis being placed on 'a subjective process of reflecting, exploring, sifting, and elucidating the nature of the phenomenon under investigation' (Douglass & Moustakas, 1985, p. 40).

In gender studies, scholars have approached the study of non-binary gender identity with a nuanced understanding of contemporary queer discourses. Halberstam, in their seminal work, conceptualises these processes as a 'continuous building and unbuilding' (2018, p. 3), encapsulating a dynamic and evolving nature of gender identity. This perspective is further expanded by Ball, who articulates the concept as an 'iterative and intimate self-making' (2021, p. 12), highlighting the personal and recursive aspects of gender identity formation. These theoretical frameworks have been instrumental in informing Ezra Baldwin's 2023 thesis, which delves into the complexities and lived experiences of non-binary individuals, grounding their research within these established discursive constructs.

Conversely, the photographer Leanne Miller, whose study dealt with the subjective experience of home invasion, defined the phases of her inquiry as 'recollecting, relating, and creating' (2013, p. 33). The film poet David Sinfield described the phases he navigated when creating a typographical voice for an abandoned Freezing Works as 'dwelling within a site, recording, and creative synthesis' (2020, p. 80).

Rene Burton (2015) initially posited, followed by Sinfield (2020), that phases in an artistic heuristic inquiry 'operate in relation to each other [and the researcher] moves fluidly between them' (Sinfield, 2020, p. 83). This perspective was further developed by Igelese Ete (2021) and then most recently by Toiroa Williams (2024).

Visual communication designers Tavares (2011), Chooi (2017), and Panaita (2018), who have written and illustrated graphic novels as thesis submissions, describe immersive ways of heuristically creating stories that contain varying degrees of autobiographical material. None of these candidates employed Moustakas' six phases of heuristic research, although they all identified broader approaches like 'immersion' (Moustakas, 1990), or the concept of 'indwelling' (Conlan, 2000), as important when accessing, then composing, narrative elements. Panaita described her heuristic trajectory as 'deeply subjective because I am sensing my way through memories and creating a process that may help to understand my personal experience, the conditions that gave rise to it, and the communicative potentials of my artistic orchestration of elements' (2018, p. 34).

Both Ventling (2018) and Najafi (2023) have employed heuristic inquiry in artistic research journeys based on theories of practice and enlightenment. Ventling employed Bonaventure's 13th-century spiritual theory that illumination is a transformational aspect in a cognitive journey in which light is subjectively experienced through engagement with materials and processes of making. Najafi's (2023) study interwove heuristic inquiry and a Persian illuminationist approach to investigate the phenomena of acculturation, displacement, self-continuity, and identity transition experienced by refugees. In Persian illuminationism, heuristic inquiry is transcended in the form of a journey, where knowledge is gained through praxis, or metaphorically through a journey where the artist and practice unify.

Effective questioning

Heuristic inquiries, including artistic ones, are heavily question-driven (Ings, 2011; Ventling, 2017, 2018). As Moustakas notes:

> Heuristic inquiry is a process that begins with a question or problem which the researcher seeks to illuminate or answer. The question is one that has been a personal challenge and puzzlement in the search to understand oneself and the world in which one lives.
>
> (Moustakas, 1990, p. 15)

Moustakas proposes that the heuristic research journey cannot be hurried or timed by a clock or calendar (for a discussion of which, see Cousins et al., 2024 [Chapter 9 in this volume]). It demands the researcher's complete presence. Although a heuristic inquiry is largely autobiographic, he suggests that 'with virtually every question that matters personally, there is also a social, and perhaps universal, significance' (Moustakas, 1990, p. 15). In the pursuit of a research question, he says that the researcher enters

> into dialogue with the phenomenon, allowing the phenomenon to speak directly to one's own experience, to be questioned by it. In this way, one is able to encounter and examine it, to engage in a rhythmic flow with it – back and forth, again and again – until one has uncovered its multiple meanings.
>
> (Moustakas, 1990, p. 16)

Kleining and Witt suggest that although heuristic research procedures are non-linear, they are dialectical. They recommend that the heuristic researcher asks their material open questions 'in a similar way one may ask a person, receiving "answers" and questioning again' (2000, para. 14).

According to Moustakas (1990), effective heuristic questions are character-ised by a desire to reveal the essence of human experiences qualitatively, and they are elucidated through creative means. An effective heuristic question, he suggests, will lead the researcher to a deeper understanding and connec-tion with the subject, creating a thirst for discovery and clarification. Although Moustakas maintains that the researcher's openness in clarifying the question will lay the foundation for discovery, in much artistic inquiry one is dealing with questioning that is neither singular nor fixed. This is because questions must respond dialogically to expressions of ideas as artefacts take conceptual and physical form. Thus, while a question about an experience may initiate an inquiry, as a project progresses questions will morph as the researcher engages with artistic data processing and critical reflection (Baldwin, 2023; Sinfield, 2020; Ventling, 2018). Significantly, as a project progresses into creative syn-thesis, questions may adopt a seemingly poetic nature. Thus, one might ask 'What is the weight of the colour of this emotion?' or 'What is the rhythm of this pause?' or 'Is the depth of this event best served with monologue or a series of images?'

Comparing heuristics in AI and artistic research

This chapter explores the intersections of heuristics within the fields of artifi-cial intelligence (AI) and artistic research. Despite their distinct disciplinary backgrounds, both fields are heavily informed by heuristic inquiry proce-dures. The following discussion is organised into seven key themes, each highlighting a specific aspect of heuristic inquiry as it manifests in AI and artistic research. The selection and order of these themes are designed to reflect the progression from abstract concepts, such as embracing the unknown, to more concrete applications, like problem-solving and pattern recognition, culminating in a discussion on certainty. This progression aims to provide a comprehensive understanding of how heuristic principles operate similarly and differently across these fields.

Being at ease with the unknown

The rise of AI indicates a notable shift in scientific exploration as it moves towards a greater acceptance of the *unknown* and an openness to engage with perplexing data. This transition represents a departure from rule-based and algorithmic systems, including the older symbolic AI. Historically, scien-tists and researchers sought to decipher the logic of the natural world through deterministic and linear methods. However, the complexity of real-world phenomena often baffled these approaches. Increasingly, ambiguity and uncertainty are not only acknowledged but also embraced as integral to understanding and exploration. This shift is evident in the work of pioneering computer scientists and cognitive psychologists, who recognised the limitations of rigid algorithmic methods and advocated for more flexible, data-driven approaches (Gigerenzer & Gaissmaier, 2011; Newell & Simon, 1972; Russell & Norvig, 2010). AI procedures aim to be inherently adaptive and capable of learning from unstructured data (LeCun et al., 2015) and utilise probabilistic models that accommodate uncertainty and variability.

Embracing *the unknown* and navigating one's way through its potential is fundamental to heuristic inquiry in artistic research (Ings, 2014; Paora, 2023; Ventling, 2018). This process involves delving into the unknown features of an experience in intuitive ways (Bach, 2002), which can be related to what Keats calls 'negative capability', a state 'when a man is capable of being in uncertainties, mysteries, doubts, without any irritable reaching after fact or reason' (1895, p. 193). In the context of heuristic research, this capability manifests as a readiness to explore and engage with the unknown, allowing the flow of novel insights, putting aside apprehension, fear, and the pursuit of anxious or rapid closure (Eisold, 2000).

This embracing of the unknown in heuristic inquiry may be aligned with the concept of latent spaces or the 'black box' in AI, where complex data are transformed into abstract, less tangible forms. Just as heuristic researchers navigate the unknown to gain insights, AI systems traverse through latent spaces, deciphering patterns and deriving meaning from data that is not immediately clear or structured.

Iterative processes

In AI, particularly within machine learning, iterative processes are integral to the development and optimisation of procedures. Heuristic models in AI engage in a cycle of generating, modifying, and restructuring data or symbols, where each iteration refines the approach based on feedback (Moussaoui & Benslimane, 2023). This involves assessing the effectiveness of each step in reaching the desired outcome, learning which paths are more promising, and eliminating less effective ones. For example, heuristic rules in antivirus software iteratively improve their detection and isolation of malware, enhancing accuracy and efficiency with each cycle (Ye et al., 2018). In artistic research, the iterative process is generally more introspective and exploratory, and involves a recursive journey of exploration, reflection, and synthesis (Najafi, 2022). Broadly, researchers engage with subject matter and enter into dialogue with their subjective experience as they begin to synthesise insights, in an attempt to deepen their understanding of the research topic. While in AI the focus is on efficiency and accuracy, in artistic research emphasis is placed on gaining a nuanced understanding and personal insight that leads to communicative artefacts. Nevertheless, both fields utilise an iterative process as researchers move from initial concepts or models towards increasingly refined and resolved outcomes.

Intuition

Intuition is a multifaceted concept with diverse definitions. Simon describes it as 'bounded rationality' (1979, p. 501), a simplified reasoning sufficient for practicality. Alternatively, Myers defines intuition as 'our capacity for direct knowledge, for immediate insight without observation or reason' (2002, p. 1) and according to Epstein, 'Intuition involves a sense of knowing without knowing how one knows' (2010, p. 296). Similarly, in heuristic artistic inquiry, intuition draws on tacit and explicit knowledge, enabling researchers to gain deep insights into their subject matter (Moustakas, 1990). This process involves a personal and subjective application of intuition, where artists engage deeply with their experiences uncovering new meanings and understandings (Ings, 2015).

In AI, intuition is often subtly embedded in heuristic algorithms, serving as a form of *artificial intuition* (Johnny et al., 2020). These procedures enable AI systems to make educated guesses. This involves an intuitive understanding of which paths to pursue and which to avoid, where the heuristic model iteratively refines its approach to align closely with the desired solution (Wu et al., 2021).

Whether deeply personal of artificial, in both artistic research and AI intuition is employed to uncover new insights.

Problem-solving

Both AI and artistic research utilise heuristics for problem-solving, although in different contexts and applications. In AI, heuristics are instrumental in simplifying complex decision-making processes, enabling systems to provide feasible solutions swiftly, especially in scenarios where exact solutions are not computationally practical (NP-hard). This concept is discussed by Simon and Newell (1958), who note that computers employ heuristic problem-solving in instances lacking specific algorithms, and this closely parallels human problem-solving methods. Additionally, heuristics in AI play a crucial role in reducing overwhelming complexities into more manageable forms, thus accelerating the problem-solving process (Simon, 1955).

On the other hand, in artistic research, heuristics guide the discovery process, aiding researchers in making intuitive decisions in complex situations where definite answers are out of reach (Yilmaz et al., 2016). Simon's (1979) principle of *satisficing* (which advocates for satisfactory rather than optimal decision-making) is particularly applicable in creative contexts where decisions often have to be made under time, resource, or information constraints (Yilmaz & Seifert, 2011).

Pattern recognition

ML models, integral to AI, rely heavily on data to identify patterns and statistical relationships, facilitating the learning and adaptive capabilities of AI systems (Flasiński, 2016). This approach marks an evolution from earlier rule-based methods to more dynamic, data-driven models. Techniques such as decision trees, support vector machines, and k-means clustering[3] have been instrumental in this paradigm shift, with deep learning excelling in tasks such as image recognition and natural language processing (Russell & Norvig, 2010). These advancements owe much to sophisticated pattern recognition algorithms that enable these systems to interpret complex datasets effectively.

In the domain of artistic research, pattern recognition plays a similarly integral role that involves the identification of resonances, themes, or recurring elements (Ventling, 2017). Kleining and Witt (2000) argue that one of the significant skills in heuristic inquiries is the ability to discover similarities, patterns, analogies, or homologies within the diverse data that are being collected and processed, and they suggest that the success of pattern recognition as a procedure can be measured by the richness of the result, its cohesive patterns, and inter-subject validity. In heuristic artistic inquiry, this skill has been discussed in relation to artefact development by Ings (2004, 2018), Panaita (2018), Mortensen Steagall (2019), Tavares (2019), and Najafi (2023).

Embracing experience

In AI, data fundamentally represents experiential knowledge, encompassing a wide spectrum of human experiences, interactions, and observations (Jordan & Mitchell, 2015). This experiential nature of data is pivotal because it provides the raw material from which AI systems learn and develop. These often vast and multifaceted datasets capture the intricacies of human behaviour, societal trends, and natural phenomena, making them integral to the learning processes in AI. Utilising statistical and neural procedures, AI translates these iterations of human experiences into computational models capable of addressing complex real-world problems. This translation process is not merely a mechanical replication but involves the infusion of human cognitive patterns into the algorithms. Russell and Norvig (2010) note how AI systems, especially in machine learning (ML), incorporate these cognitive residues in their procedures, effectively blending human-like intuition with computational efficiency.

In artistic research, heuristic inquiry enables a transformative process, where personal knowledge and experience lead to universal insights. This mirrors how AI, through its learning procedures, transforms experiential data into generalisable knowledge, capable of addressing broad, real-world issues. The process is not purely analytical: it also involves a creative synthesis of data, paralleling the intuitive and deeply reflective nature of heuristic inquiry in artistic research. Moreover, just as heuristic inquiry in artistic research embraces the complexity and ambiguity inherent in human experiences, AI's use of experiential data embraces the multifaceted nature of real-world data, weaving it into sophisticated models that reflect nuanced human experiences and cognitive patterns. This similarity underscores a shared underlying assumption that deep understanding and innovation emerge out of engaging intimately and creatively with complex, experiential data.

Certainty and uncertainty

In our previous discussion on uncertainty, we explored how the rise of AI and artistic research has led to a greater acceptance of ambiguity and openness to engage with perplexing data. AI approaches differ from traditional algorithmic methods in their handling of ambiguity and uncertainty by acknowledging and embracing these elements as integral parts of the problem-solving process.

Certainty in AI and in artistic research can be discussed through the phenomena of underfitting and overfitting.

Underfitting in AI occurs when a model is too simple and fails to capture the complexity or patterns in the data. This results in poor performance on both training and new datasets (Russell & Norvig, 2010). This may be likened to conducting insufficient research in a creative endeavour, where a lack of depth and exploration leads to superficial or incomplete understandings and outcomes. It may also be associated in artistic research, with instances when the researcher becomes too self-centred. If they avoid external feedback, they might be underfitting the data critical to their research. In an artistic inquiry the researcher must negotiate a balance of the self and the arena of practice without tipping too far towards solipsism (Barrett & Bolt, 2014), or towards the overly objectified (Sela-Smith, 2002).

Conversely, overfitting in AI refers to a model that is excessively complex, fitting too closely to the training data, and capturing noise along with the underlying pattern. This leads to a model that performs well on training data but poorly on new, unseen data, essentially because it is too sure of its training data to generalise effectively (Goodfellow et al., 2016). In artistic research, overfitting is akin to being overly convergent and certain about one's findings or creative direction, to the extent that there is excessive focus on specific details or a single perspective. In discussing this phenomenon, Polanyi suggests that the researcher must linger in ambiguity to overcome 'sharp outlines of certainty, only to dissolve again in the light of second thoughts or of further experimental observations' (1966, p. 30).

Conclusion

This chapter has considered the nature of heuristics in the realms of AI and artistic research. The comparison reveals a nuanced understanding of how heuristics function within seemingly disparate domains, each with its unique demands and characteristics, yet both connected by underlying concepts.

In the field of AI, heuristic methods have proven essential for tackling complex, data-rich environments. These methods, including algorithmic approaches to neural network-based systems, embody a form of artificial intuition, allowing AI systems to navigate vast datasets and uncover patterns within them (Goodfellow et al., 2016; Russell & Norvig, 2010). This aspect of AI highlights the integration of human cognitive patterns into computational models, that enable machines to perform tasks with a degree of human-like intelligence and intuition.

Heuristic inquiry as it is employed in artistic research draws some of its distinctiveness from the work of Clark Moustakas (Douglass & Moustakas, 1985; Moustakas, 1967, 1990) and the thinking of John Wood (2000). These theorists from the Social Sciences and Design emphasise a comparatively introspective and subjective heuristic encounter, where value is placed on personal experiences, intuition, flexibility, and emotional engagement. This approach underlines the importance of the self in the research process, where the artistic scholar is both a participant and an observer who navigates the tension between subjective experience and objective analysis (Ings, 2015).

The comparative analysis of heuristic inquiry in these fields reveals several similarities. Both domains engage deeply with uncertainty and ambiguity, recognising these elements as sources of innovation and understanding. This engagement is evident in the iterative nature of the processes involved, whether refining algorithms in AI based on feedback loops or in deepening understanding through reflection and synthesis in artistic research (Moussaoui & Benslimane, 2023; Najafi, 2022).

Moreover, both AI and artistic research demonstrate a preference for functioning outcomes over absolute precision. In AI, this is reflected in the development of heuristic models that prioritise efficiency and effectiveness, while in artistic research, it is manifested in a reliance on intuition and educated guesses in the pursuit of elegant solutions rather than absolute truth (Wood, 2000).

The chapter underscores the significance of human cognitive abilities, whether manifested through artificial intuition in AI or in the intuitive insight of a researcher. It highlights the importance of flexible, approximate, problem-solving approaches in two very different disciplines, where researchers embrace uncertainty, value iterative learning, and recognise the positive role of intuition and creativity. In shedding light on similarities and differences in how heuristic approaches are employed, the chapter anticipates continued interdisciplinary research between science and the arts, and an increasing understanding such that shared insights from diverse fields might inform and enrich each other, and result in fostering a deeper appreciation of both.

Notes

1 The difficulty of solving a particular problem is related to the computational complexity. This means time and memory required for the execution of a certain operation. Computational complexity depends on the number of elements and is often expressed with respect to estimated upper bounds employing the Big-O notations introduced by Bachmann (1894). The point of these notations was to provide some indication of how an algorithm would function in the worst possible scenario as input sizes grow.
2 Expert systems – computer programs that mimic human expert decision-making in specific fields – use a knowledge base and heuristics to offer practical solutions (Jackson, 1986). Like humans estimating travel times with approximate guesses, these systems simplify complex problems for quicker, effective resolutions (Russell & Norvig, 2010).
3 K-means clustering is a data partitioning method that divides a dataset into k clusters by minimising the variance within each cluster. It was originally proposed by Stuart Lloyd in 1957 and later named 'k-means' by James MacQueen in 1967.

References

Alpaydin, E. (2020). *Introduction to machine learning*. MIT Press.
Bach, L. (2002). Heuristic scholar: Heuristic inquiry and the heuristic scholar. *Counterpoints, 183*, 91–102. https://www.jstor.org/stable/42976833
Bachmann, P. (1894). *Zahlentheorie: Die analytische Zahlentheorie* [Number theory: The analytical number theory] (Vol. 2). Teubner.
Baldwin, E. (2023). *Transcendence: An exploration of collage as a voice for non-binary identity* [Master's thesis, Auckland University of Technology]. Tuwhera Open Access Theses & Dissertations. https://hdl.handle.net/10292/16581
Ball, J. (2021). *Collage as queer methodology: The pleasures and politics and queer photographic representations* [Doctoral dissertation, Curtin University]. espace. https://hdl.handle.net/20.500.11937/83186
Barrett, E., & Bolt, B. (2014). *Practice as research: Approaches to creative arts enquiry*. Bloomsbury Publishing.
Burton, R. (2015). *A creative consideration of climate adaptation as a social and ecological palimpsest* [Master's thesis, Auckland University of Technology]. Tuwhera Open Access Theses & Dissertations. https://hdl.handle.net/10292/9138
Cacchiani, V., Iori, M., Locatelli, A., & Martello, S. (2022). Knapsack problems – An overview of recent advances. Part II: Multiple, multidimensional, and quadratic knapsack problems. *Computers & Operations Research, 143*, 105693. https://doi.org/10.1016/j.cor.2021.105693
Chooi, D. (2017). *'Homebound': The illustrated graphic novel as an autobiographic voice for an immigrant Asian gay male in New Zealand* [Master's thesis, Auckland University of Technology]. Tuwhera Open Access Theses & Dissertations. https://hdl.handle.net/10292/10551

Cioffi, R., Travaglioni, M., Piscitelli, G., Petrillo, A., & De Felice, F. (2020). Artificial intelligence and machine learning applications in smart production: Progress, trends, and directions. *Sustainability, 12*(2), 492. https://doi.org/10.3390/su12020492

Conlan, D. (2000). Heuristic research: With thanks and apologies to Clark Moustakas. In P. Willis, R. Smith, & E. Collins (Eds.), *Being, seeking, telling: Expressive approaches to qualitative adult education research* (pp. 12–31). Post Pressed.

Cousins, G., Humphris, A., Kingi, A., Oram, L., & Tudor, K. (2024). Heuristic research in a time-limited context. In W. Ings & K. Tudor (Eds.), *Heuristic enquiries: Research across disciplines and professions* (pp. xx–xx). Routledge.

Crevier, D. (1993). *AI: The tumultuous history of the search for artificial intelligence.* Basic Books. https://doi.org/10.5555/151188

Doshi-Velez, F., & Kim, B. (2017). *Towards a rigorous science of interpretable machine learning* (arXiv:1702.08608). arXiv. https://arxiv.org/abs/1702.08608

Douglass, B. G., & Moustakas, C. (1985). Heuristic inquiry: The internal search to know. *Journal of Humanistic Psychology, 25*(3), 39–55. https://doi.org/10.1177/0022167885253004

Dridi, S. (2021). *Supervised learning – A systematic literature review.* https://files.osf.io/v1/resources/tysr4/providers/osfstorage/624a442a7a7d9e04500608ce?action=download&direct&version=3

Dube, T., Raines, R., Peterson, G., Bauer, K., Grimaila, M., & Rogers, S. (2012). Malware target recognition via static heuristics. *Computers & Security, 31*(1), 137–147. https://doi.org/10.1016/j.cose.2011.09.002

Duncan, M. (2004). Autoethnography: Critical appreciation of an emerging art. *International Journal of Qualitative Methods, 3*(4), 28–39. https://doi.org/10.1177/160940690400300403

Eisold, K. (2000). The rediscovery of the unknown: An inquiry into psychoanalytic praxis. *Contemporary Psychoanalysis, 36*(1), 57–75. https://doi.org/10.1080/00107530.2000.10747045

Epstein, S. (2010). Demystifying intuition: What it is, what it does, and how it does it. *Psychological Inquiry, 21*(4), 295–312. https://doi.org/10.1080/1047840X.2010.523875

Ete, I. (2021). *Naatapuitea: An artistic interpretation of traditional and contemporary Samoan musical structures, instrumentation and koniseti* [Doctoral thesis, Auckland University of Technology]. Tuwhera Open Access Theses & Dissertations. https://hdl.handle.net/10292/14792

Flasiński, M. (2016). *Introduction to artificial intelligence.* Springer. https://doi.org/10.1007/978-3-319-40022-8

Gigerenzer, G., & Gaissmaier, W. (2011). Heuristic decision making. *Annual Review of Psychology, 62*(1), 451–482. https://doi.org/10.1146/annurev-psych-120709-145346

Goodfellow, I., Bengio, Y., & Courville, A. (2016). *Deep learning.* MIT Press.

Griffiths, M. (2010). Research and the self. In M. Biggs & H. Karlsson (Eds.), *The Routledge companion to research in the arts* (pp. 167–185). Routledge.

Guidotti, R., Monreale, A., Matwin, S., & Pedreschi, D. (2020). Black box explanation by learning image exemplars in the latent feature space. In U. Brefeld, E. Fromont, A. Hotho, A. Knobbe, M. Maathuis, & C. Robardet (Eds.), *Machine learning and knowledge discovery in databases* (Vol. 11906, pp. 189–205). Springer. https://doi.org/10.1007/978-3-030-46150-8_12

Halberstam, J. (2018, October). Unbuilding gender. *Places Journal*. https://doi.org/10.22269/181003

Hamilton, J. (2011). The voices of the exegesis. In F. L. Justice & K. Friedman (Eds.), *Pre-Conference Proceedings of Practice, Knowledge, Vision: Doctoral Education in Design Conference* (pp. 340–343). School of Design, Hong Kong Polytechnic University. https://eprints.edu.au/41832/

Harguess, J., & Ward, C. M. (2022). Is the next winter coming for AI? Elements of making secure and robust AI. *2022 IEEE Applied Imagery Pattern Recognition Workshop (AIPR)*, 1–7. https://ieeexplore.ieee.org/abstract/document/10092230/

Hoyle, E. (2023). Untitled grief: An application of heuristic inquiry. *Rangahau Aranga: AUT Graduate Review*, 2(3). https://doi.org/10.24135/rangahau-aranga.v2i3.208

Hruschka, H. (2021). Comparing unsupervised probabilistic machine learning methods for market basket analysis. *Review of Managerial Science*, 15(2), 497–527. https://doi.org/10.1007/s11846-019-00349-0

Ings, W. (2006). *Talking pictures: The creative utilisation of structural and aesthetic profiles from narrative music videos and television commercials in non-spoken film texts* [Doctoral thesis, Auckland University of Technology]. Tuwhera Open Access Theses & Dissertations. https://hdl.handle.net/10292/346

Ings, W. (2011). Managing heuristics as a method of inquiry in autobiographical graphic design theses. *International Journal of Art & Design Education*, 30(2), 226–241. https://doi.org/10.1111/j.1476-8070.2011.01699.x

Ings, W. (2014). Embodied drawing. A case study in narrative design. *Artifact: Journal of Design Practice*, 3(2), 2.1–2.10. https://intellectdiscover.com/content/journals/10.14434/artifact.v3i2.3983/art.3.2.2.1_

Ings, W. (2015). The authored voice: Emerging approaches to exegesis design in creative practice PhDs. *Educational Philosophy and Theory*, 47(12), 1277–1290. https://doi.org/10.1080/00131857.2014.974017

Ings, W. (2018). Heuristic inquiry, land and the artistic researcher. In M. Sierra & K. Wise (Eds.), *Transformative pedagogies and the environment: Creative agency through contemporary art and design* (pp. 55–80). Common Ground Research Networks.

Jackson, P. (1986). *Introduction to expert systems*. Addison-Wesley.

James, G., Witten, D., Hastie, T., & Tibshirani, R. (2021). *An introduction to statistical learning: With applications in R*. Springer. https://doi.org/10.1007/978-1-0716-1418-1

Johnny, O., Trovati, M., & Ray, J. (2020). Towards a computational model of artificial intuition and decision making. In L. Barolli, H. Nishino, & H. Miwa (Eds.), *Advances in intelligent networking and collaborative systems* (Vol. 1035, pp. 463–472). Springer. https://doi.org/10.1007/978-3-030-29035-1_45

Jordan, M. I., & Mitchell, T. M. (2015). Machine learning: Trends, perspectives, and prospects. *Science*, 349(6245), 255–260. https://doi.org/10.1126/science.aaa8415

Jünger, M., Reinelt, G., & Rinaldi, G. (1995). The traveling salesman problem. *Handbooks in Operations Research and Management Science*, 7, 225–330.

Keats, J. (1895). *The letters of John Keats*. Reeves & Turner.

Klein, J. (2010). What is artistic research? https://www.researchcatalogue.net/view/15292/15293

Kleining, G., & Witt, H. (2000). The qualitative heuristic approach: A methodology for discovery in psychology and the social sciences. Rediscovering the method of introspection as an example. *Forum Qualitative Sozialforschung/Forum: Qualitative Social Research, 1*(1). https://doi.org/10.17169/fqs-1.1.1123

Kuhn, M., & Johnson, K. (2013). *Applied predictive modeling.* Springer. https://doi.org/10.1007/978-1-4614-6849-3

LeCun, Y., Bengio, Y., & Hinton, G. (2015). Deep learning. *Nature, 521*(7553), 436–444. https://doi.org/10.1038/nature14539

Lesage, D. (2009). Who's afraid of artistic research? *Art & Research, 2*(2), 1–10.

Mansingh, G., Osei-Bryson, K.-M., Rao, L., & McNaughton, M. (2016). Data preparation: Art or science? *2016 International Conference on Data Science and Engineering (ICDSE),* 1–6. https://ieeexplore.ieee.org/abstract/document/7823936/

Matai, R., Singh, S. P., & Mittal, M. L. (2010). Traveling salesman problem: An overview of applications, formulations, and solution approaches. In D. Davendra (Ed.), *Traveling Salesman Problem, Theory and Applications, 1*(1), 1–25. https://doi.org/10.5772/12909

Merenda, M., Porcaro, C., & Iero, D. (2020). Edge machine learning for AI-enabled IOT devices: A review. *Sensors, 20*(9), 2533. https://doi.org/10.3390/s20092533

Miller, L. (2013). *The visceral metaphor: A contemplation on the invaded self* [Master's thesis, Auckland University of Technology]. Tuwhera Open Access Theses & Dissertations. https://hdl.handle.net/10292/6731

Mortensen Steagall, M. (2019). *The process of immersive photography: Beyond the cognitive and the physical* [Doctoral thesis, Auckland University of Technology]. Tuwhera Open Access Theses & Dissertations. https://hdl.handle.net/10292/12251

Moussaoui, H., & Benslimane, M. (2023). Reinforcement learning: A review. *International Journal of Computing and Digital Systems, 13*(1), 1465–1483. https://doi.org/10.12785/ijcds/1301118

Moustakas, C. (1967). Heuristic research. In J. Bugental (Ed.), *Challenges in humanistic psychology* (pp. 100–107). McGraw-Hill.

Moustakas, C. (1990). *Heuristic research: Design, methodology, and applications.* Sage.

Myers, D. G. (2002). *Intuition: Its powers and perils.* Yale University Press.

Najafi, H. (2022). Persian illuminationism as a heuristic methodology in creative practice-led research (M. Mortensen Steagall, Trans.). *Revista GEMInIS, 13*(2), 36–45. https://doi.org/10.53450/2179-1465.RG.2022v13i2p36-45

Najafi, H. (2023). *Displacement of self-continuity: An illuminative, heuristic inquiry into identity transition in an animated short film* [Doctoral thesis, Auckland University of Technology]. Tuwhera Open Access Theses & Dissertations. https://hdl.handle.net/10292/15784

Newell, A., & Simon, H. A. (1972). *Human problem solving* (Vol. 104). Prentice-Hall.

Panaita, E. (2018). *An exegetical consideration of upgraded gods* [Master's thesis, Auckland University of Technology]. Tuwhera Open Access Theses & Dissertations. https://hdl.handle.net/10292/11510

Paora, T. I. (2023). *Takatāpui – Beyond marginalisation: Exploring Māori gender, identity and performance* [Doctoral thesis, Auckland University of Technology]. Tuwhera Open Access Theses & Dissertations. https://hdl.handle.net/10292/16962

Peacock, F. (2023). A heuristic inquiry into my use of Theraplay® with children experiencing the impact of relational and developmental trauma. *European Journal for*

Qualitative Research in Psychotherapy, 13. https://www.ejqrp.org/index.php/ejqrp/article/view/200

Polanyi, M. (1966). *The tacit dimension*. Doubleday.

Provost, F., & Fawcett, T. (2013). *Data science for business: What you need to know about data mining and data-analytic thinking*. O'Reilly Media.

Russell, S. J., & Norvig, P. (2010). *Artificial intelligence: A modern approach*. London.

Sarker, I. H. (2022). AI-based modeling: Techniques, applications and research issues towards automation, intelligent and smart systems. *SN Computer Science, 3*(2), 158. https://doi.org/10.1007/s42979-022-01043-x

Schmidhuber, J. (2015). Deep learning in neural networks: An overview. *Neural Networks, 61*, 85–117. https://doi.org/10.1016/j.neunet.2014.09.003

Schuster, P. (2000). Taming combinatorial explosion. *Proceedings of the National Academy of Sciences, 97*(14), 7678–7680. https://doi.org/10.1073/pnas.150237097

Scrivener, S. (2000). *Reflection in and on action and practice in creative production doctoral projects in art and design*. Working Papers in Art and Design 1. https://www.herts.ac.uk/__data/assets/pdf_file/0014/12281/WPIAAD_vol1_scrivener.pdf

Sela-Smith, S. (2002). Heuristic research: A review and critique of Moustakas's method. *Journal of Humanistic Psychology, 42*(3), 53–88. https://doi.org/10.1177/00267802042003004

Simon, H. A. (1955). A behavioral model of rational choice. *The Quarterly Journal of Economics*, 99–118. https://doi.org/10.2307/1884852

Simon, H. A. (1979). Rational decision making in business organisations. *The American Economic Review, 69*(4), 493–513. https://www.jstor.org/stable/1808698

Simon, H. A., & Newell, A. (1958). Heuristic problem solving: The next advance in operations research. *Operations Research, 6*(1), 1–10. https://doi.org/10.1287/opre.6.1.1

Sinfield, D. (2020). *Typographical voices: Poetic reflections on the Pātea Freezing Works* [Doctoral thesis, Auckland University of Technology]. Tuwhera Open Access Theses & Dissertations. https://hdl.handle.net/10292/13601

Snyder, L. J. (2012). *Qualitative research ethics: An heuristic inquiry exploring the meaning and application of ethics in qualitative research* [Doctoral thesis, University of Calgary]. PRISM. https://hdl.handle.net/1880/51588

Tavares, T. (2011). *Carnival land: A performance of metaphors* [Master's thesis, Auckland University of Technology]. Tuwhera Open Access Theses & Dissertations. https://hdl.handle.net/10292/1318

Tavares, T. (2019). *Paradoxical realities: A creative consideration of realismo maravilhoso in an interactive digital narrative* [Doctoral thesis, Auckland University of Technology]. Tuwhera Open Access Theses & Dissertations. https://hdl.handle.net/10292/12958

Ventling, F. D. (2017). *Illuminativa – The resonance of the unseen* [Doctoral thesis, Auckland University of Technology]. Tuwhera Open Access Theses & Dissertations. https://hdl.handle.net/10292/7037

Ventling, F. D. (2018). Heuristics – A framework to clarify practice-led research. *DAT Journal, 3*(2), 122–156. https://doi.org/10.29147/dat.v3i2.88

Williams, T. (2024). *Tangohia mai te taura – Take This Rope: Exploring Māori documentary-making approaches to elevate whānau narratives* [Doctoral thesis, Auckland University of Technology]. Tuwhera Open Access Theses & Dissertations. https://hdl.handle.net/10292/17323

Wilt, C., Thayer, J., & Ruml, W. (2010). A comparison of greedy search algorithms. *Proceedings of the International Symposium on Combinatorial Search, 1*(1), 129–136. https://doi.org/10.1609/socs.v1i1.18182

Wood, J. (2000). The culture of academic rigour: Does design research really need it? *The Design Journal, 3*(1), 44–57. https://doi.org/10.2752/146069200789393599

Wu, Y., Song, W., Cao, Z., Zhang, J., & Lim, A. (2021). Learning improvement heuristics for solving routing problems. *IEEE Transactions on Neural Networks and Learning Systems, 33*(9), 5057–5069. https://doi.org/10.1109/TNNLS.2021.3068828

Ye, Y., Li, T., Adjeroh, D., & Iyengar, S. S. (2018). A survey on malware detection using data mining techniques. *ACM Computing Surveys, 50*(3), 1–40. https://doi.org/10.1145/3073559

Yilmaz, S., Daly, S. R., Seifert, C. M., & Gonzalez, R. (2016). Evidence-based design heuristics for idea generation. *Design Studies, 46*, 95–124. https://doi.org/10.1016/j.destud.2016.05.001

Yilmaz, S., & Seifert, C. M. (2011). Creativity through design heuristics: A case study of expert product design. *Design Studies, 32*(4), 384–415. https://doi.org/10.1016/j.destud.2011.01.003

Zadeh, L. A. (1988). Fuzzy logic. *Computer, 21*(4), 83–93. https://doi.org/10.1109/2.53

Zheng, A., & Casari, A. (2018). *Feature engineering for machine learning: Principles and techniques for data scientists*. O'Reilly Media.

9

CATALYST AND CONSTRAINT

The question of time in heuristic research

Guy Cousins, Alana Humphris, Anna Kingi, Luke Oram, and Keith Tudor

Introduction and background

This chapter considers the question or issue of time in heuristic research, specifically in the context of research undertaken in a context of limited time. The first four authors were all master's students who wrote their dissertations (on different topics) as the final piece of work on a degree course (the Master of Psychotherapy at Auckland University of Technology); the fifth author was their academic supervisor. In the year the students wrote their dissertations (2023), the tariff of the course had changed from that of a 60-point paper (representing 600 hours of study) to a 45-point course (representing 450 hours of study). This, together with the requirement to complete the course, including submitting a dissertation of 10,000 words (a reduction from the previous requirement of 15,000 words) within eight months provided a clear and present focus for both students and supervisor, and created some anxiety. Some of us made a connection between this timeframe and a foreshortened gestation period and premature birth. Early on in our experience(s), we all became aware of the impact of time on the research and were interested to reflect on this together. However, as none of us wanted to add to the pressure of time the students were feeling, we all decided to leave this particular and collaborative heuristic enquiry until after the students had submitted their dissertations (Cousins, 2024; Humphris, 2024; Kingi, 2024; Oram, 2024), though, not surprisingly, some aspect of the pressure or limit of time came into all of them. When looking back on our experience of time we all encountered a sense of anxiousness, pressure, or constraint (which here, as elsewhere in the chapter, we comment on individually):

DOI: 10.4324/9781003507758-13

As I dove inwards, accessing the tacit knowledge and intuition from the many versions of myself, I found a great void of endless experience, moments, and emotions. I floated in a bath of overwhelm and resistance, where time stood still. I felt the external force of a sharp jolt forward from my supervisor to get something down on paper as time was running out. Great feelings of inadequacy were pushed aside so I could adhere to the time requirements. The feelings of inadequacy became the pivoting moment in the research project, a marker of the experience of a mother training to be a psychotherapist in modern society.

(Alana)

Accessing my intuitive knowing within an institutional time construct proved to be a consistent pressure that threatened the potential transformative effects of heuristic inquiry. In my own heuristic wonderland, I wished to be like the Mad Hatter and fully immerse myself in creative experiencing, where it was *always* 6 o'clock – teatime! I eventually realised that I also would need to embody the anxiousness of the time-obsessed White Rabbit, to fully arrive at the prescribed destination in the research timeline and complete the dissertation for assessment.

(Anna)

There was a constant sense of attempting to distil and synthesise, particularly while balancing the need to immerse myself deeply within the research process and work within time constraints… Over time, the ideas metamorphosed, slipping through my fingers like sand and settling onto the ground. The sand formed intricate shapes and small hills, hinting at the emergence of subtle themes. I learned to allow the process to unfold naturally, trying to put any sense of haste to one side.

(Guy)

I struggled to give incubation the time it deserved, but I also wonder if my understanding – and Moustakas' (1990) conception of the incubation phase – was a little unrealistic, and inflexible. Moustakas defines incubation as a period, evoking visions of a linearly defined, cohesive stretch of time. Upon reflection, I realise that I experienced incubation as small moments; microcosms within the greater process.

(Luke)

As the students' supervisor, Keith experienced the time limit of working with each of them across eight months, a little differently, from the drafting of their initial proposal to the submission of their dissertation.

Whilst I didn't experience any pressure to rush or push them through Moustakas' phases (not least as I am critical of the use of his theory in that way), I did feel more responsibility than I usually do to help them to complete the research in the given timeframe. I think this manifested at times in me being more focused than previously, e.g., perhaps asking more questions such as 'How are you doing?', 'What do you want from this [supervisory] meeting?', 'What do you need over the next month?', and so on.

(Keith)

In his work, Moustakas encourages researchers to invest 'full energy and resourcefulness over an extended period of time' (1990, p. 40) and to 'immerse themselves in a timeless moment, fully experiencing it' (1990, p. 44). He also asserts that 'The heuristic research process is not one that can be hurried or timed by the clock or calendar' (1990, p. 6). Thus, having an intended and limited period of time to complete a heuristic enquiry, being compromised by experiencing timeless moments, and being on a clock or having a specific calendar and deadline creates a certain tension. It was in and from this tension that we identified the themes we explore in this chapter: that of a time limit being both a catalyst for, and a constraint on, heuristic enquiry.

The first part of the chapter offers some reflections on the nature of time and of heuristics; the second and main part of the chapter considers the phases of heuristic enquiry with regard to which we discuss whether time was a catalyst or a constraint – or both. As Guy recalls:

Time catalysed me, energising different aspects of my work. Although the constraints initially felt like an unwelcome burden, they ultimately forced me to focus. Since time was integral to my research topic, I can see how it possesses complex dimensions that take on different meanings based on the type of immersive processes involved in research. For instance, the perception of time may vary subjectively when engaged in right- versus left-hemisphere activities, especially during immersion or explication phases, and so on. Moreover, having a time constraint as a prominent feature in the research raises an interesting question about how a concept like time can be integrated into the unconscious processes of heuristic research, eventually emerging as a salient feature in the research findings.

Here we consider time and time limits with regard to the *phases* of heuristic enquiry as identified by Douglass and Moustakas (1985) and Moustakas (1990); elsewhere, we consider time and time limits with regard to the *concepts* that inform heuristic methodology (Tudor et al., 2024).

Time and heuristics

There is something lyrical about the way Moustakas addresses time. In his conception, the heuristic journey is almost mythic, and somewhat heroic. It is a search for a kind of sempiternal truth, but the quest itself occurs outside of time, unhurried by clock or calendar. Much like the gilded hero, the researcher is driven by a single-minded question, committed to 'endless hours of sustained immersion' (1990, p. 13), as monomaniacal as Melville's (1922) Captain Ahab. Indeed, in his major work on heuristic research, Moustakas refers to 'endless hours' and 'endless time', 'timeless immersion' (twice), and a 'timeless world'; refers to the researcher (and in one case the therapist) being 'in their own time' and working to 'their own timetable'; and rallies the researcher to abandon temporality in their search, and to be ruled instead by a sense of 'inner experiential time' (1990, p. 36). Sela-Smith calls the heuristic search a 'leap into the darkness' (2002, p. 70). Writing about the importance of the freedom of exploration and enquiry for heuristic research, Frick, another early humanistic psychologist and heuristic researcher in the field of symbolic growth experience, comments that: 'This [freedom] allowed the essence of the experience to reveal itself *over time*' (1990, p. 79, our emphasis). Much of this sounds like succumbing to a kind of illimitable insanity, a need to become, as Kurt Vonnegut so eloquently puts it, 'unstuck in time' (1969, p. 23).

Heuristics is essentially concerned with, and facilitative of, discovery (Douglass & Moustakas, 1985; McLeod, 2003; Moustakas, 1990; Souba, 2011); time is the unit of that discovery, and, therefore, is both a moment or point as well as a marking a length (i.e., eight months, a three-day writing retreat, and so on). Accordingly, heuristic research is not based on the usual form of research hypothesis, based on an a priori underplacing (hupo = under + thesis = placing), but, rather, is an exploration to discover what lies in the dark, just outside our reach, and in that sense is an a posteriori metathesis (meta = after).

Time has its own way of defying linearity which refuses to be constrained by description. In this sense, time is simply an imitation of eternity (van Ruusbroec & de Baere, 2014). It evokes the Urdu concept of *nafas*, the world renewed with each breath. In a way, the heuristic endeavour is like trying to traverse the fourth dimension, a place where moments past, present, and future converge. This is the milieu into which Moustakas asks us to free-fall and to which Sela-Smith impels us to surrender. We immerse ourselves in Rumi's (2009) ever-running river, trying to grasp what we can while keeping our breath. As Hegel (1807/2019) acknowledges, even the moment of absolute knowing is betrayed by perpetual motion.

How do we know when to step out of this river, which flows eternally back to the sea? Moustakas asks us to ignore time, but, as time is the only difference between diving and drowning, it may be better to find a way of embracing time or, at least, to be time-conscious (Elton Wilson, 1996). To assume that a story has a natural conclusion is to believe the dogma of eternal return: that the story even *has* an ending, that the plot isn't constantly in flux, that the question will always have the same answer. Heuristic enquiry is a muse unto itself; as Dahlberg et al. put it: the researcher 'conduct[s] one's research on behalf of the phenomenon' (2008, p. 98), following intuition to what Sultan describes as 'the place where things matter' (2019, p. 79). Perhaps, this gives us two options: either to choose a point of abandonment, as Valéry (McGrath & Comenetz, 2013) does; or to recognise the scarcity of time as fundamental to the human condition, as Taft (1933) proposes. Reflecting on the near-endless nature of his project, Luke adds,

> My heuristic project required me to trace the outlines of a father I had known for four decades, but in doing so, I had to unpack two lives: his and mine. That was just the start. My immersion was in a generational river which flowed from his ancestral past to the unending bloodline of his future. In a way, I was telling a story that would never end, mapping a river that would flow ever to the sea. The best I could offer was a snapshot of a man who was being eternally reborn in my mind, someone constantly evolving. It was a successful project in that it transformed my view of my father, but it was also maddeningly incomplete, just a sketch of Osiris the god of resurrection *in hoc momento*.

This is a dialogue with eternity, something entirely circular: an attempt to catch the universe with a fishing net. In this sense, the issue for Luke and many others was not that he/they would hurry the heuristic process; quite the opposite. For some, perhaps many, the risk was getting lost in the infinite, stranded in an eternal now. In heuristic research, limitless or endless immersion, with no reference to a clock or calendar, threatens to become all-encompassing, and indwelling an untethered obsession. The quest threatens to become Promethean: creative and self-punishingly cyclical. However, as Luke put it, 'Luckily for most of us, the clock tends to run out first.'

Time also appeared as a construct and/or phenomenon *in* the four different master's dissertations:

> The heuristic process and institutional requirements drew me towards a linear parallel of the creation of life – conception, gestation, labour, and birth – an expected and predetermined timeline. Within gestation, was a non-linear entanglement in time as I reached inward exploring the past, present, and future, growing my knowing. The gestation was cut short, labour was induced by regulations and requirements. Labouring through the pain, the birth felt premature.
>
> (Alana)

Adopting the heuristic attitude of curiosity and openness to serendipitous discovery meant that I experienced time as naturally cyclical in powerful moments of transformation. During the inquiry I would revisit, remember, and re-experience the past, which led to an eventual integration of split off experiences, into a new whole way of being or understanding in the present. This was achieved by recording spontaneous data without delay, which felt like I was leaving cryptic clues about my experience of the phenomena for my future researcher self. Seemingly irrelevant data gathered in April turned out to be fundamental lynchpins of discovery during creative synthesis in October.

(Anna)

There were times in my heuristic project where I felt wrenched from linearity into liminality. I was studying the image of my father, an endeavour that required traversing past, present, and future. At times, the project felt like the alchemic *ouroboros*, the serpent devouring its own tail. As I pursued one thread, another one opened. A dialogue led to a tangent; the mandala that was the man bloomed perpetually. Time became irrelevant, immersion more like delirium. It was near-impossible to stop. In fact, there was an acute sense that, if there wasn't a deadline to meet or a dissertation to lodge, this project could have unravelled forever.

(Luke)

For Guy, the experience of time was closely related to a process of immersion and emersion:

During these moments of deep immersion, time could vanish, plunging me into a strange vortex where the ordinary world fell away. After emerging from this state, I often felt disoriented and adrift from the world around me. However, gradually, the rhythms of life would reintegrate, and the once-absent world would reassert itself. Yet I was left with a lingering sense that the world had momentarily fallen away. This aspect of time became integral to my study: it highlighted an experience of a break in going on being (Winnicott, 1963), a rekindling of a more primitive experience that may have predated the earliest impingement of the concept of time.

The experience of time-limited heuristic research in terms of heuristic phases

In this part of the chapter, we consider the experience of heuristic research in a time-limited context in terms of Moustakas' (1990) phases of heuristic enquiry, i.e., initial engagement, immersion, incubation, illumination, explication, and creative synthesis.

In the context of heuristic research, where time exhibits a mutable quality that shifts with the evolving focus of each phase, the unfolding experience manifests as something both strange and dynamic. As Guy notes:

> Time possesses a peculiar quality. Its palpable presence morphs and shifts, sometimes revealing its stretchable and compressible nature. There are phases where I sense time accelerating, propelling me with urgency. At other times, it seems to drag on endlessly, as I shift into a different cognitive state that is more analytical and linear.

Navigating through Moustakas' original identification of six phases, we discuss each one. Aligning with Tudor (2022), we propose that illumination is more a moment, or a number of moments that appear throughout the journey of enquiry, and thus is not technically a phase. Similarly, we consider that creative synthesis is often the final and whole product (such as a dissertation, thesis, chapter, article, or artifact), rather than a final phase or part of the product or output. Finally, as we view validation as a concept and a process more than a phase, we address the impact of time on this elsewhere (Tudor & Oram, 2024).

With these distinctions, our exploration of heuristic phases sheds light on the unique emphasis each carries. The researcher's trajectory involves an ongoing dialogue with temporal dimensions, unveiling the intricate interplay between the timeless and time constraints. While heuristics doesn't strictly follow a linear trajectory, it does have a starting point emerging from the researcher's interiority.

Initial engagement

This first phase of heuristic enquiry, as described by Moustakas, involves the recognition that 'Within each researcher exists a... question... the question lingers within the researcher and awaits' (1990, p. 27). This anthropomorphised question lives in the present tense: it *exists*; it lingers; and waits to be discovered. Temporally speaking, Moustakas is describing something that may have always been; something from the realm of time immemorial; something atavistic. One gets a sense that the research question is not so much created or anticipated as it is unearthed by the researcher, just as an archaeologist finds and excavates strata. Sela-Smith (2002) describes the question as an unknown that seeks to be known.

Perhaps what Moustakas is saying is that our initial engagement is not so much a discovery as a *re*-discovery of something that has always been; something that has been waiting for the right time to appear, or as Shakespeare puts it: 'When time is ripe, which will be suddenly' (1598/2019, Act I, Scene 3, l. 632). In the grand scheme of time, initial engagement means more than just simple articulation; it is the ushering in of a season of harvest, a ritual space carved out to answer a call: 'A time to plant and a time to uproot' (*New International Version*, 1973/2011, Ecclesiastes 3:2).

As both Moustakas (1990) and Sela-Smith (2002) intimate, the heuristic researcher's question already exists on some level; Sela-Smith (2002) says it is near-impossible to notice. Whether it be a growing dissonance, or a vague fragrance, one only needs to tune in with intention to hear the call from *terra interior*. One only needs to turn inwards and say, '*Now* is the time.'

However, this is also the researcher's first encounter with the immemorial nature of the project. They soon realise that they do not have the luxury of creating a boundaried research question from scratch, with realistic parameters including timelines. One researcher (Guy) wandered through the familiar corridors and dimly lit cellars of his childhood, recalling boarding school, allowing the nostalgia of the past to intertwine with his present thoughts. A second (Luke) considered his father, his intuition leading him further up a genealogy that threatened to tangle with the gods. A third (Anna) considered hope, which springs eternal and is silently present in each psychotherapy session. As a fourth (Alana) considered her motherhood, she found herself tuning into that of her own mother, and her mother before her… and the great chorus of Papatūānuku, mother earth, and the mythical cycles of birth and rebirth.

Initial engagement is a lot like screaming into a timeless void. Moreover, this sense of overwhelm is just the beginning; the first opening of Pandora's Box based on a curiosity which, unbeknowingly, threatens to unleash chaos. All the researcher knows is that the time to explore the timeless is now. Perhaps the most terrifying prospect of this journey is time itself. The great irony of initial engagement, this first tussle with the infinite and scopeless, is that it often arrives amidst discussions of deadlines, timelines, word counts, and schedules. Initial engagement asks us to confront both the catharsis – and, therefore, catalyst – as well as the constraint of time before we even take our first step.

In Anna's initial engagement, time passed as resistance blocked movement into the subsequent phases. Time felt stagnant, like a dam during a rainstorm wherein the pressure builds until the water is released and can flow. Paradoxically, achieving a flow required a surrender to the fixity or blockage (in this case, of stagnation and pressure), which involved, as Sela-Smith (2002) acknowledges, an essential relinquishing of perceived control and surrender to the unknown. As Anna puts it:

> I negotiated my own surrender to both a limitless time (how and when each stage would feel met enough) and a time limit (imposed by the external reality of time-limited research). An exploration in a heuristic self-search inquiry timeline and an internal reference and tacit dimension

timeline. I was time-limited, and word-limited – so I adjusted my engage-ment with the phases and how they would be explored and experienced within the research. Thus, in my dissertation, I wrote four chapters high-lighting four of the phases, while considering the other two phases as expe-rienced throughout the process.

Immersion

Discussing methods of organising and synthesising data, Moustakas asserts that 'The task involves timeless immersion inside the data, with intervals of rest and return to the data until intimate knowledge is obtained' (1990, p. 49). He also suggests that 'Virtually anything connected with the question becomes raw material for immersion, for staying with and for maintaining a sustained focus and concentration' (1990, p. 28). At least one of the researchers found the time limit of the prescribed study period a considerable constraint; as Guy recalls:

> I could not shake the feeling of injustice at being deprived of such extended immersion. At the same time, despite initial fears that I needed longer time than available for immersion, with hindsight, I realised that most of the insights surfaced within just a few days. This was at 'peak immersion' where thoughts that had been gestating emerged creatively and spontane-ously. I was utterly absorbed and disconnected from the daily world.

Writing in a letter to his protégé Franz Xaver Kappus, a man beset with 'beau-tiful anxiety about life', the poet Rilke offers this advice:

> Be patient toward all that is unsolved in your heart and try to love the ques-tions themselves… the point is, to live everything. Live the questions now. Perhaps you will then gradually, without noticing it, live along some dis-tant day into the answer.
>
> (Rilke, 1929/1992, p. 3)

There are strains of the paradoxical idiom 'Hurry up and wait' in this counsel. It is like the Hebraic 'Now and not yet' (*New International Version*, 1973/2011, Hebrews 11:1), the theological hypothesis that divine knowledge is both upon us and still waiting to be discovered. In his advice to Kappus, Rilke (1929/1992) weaves temporal threads: live in your present doubt, let the pro-cess unfold, and submit to a distant resolution as an ever-receding horizon. The entity in charge here is Cronos, the god of time: he who will not be hur-ried. Of course, it is an irony that, from Chronos, we derive chronological time, for many marked by the clock, and the ticking and marking of time. In order to counter hurry – and 'Hurry[ing] Up' (Kahler with Capers, 1974) – we need to draw on another Greek work for time: kairos, which refers to the right or appropriate time (Smith, 1969; Tudor, 2001).

When it comes to heuristic immersion, Moustakas (1990) asks us to do the same. Once the research question has come into view, he suggests that the investigator's next step is to inhabit it: to become, as it were, a slave to immersion. It is no wonder the word itself conjures ideas of drowning (submerged) or being consumed (immerged). This is what it means to live the question in every waking moment, in each thought and sensation. Even when collecting data, Moustakas advocates a 'timeless' immersion in it/them (1990, p. 47). His prescription for immersion is near-amaranthine; in his conception, it is a state that transcends conscious time, bleeding into dream-life and the quietude of sleep. In his critique of behavioural approaches, Rogers comes close to describing this intemporal journey, imagining a dedicated 'free reign to phenomenological thinking' (1965, p. 192), unfettered by methodology or hypothesis. Reflecting on her experience of immersive time Anna writes:

> During my busiest waking hours of this phase, I was anxious about missing full immersion in my inquiry. Interestingly, hope became a prominent feature in my dreams. It seemed that when I was most absorbed with other life commitments, the subject of my inquiry relentlessly pursued me at night, in absence of me consciously perusing it during the day.

In immersion, we not only meet what Levine refers to as the 'great "don't know"' (1991, p. 11), we are asked to patiently inhabit it, to wait without thought. Doubt and uncertainty become our compass. Imagination, which Sagan (1987) calls the source of hope, inspiration, and frustration, becomes our milieu.... and we wait. Somehow, amidst the thrum of a saturated life and the societal privileging of fast answers, we wait. Moustakas tells us to check our clocks and calendars at the door. Perhaps... gradually... distant. Rilke's (1929/1992) maddening words become our only solace; but we also inhabit a curious now, a bare attention to whatever arrives. We don't know when to leave. In kairos, we wait for the call of Cronos, ushering us on to the next phase.

This mindset is catalytic, counter-cultural even. Perhaps it makes us feel a little insane, existing somehow outside of this chronological realm. Moustakas (1990) describes his immersion in near-schizophrenic terms: he wandered moonlit streets, consumed by a single-minded preoccupation. His life became an exercise in frequency bias; his obsession sidling its way into his every waking thought.

It may also be a fantasy. Because this sacred space will always be somewhat polluted. In the academic sphere, institutional deadlines bang their fists against our closed doors, reminding us that time is not as appropriate, unmediated, or unquantifiable as we think. Our families, initially sympathetic to our pilgrimage, begin to wonder about our return from a foreign plane. Time is never as forgiving as we would like; its restriction ever more real. There is a constriction here, which is the call of reality. In its pure sense, immersion skirts with madness, the kind that renders a prophet unwelcome in his own country or hometown. Alana recalls,

> My research was related to the experience of psychotherapy training as a mother. As I attempted to capture some element of these two transient life-long experiences intertwined in my life, it was overwhelming. The topic already existed in my psyche, in my realm, in my experience, meaning the immersion phase had no beginning moment in time. I must live and write at the same time. Immersed in the topic in all senses of the word, I lived, breathed, studied, and conversed it. I felt most drawn to tune in to my existing 'tacit knowledge'.

Incubation

According to Moustakas, 'Incubation is the process in which the researcher retreats from the intense, concentrated focus on the question' (1990, p. 14). In incubation, the research question, subject, issue, and/or enquiry takes root in the tacit dimension, enabling the unconscious mind to contribute to the development of ideas. There is a surrender to wisdom that lies beyond our conscious control. In the unconscious realm, we are outside of linear time. Consequently, safeguarding becomes important. Researchers must devise methods to preserve this delicate process and prevent any form of 'contamination'. The sense of incubation suggests a state of stillness, removed from external influences, and a nest(l)ing away from the constraints of time. Ideally, it requires a withdrawal from the external world.

Yet, how does a researcher fully immersed in the identity of the topic withdraw themselves in order to incubate? As someone who identifies as having obsessive-compulsive disorder, Ozertugrul (2017) did not. As someone who experiences chronic pain, Maya-Chipman (2023) could not. As a training psychotherapist and a mother, Alana could and would not:

> There was no ability to 'withdraw' from the topic as I lived it fully and could not remove or take back my immersion or begin incubation in the realms of psychotherapy training or motherhood. This stage felt like I was doing nothing towards the project as I felt unsure how to engage in these phases. I struggled with how little or how long to attempt to 'incubate' before I must write something down. I attempted to block out a portion of time to 'deliberately withdraw' for a weekend. I stepped away from parenting responsibilities and studies. But I could not step away from my

identity in both roles, so this too contributed new knowledge to the research. I can't not be a parent; I can't come out of the experience then to write about it.

Even for those who may be able to move out of incubation, there is a question of how we know when our time is up. Moustakas has an idea: 'One completes the quest when one has an opportunity to tell one's story to a point of natural closing' (1990, p. 38). However, this seems somewhat Quixotic, the poor cousin of 'You'll know it when you see it'. In her research primer on *Heuristic Inquiry*, Sultan (2019) adopts the infinity symbol to represent the heuristic journey, implying a constant process of creation and re-creation. Sometimes, despite your best attempts at single-mindedness, your original research question threatens to become infinite. Like Theseus navigating the labyrinth, heurism is an often-exasperating pilgrimage of left turns and circular returns. Sela-Smith (2002) suggests that we surrender to this process, admitting that, before we are found, we must be lost. However, what she neglects to mention is that it's possible that we never find – and are never found. This is the challenge of heuristics as discovery: we have to risk getting and being lost in order to find – and that is compromised by having a chronometer ticking. Nevertheless, with time in mind, heuristics could perhaps be better described as a dialogue with eternity, and the discovery of moments of eternity (O'Hara, 2002).

Illumination

Whist illumination is one of the six phases of heuristic research design described by Moustakas, he describes it experientially as a natural awakening process wherein and wherefrom previously hidden qualities or themes inherent in the research question break through into conscious awareness, sometimes in 'shocking' ways (1990, p. 16). Reading Moustakas' research design, it is clear that this phase – or, perhaps better, process – is crucial both to the discovery that is heuristics, and to the subsequent 'phases' of explication and creative synthesis. However, regarding it as a phase, especially in time-limited research, gives rise to a tension when constructing the timeline for a standard research proposal as it implies that such illumination will occur in a particular chronological sequence, and an anxiety if illumination fails to occur within the allocated time.

Sela-Smith (2002) suggests that illumination is not something that can be planned; instead, it occurs in serendipitous moments in which some reorganisation of newly conscious knowing makes a strong impression on the researcher, leading to deep transformation. In order to manage the reality that illumination cannot be forced artificially by a research timeline (but is crucial to one's final product), Sultan (2019) suggests that a consistent adoption of the discovery-orientated heuristic attitude of openness and curiosity will best capture the serendipitous nature of illumination. More recently, Tudor argues that illumination is more accurately viewed as a process or series of moments, which:

> Do not occur conveniently between the heuristic stages or phases of incubation and explication and so should not be viewed as forming a certain and invariant part of a stage theory but, rather, as illuminative, 'eureka' moments through the research.
>
> (Tudor, 2023, p. 121)

The time frame of any research encourages movement through the phases of a research project from initial application and proposal to final presentation, defence, lodgement, and/or publication. Nevertheless, to force illumination contradicts the basis of heuristics as discovery. This view of illumination allows a surrendering to an acceptance that such illuminations may or may not come, but the researcher should trust time, and illumination will happen in time. Indeed, Tudor (2017) describes a powerful moment of illumination occurring in his doctoral viva/oral examination. Alana recalls,

> I was surprised when illumination occurred during the incubation phase. In my organic unplanned self-dialogue whilst driving and reflecting on both the process of writing and engaging with the topic, it struck me in an a-hah lightbulb moment, and I began to cry with relief just as Archimedes cried Eureka!

Anna experienced moments of illumination as transformative shifts in embodied emotional states which preceded a conscious comprehension of knowledge in new and different ways:

> They were moments of integration of previously split experiences, into a perspective of the 'whole' which ultimately brought me closer to my focus of inquiry. For me, illumination felt like coming home to a place of deep knowing.

Luke describes the unpredictable nature of illumination:

> There came a point in my heuristic project where I thought I might be going insane. I had reached a point of dissociation, not in a sense of becoming dislocated from feelings, memories, or identity, but from a sense of coherent time. For the first time in my life, I was scrutinising my father with a relentless lens, studying him as both a known entity and a stranger. To be heuristic meant to deconstruct him down to an atomic level, to not

take anything for granted. In this place, illuminations came raining down like psychic imps; long-forgotten smells, flashes of sepia-toned memory, words, and phrases. At the same time, I had to doubt everything I knew about the man, to consciously push past everything I knew about him to make room for all that was tacit. Amidst all this, I had to unravel my own DNA, knowing that he also existed within me.

Explication

Having been engaged and immersed in discovery of the implicit and the tacit, and, hopefully, having had time to incubate (if that's possible), this phase describes the process in which the heuristic researcher makes things explicit; as Moustakas puts it: the purpose of this phase is 'to fully examine what has awakened in consciousness, in order to understand its various layers of meanings' (1990, p. 31). This involves unfolding, expanding, displaying, disentangling, and explaining (Tudor, 2017).

With regard to time, this phase can be seen as a culmination of time periods and one which requires focused time for the laying out of the ghosts past and present, for discovering and highlighting experience and phenomena, as well as possible patterns with the potential to find new meaning for the future. It also marks the beginning of the end of the heuristic process – at least for now – and is the basis for the final phase or process of synthesis. That said, if the researcher moves too quickly to explicating their research, not least in response to external time constraints, they may need to return, re-engage, and re-immerse, a process that has implications for the internal and external validity of the research.

Ultimately, explication is an excavation of experience, phenomena, memory, and time. It requires wrecking balls in the halls of *Memoria*, the place where Hillman (1983) situates memory, imagination, and the unconscious. It enacts a temporary kind of insanity. The words of Solomon resound in your head: 'There is a time to tear down and a time to build up' (*New International Version*, 1973/2011, Ecclesiastes 3:3). Somehow, for a second, you manage to exist between the two acts. What is left is the stuff of explication: the psychic detritus that becomes the grist for synthesis. Even then, Moustakas (1990) warns that the job may not be done. You must stare at this rubble, these layers of meaning, and ask yourself, 'Have I reached the foundation?' Of course, the question is also moot: time reveals itself as a constraining force – the project of the self is a life-long undertaking. In the time afforded to you, you may only manage to level one wing of the house. Nevertheless, eventually, whether prompted by the clock, or the striking of substratum, you begin to rebuild, gathering the stuff of explication and reconstructing the time-space continuum with careful intent. Discussing her recognition of this state, Alana recalls that

It was time to begin the 'end' as time was running out. Resistance raged in my tacit dimension, recognising this as something I had experienced before: nurturing the foetus for many months and the excavation of the womb before it was ready.

Creative synthesis

Douglass and Moustakas describe the process of creative synthesis as one in which 'researchers face the challenge of creating a new reality, a monolithic significance that encapsulates the very essence of heuristic truth' (1985, p. 52). Sela-Smith describes it as 'an amazing time of synchronicity, harmony, connection, and integration' (2002, p. 69) which can be likened to an intimate union of the heuristic researcher and their enquiry. However, this union must find its ending before the due date and result in a product to be assessed and published. In this, the researcher must hold the tension between an imagined future and the demands of the present. Writing about the nature of work, Whyte suggests that it requires 'the ability to sustain an alchemical, almost lover like relationship that touches both the concrete essence of the present and the longed for mystery of the future to which the work leads us' (2014, p. 158).

The process of creative synthesis blurs boundaries between phases such as immersion, incubation, and explication; and serves both as a distinct phase and an ongoing process in the research journey (Chue, 2021). Time, perceived as external pressure, can feel like an aggressive intrusion and, therefore, a constraint on both synthesis and creativity. Nevertheless, it can also function as an alchemical catalyst akin to a pressure valve compressing and compelling change, thereby forcefully reshaping and reordering experiences and ideas. In this crucible of constraints, the researcher assumes the role of an alchemist, crafting unexpected forms. This dynamic interaction with time serves as a forge for innovation, pushing boundaries and shaping perspectives. As we navigate the temporal constraints, our perspective evolves, shifting from a contemplative and reflective stance to that of producer and creator. There is a passionate beauty found in the intensity created by a deadline, as previous concepts of self dissolve during the alchemical coming together of researcher, methodology, and topic of enquiry (Sultan, 2019).

Anna maintains that it was during creative synthesis that she most acutely experienced time as a catalyst. She recalls that

Approaching the external submission date created an inner potent surge of creative and *future* orientated energy during my writing hours each dawn. I deeply considered how my discoveries and transformations could cumulate in a story embedded in wholes (Sela-Smith, 2002) for the purpose of reaching into transpersonal realms. I wrote with homage to the brave self-honesty of previous heuristic researchers that inspired me with their transformative discoveries. I also wrote with intention to invite psychotherapists to reflect on their own experiences of hope in their daily practice, especially at a time in history such as this.

For her part, Alana remembers feeling that

Time was on my side in this phase, as it was forming from the very first mind-map of terms as I identified my associations with the topic. It was whittled down into a culmination of words to form a poem in an attempt to encapsulate the prominent themes of the research. The heuristic process and concepts had formed my creative synthesis.

For the student authors of this chapter, creative synthesis included writing, seeking feedback, and revising the final chapters of their dissertations, bearing in mind the assessment criteria by which their work would be marked, would include: 'reflect[ing] on and evaluat[ing] the significance of the research in the discipline area' (Auckland University of Technology, 2023, p. 127). Although heuristic self-search enquiry can appear to be overly self-referential, this criterion requires students to articulate their unique discoveries as contributions to the discipline, in this case, of psychotherapy, which requires, as Douglass and Moustakas propose, going 'from the specific to the general and from the individual to the universal' (1985, p. 52). This requires the researcher and their enquiry to move from feeling to action (Tudor, 2023), and, with regard to time, to face forward into a time that is yet to come.

Conclusion

Garfield (2016) notes that the word 'time' remains the most used noun in the English language, a stark reminder of what an unassailable and aggressive presence it is in our lives. Yet, arguably, one of the most catalytic things about heuristic research is that it demands a defying of time, almost an existence outside of it. When both Moustakas and Sela-Smith ask the heuristic researcher to surrender to the process, they are inciting a revolutionary act: to step outside a world that is constrained and delineated by clock and calendar. This abandoning of the pervasive structure of time is also a meditative act. In this way, it is our first real taste of extratemporal freedom. It is also a stand against the very scaffolding of society. Heuristic research also involves embracing the abstraction of things that may exist a priori in the unconscious realm, and taking on a pre-existing form that exists before the particular timeframe of the research study.

The pressure of time restrictions evokes, even provokes, strong feelings and thoughts and, as has been noted, a sense of constraint. At the same time, the same pressure may, through its forceful energy, catalyse moments of discovery. A time-conscious attitude (Elton Wilson, 1996) involves cultivating a creative relationship with time, i.e., harnessing its energy while, at moments, through careful management of boundaries, setting aside linear (chronological) clock time to embrace an inner experiential temporality (Kairos).

Across the research projects discussed here, the collective experience suggests that to undertake a heuristic self-search enquiry in a time-limited context requires both autonomy as well as adaptability. It requires researchers who are open to undertaking the enquiry and reflecting on the experience in depth. It also requires a supportive yet challenging and boundaried supervisor who is an ally in observing timekeeping requirements. In dealing with time and time limits, and experiencing them as both a catalyst and constraint, together we discovered that this drew from us what we consider to be heuristic qualities and/or attitudes of reflexivity and criticality, openness and non-defensiveness, sensitivity and robustness, patience and alacrity, discipline and flexibility, and autonomy and authenticity.

References

Auckland University of Technology. (2023). *Postgraduate handbook 2023*. https://tinyurl.com/y6ksjk2b

Chue, D. (2021). *Falling into the abyss: A heuristic self-inquiry into a psychotherapist's experience of abrupt endings* [Master's dissertation, Auckland University of Technology]. Tuwhera Open Access Theses & Dissertations. https://hdl.handle.net/10292/14790

Cousins, G. (2024). *In search of the boarding school self: A heuristic inquiry* [Unpublished master's dissertation]. Auckland University of Technology. http://hdl.handle.net/10292/17753

Dahlberg, K., Dahlberg, H., & Nyström, M. (2008). *Reflective lifeworld research* (2nd ed.). Studentlitteratur AB.

Douglass, B. G., & Moustakas, C. (1985). Heuristic inquiry: The internal search to know. *Journal of Humanistic Psychology*, *25*(3), 39–55. https://doi.org/10.1177/0022167885253004

Elton Wilson, J. (1996). *Time-conscious psychological therapy*. Routledge.

Frick, W. B. (1990). The symbolic growth experience: A chronicle of heuristic inquiry and a quest for synthesis. *Journal of Humanistic Psychology*, *30*(1), 64–80. https://doi.org/10.1177/0022167890301004

Garfield, S. (2016). *Timekeepers: How the world became obsessed with time*. Canongate Books.

Hegel, G. W. F. (1807/2019). *The phenomenology of spirit* (P. L. Fuss & J. D. Dobbins, Trans.). University of Notre Dame Press.

Hillman, J. (1983). *Healing fiction*. Spring Publications.

Humphris, A. (2024). *Motherhood and psychotherapy training: A heuristic self-search inquiry into a trainee's experience* [Unpublished master's dissertation]. Auckland University of Technology. http://hdl.handle.net/10292/17878

Kahler, T., & Capers, H. (1974). The miniscript. *Transactional Analysis Journal*, *4*(1), 26–42. https://doi.org/10.1177/036215377400400110

Kingi, A. (2024). *Glimmer: A heuristic self-search inquiry into a beginning psychotherapists experience of hope* [Unpublished master's dissertation]. Auckland University of Technology.

Levine, S. (1991). *Guided meditations, explorations and healings*. Anchor Books.

Maya-Chipman, T. (2023). *Navigating the wilderness – A heuristic self-search inquiry into the lived experience of chronic pain* [Master's dissertation, Auckland University of Technology]. Tuwhera Open Access Theses & Dissertations. https://hdl.handle.net/10292/17183

McGrath, H. P., & Comenetz, M. (2013). *Valéry's graveyard: Le Cimetière marin: Translated, described, and peopled*. Peter Lang.

McLeod, J. (2003). *Doing counselling research* (2nd ed.). Sage.

Melville, H. (1922). *Moby Dick*. Dodd, Mead & Company.

Moustakas, C. (1990). *Heuristic research: Design, methodology, and applications*. Sage.

New International Version. (1973/2011). BibleGateway.com. https://www.biblegateway.com/versions/New-International-Version-NIV-Bible/#booklist

O'Hara, M. (2002). Moments of eternity: What Carl Rogers has to offer brief therapists. In J. K. Zeig (Ed.), *Brief therapy: Lasting impressions* (pp. 337–366). The Milton H. Erickson Foundation Press.

Oram, L. (2024). *Remaking the Imago Paterna: How psychotherapy helps a son reimagine the father* [Unpublished master's dissertation]. Auckland University of Technology. http://hdl.handle.net/10292/17754

Ozertugrul, E. (2017). Heuristic self-search inquiry into one experience of obsessive–compulsive disorder. *Journal of Humanistic Psychology*, *57*(3), 215–236. https://doi.org/10.1177/0022167815592503

Rilke, R. M. (1929/1992). *Letters to a young poet*. New World Library.

Rogers, C. R. (1965). Some thoughts regarding the current philosophy of the behavioral sciences. *Journal of Humanistic Psychology*, *5*(2), 182–194. https://doi.org/10.1177/002216786500500207

Rumi, J. (2009). *Mystical poems of Rumi*. University of Chicago Press.

Sagan, C. (1987, Fall). The burden of skepticism. *Skeptical Inquirer*, *12*(1). https://skepticalinquirer.org/1987/10/the-burden-of-skepticism/

Sela-Smith, S. (2002). Heuristic research: A review and critique of Moustakas's method. *Journal of Humanistic Psychology*, *42*(3), 53–88. https://doi.org/10.1177/00267802042003004

Shakespeare, W. (1598/2019). *The first part of King Henry IV* (2nd ed.; J. Weil & H. Weil, Eds.). Cambridge University Press.

Smith, J. E. (1969). Time, times, and the 'right time'; Chronos and kairos. *The Monist*, *53*(1), 1–13. https://www.jstor.org/stable/27902109

Souba, W. (2011). The language of discovery. *Journal of Biomedical Discovery and Collaboration*, *6*, 53–69. https://doi.org/10.5210/disco.v6i0.3634

Sultan, N. (2019). *Heuristic inquiry: Researching human experience holistically*. Sage.

Taft, J. (1933). *The dynamics of therapy in a controlled relationship*. Macmillan.

Tudor, K. (2001). Change, time, place and community. In P. Lapworth, C. Sills, & S. Fish (Eds.), *Integration in counselling and psychotherapy* (pp. 142–151). Sage.

Tudor, K. (2017). The fight for health: An heuristic enquiry (2010). In K. Tudor, *Conscience and critic: The selected works of Keith Tudor* (pp. 143–168). Routledge.

Tudor, K. (2022). Supporting critical self-enquiry: Doing heuristic research. In S. Bager-Charleson & A. McBeath (Eds.), *Enjoying research in counselling and psychotherapy* (pp. 57–79). Springer. https://doi.org/10.1007/978-3-031-13942-0_4

Tudor, K. (2023). Critical heuristics: From 'I who feels' to 'We who care – and act'. In K. Tudor & J. Wyatt, (Eds.), *Qualitative research approaches for psychotherapy: Reflexivity, methodology, and criticality* (pp. 115–132). Routledge.

Tudor, K., & Oram, L. (2024). *Time: The hidden context of heuristic research.* Manuscript in preparation.

van Ruusbroec, J., & de Baere, G. (2014). *The complete Ruusbroec: English Translation with the Original Middle Dutch Text.* Brepols.

Vonnegut, K. (1969). *Slaughterhouse-five, or, the children's crusade: A duty-dance with death.* Dell.

Whyte, D. (2014). *Consolations: The solace, nourishment and underlying meaning of everyday words.* Many Rivers Press.

Winnicott, D. W. (1963). Communicating and not communicating leading to a study of certain opposites. In *The maturational processes and the facilitating environment* (pp. 179–192). International Universities Press. https://doi.org/10.4324/9780429482410-17

10

DISCOVERING HEURISTIC SUPERVISION

A collaborative enquiry

Keith Tudor and Welby Ings

Introduction

This chapter offers our discoveries about heuristic supervision of academic dissertations and theses. We begin by referring to our separate engagement(s) in the subject, and our joint interest in undertaking and promoting heuristic research. We then consider the results of a discussion between seven heuristic researchers who, one evening during the residential writing retreat that facilitated much of this book (see 'Gathering in'), shared their thinking about what constitutes effective supervision. Their thinking was prompted by the question: 'Speaking from embodied experience, what qualities create effective supervision for a postgraduate heuristic enquiry?'

The discoveries made during this discussion focus on: community support and expectations; the supervisory relationship (characterised by love, warmth, and trust; the journey, space, and time; and challenge); the nature of the supervisor (in terms of holding boundaries, being a witness, and being willing to share their experiences); and the qualities of the supervisee (namely their emotional readiness).

In writing this chapter, we express our gratitude to the seven researchers and co-participants who gave us permission to include excerpts from our discussion: Akbar Ghobakhlou, Elizabeth Hoyle, Alana Humphris, Anna Kingi, Luke Oram, Tangaroa Paora, and Derek Ventling. They have read and approved the quoted material, the inclusion of their names, and what has been synthesised from our shared reflection. Their insights, commitment to understanding effective supervision of heuristic inquires, and generosity enable us all.

DOI: 10.4324/9781003507758-14

Initial engagement(s) with heurism and supervision

As we have our own, individual histories with heurism, supervision, and heuristic supervision, we present these before offering a brief review of the literature on heuristic supervision. These represent our initial engagement(s) with the subject of our enquiry.

Welby

When I was growing up, I encountered supervision as a problem. As an unruly child who was eventually expelled from school and later suspended from Teacher's College, I experienced supervision as a form of imposed monitoring that I came to associate with the maintenance of institutional order. After leaving university at 19, I worked as a film director, a teacher, teacher educator, and political activist. However, although these commitments still accompany my practice, the last 27 years of my life have been spent oscillating between the film industry and helping people to grow their research skills inside universities. During this time, I have supervised over 90 postgraduate theses, of which 35 have been doctoral projects. These research journeys have been realised across a spectrum of disciplines including public policy, media studies, creative writing, Indigenous studies, education, queer studies, and the visual and performing arts.

The first time I encountered supervision as something more than monitoring was in the form of a script supervisor. When you are directing films, a script supervisor frees you up so you can become more deeply embodied inside an immediate focus on actors' performances and the visual tone of what is being recorded. A script supervisor sits just behind your shoulder, preparing and checking continuity breakdowns, logging what is filmed, and checking with you that no important dialogue has been overlooked. Essentially, they are enablers who engage in an attentive, ongoing, critical dialogue with you. They help you to make the best work that you can.

I encountered their academic equivalent in a mentor I was fortunate enough to work with when I embarked on my practice-led doctoral thesis (Ings, 2006). This supervisor was both a scholar and a deeply considered educator. He was important because at the time, practice-led design PhD theses were still relatively rare and most methodological considerations were centred around the construct of reflective practice (Mace, 1997; Schön, 1983, 1987; Scrivener, 2000). However, in the study I wanted to resource a fictional work with autobiographical material. Methodologically this required more than an external process of taking action, reflecting on it, and then taking action again. The study was predicated on self-search, both into memory and into the emerging 'self' of the film. I had stumbled across Douglass and Moustakas' (1985) article on heuristic enquiry as an internal search to know;

this suggested a helpful alternative because it enabled me to embark on a journey that merged indwelling and creative synthesis. Heuristics made sense, and when adapted from humanistic psychology, it enabled me to navigate deeper levels of artistic consideration.

Almost a decade later I encountered Keith in a discussion about learning and how humanity and rigour work within this. He talked about people with vulnerable experiences and how supervision was something beyond monitoring. I was struck by the practical, compassionate strength of his thinking. His feet were on the ground and his heart was committed to enhancing research journeys. Then I found out that we both worked with heuristic enquiry. Our collaboration and resulting friendship have been a natural consequence of this.

Keith

I was first introduced to supervision as a social worker in the late 1970s. When I was first at university (1973–1976), I benefitted from weekly tutorials (see Palfreyman, 2008), which were both demanding and stimulating, taught me the discipline of writing, and encouraged intellectual rigour: meetings and process I would now view as academic supervision. When I worked as a temporary probation officer (1976–1977), a student social worker (1977–1979), a counsellor (1981–1985), and a psychiatric social worker (1987–1990), I received supervision, although this was more managerial than supervision that really developed me personally, formatively, and/or professionally. It was only when (in 1985) I began training in psychotherapy that I experienced supervision which was not only helpful in my work with clients, but also accounted for me as a person. A few years after qualifying as a psychotherapist (in 1994), I began training as a supervisor, was accredited as such (in 2000), and went on to co-design and co-facilitate supervision training courses (Tudor & Worrall, 2007). In doing so, I became particularly interested in the extent to which the philosophy that underpins a particular practice is – or is not – reflected in the supervision of that practice (Tudor, 2009; Tudor & Worrall, 2004).

In 2006/2007 I embarked on a doctorate for which I drew on heuristics as an organising framework (Tudor, 2010). While I didn't have an academic supervisor who was familiar with heuristics, my two viva examiners were, and they helped me to take the final submission to another level of enquiry. This was a process I discussed in a subsequent publication (Tudor, 2017). Since becoming an academic at Auckland University of Technology, I have promoted heuristics as a research method and methodology; supervised a number of master's dissertations as well as three doctoral theses based on heuristic enquiry into various subjects in the field of psychotherapy; co-facilitated a monthly open discussion forum on heuristics for students

(2018–2020); and published three chapters on the subject (Tudor, 2017, 2022, 2023).

I knew of Welby through his work and, more directly, in some meetings at the university we both attended, but it wasn't until I was undertaking some research into the use of heuristics in disciplines other than psychotherapy that I became aware of his interest in, support of, and publications about heuristic enquiry in art and design (e.g., Ings, 2011, 2014, 2018). I made contact with him; we met and found that we had several areas of interest in common; and he was generous enough to act as a reviewer for one of my student's doctoral proposal. Two years ago, I suggested this project, and the rest, as they say, is history.

A view of literature

As with other forms of research, students and researchers engaged in heuristic enquiry are interested in what is already known about the subject, although some forms of heuristic enquiry are less concerned that such reviews are systematic (as are favoured in empirical research). Acknowledging Douglass and Moustakas' (1985) recognition of the significance of subjectivity, and Moustakas' (1990) emphasis on heuristics as discovery, Tudor refers to an 'initial literature view' (2022, p. 71) as being more congruent with the heuristic approach. In this spirit, we offer this brief view of the literature based on a search of the term 'heuristic supervision' in Google Scholar (to the first 100 entries), which unsurprisingly (at least to us) revealed very little literature on heuristic supervision. (That is, what such supervision actually looks like, and/or whether it's useful in facilitating the heuristic enquiry of others.) The search also revealed that what little literature there is on heuristic supervision is found in the psychological sciences (psychoanalysis and psychotherapy) and humanities (art and design).

In a rare article which promises a heuristic model of supervision (in the context of psychoanalytic supervision), Zachrisson states that: 'In an abstract, heuristic model, however, keeping factors isolated helps us to perceive tensions and contradictions which we have to face. It also helps us better understand and conceptualize the dynamics at hand' (2011, p. 949). Apart from the fact that the author offers little or no detail about their heuristic model, their view of heuristics appears somewhat abstract, isolated, and isolating, rather than process-oriented and holistic. Yerushalmi's (2019) article on 'Negative capability, heuristics and supervision' offers a view of supervision that is closer to our understanding of heuristics, but it is also very specific to psychoanalysis and is not easily applicable to other therapeutic approaches, let alone other disciplines.

Also writing in the field of therapy, Merry offers a clear commentary on supervision, which he views as a form of heuristic research and of helping and enquiry 'that has as primary goals, reflexive self-monitoring, person meaning-making, and increased self- and other-awareness' (2004, p. 189). His work, is, therefore, applicable across disciplines (see Freeth, 2004; Townsend, 2004). Merry considers Moustakas' (1990) phases of heuristic enquiry as parallel to the supervisory process of therapists – and, we might say, of research students – although neither of us advocate following those stages (see Chapter 11). Merry, also comments that he follows Moustakas' method 'in spirit rather than in detail' (2004, p. 194). Using the opportunity of writing the chapter to immerse himself in his experience of supervision, both as a supervisor and a supervisee, Merry identifies what he refers to as a number 'personal implications', which, following Rogers' (1961/1967b), we view as generalisable:

1 That supervision provides an opportunity for relating to people at 'existential or relational depth' (Merry, 2004, p. 194). This is a point we address below in our comments on Ings' (2011, 2014) contributions to the literature.
2 That because supervision has a time boundary, it means that the supervisor and supervisee/student can manage what can be quite an intense emotional and intellectual involvement (see also Chapter 8).
3 That, in supervision, the creation – or co-creation – of some order from chaos may be more important than being empathic, a point also addressed in this chapter.
4 That supervision as a reflective process also needs 'external dialogue and exchange' (Merry, 2004, p. 195). This we feel speaks to the importance of the supervision of supervision or, at least, of having reflective colleagues and/or a community around the supervisor. This may occur throughout the supervision journey, including examination.

(see Tudor, 2010)

In an article on managing heuristics as a method of inquiry specifically in the case of autobiographical design master's and doctoral theses, Ings (2011) considers the implications for supervision. The first point he makes links the nature of heuristic enquiry (with its emphasis on subjectivity and the self), to the role of the supervisor:

This is a challenging issue for supervisors. In many cases, when working with a candidate employing a heuristic inquiry, it is useful to remind oneself that such an inquiry is an orchestration of questions. If feedback is framed as questions (rather than advice), and a response is not asked for as an instant response, there is a higher chance that reflection may be taken back into, and reprocessed inside the self.

(Ings, 2011, p. 77)

He also discusses the responsibility the supervisor of autobiographical projects has to consider the emotional as well as intellectual level of the student/ researcher: 'not all students who are intellectually ready to undertake creative production theses are emotionally prepared for the challenges of autobiographical approaches' (Ings, 2011, p. 78). Moreover, once engaged with the student, the supervisor of such projects also carries responsibility for 'Creating an environment for risk-taking' (2011, p. 80), which, in these risk-averse times and in institutions increasingly concerned with health and safety, is challenging for all parties.

In a second article on the subject, Ings considers the advantages and disadvantages of such autobiographical, practice-led theses, making the point that 'the vulnerability [that] gives authority to autobiographic inquiries… requires careful and attentive supervision' (2014, p. 681). Self-enquiry – and especially heuristic self-search inquiry (à la Sela-Smith, 2002) – is self-revealing and self-exposing, and both the personal material and the subject/ person need to be curated and cared for, not least, by and in supervision. As Ings puts it: 'The truth is high-risk inquiries require substantial investments from all parties, and it has been my experience that [videoconferencing] and email do not serve the research relationship well in times of uncertainty' (2014, p. 685). Ings also makes an important point that research ethics guidelines focus on protecting participants rather than the researcher and, in effect, tend not to consider or understand the researcher as a participant. He also recognises that, 'as a supervisor, of autobiographical, practice-led theses, one is not neutral' (2014, p. 689). In other words, the supervisor has an initial – and ongoing – engagement with the focus of inquiry (Moustakas, 1990). This may be related to the subject area; it is always to the subject/person:

> My role as a supervisor shifts with the journey of the thesis. I am at times a mentor, a critic, a proactive planner, a reasoned objector, and occasionally, a shoulder to cry on. This is not soft supervision. It is simply responsive. It recognises that the import of the self into a research project is more than an intellectual decision. It is also an act of faith with emotional consequences.

(Ings, 2014, p. 689)

The second aspect of heuristic supervision in which we are interested is the extent to which the supervision of heuristic research requires the supervisor themselves to be heuristic and/or to be supervising heuristically, that is, supervising and/or teaching 'in the manner of' the method (see Tudor, 2009), or walking the talk. For instance, we note a number of students thanking their supervisors for their heuristic supervision (e.g., He, 2023; Liu, 2004; Wang, 2008) or referring to heuristic supervision (e.g., Khattab et al., 2021), but not defining or describing it in any way. Interestingly, one of the participants in the writing retreat spoke appreciatively of one of his supervisors, saying 'He actually believed in the paradigm' (Akbar).

So…

On the day we met

The sky was cloudy. Down on the beach you could see the tide crawling slowly outwards, retreating with the pull of an invisible moon. Dusk had arrived and it was slowly dissolving into night.

It had been a long day, the first of the writing retreat and we were nestled into circle of assorted sofas – ten researchers in a small room. We had all undertaken heuristic inquiries. Some of us were graduates, some were students completing master's or doctoral theses, and some of us were supervisors. We researched across a spectrum of disciplines, from computer science, documentary practice, design, education, Indigenous studies, and psychotherapy to social care. We had just shared a meal together and, in the civilised grace of reflective company, now shared a space, 90 minutes, and a question. Given that little had been written about the institutional care of heuristic approaches to dissertation or thesis development, we asked the question:

> Speaking from embodied experience, what qualities create effective supervision for a postgraduate heuristic enquiry?

From the contents of the discussion, we identified the following themes:

- The context of community support and expectations.
- The supervisory relationship – characterised by love, warmth, and trust; the journey, space, and time; and challenge.
- The person of the supervisor – which, from this discussion, focused on holding boundaries; being a witness; and being willing to share their experiences.
- The emotional readiness of the supervisee.

We begin with the context within which the research takes place, specifically the responsibilities of the researcher and the context of community support that surrounds them. We do this because this was a major theme which emerged from the students/participants, and we want to offer something of a balance to the usual focus in heuristic research on the self (for a critique of which, see Ings, 2011, and Tudor, 2023).

Our discoveries

Community support – and expectations

Tangaroa: I made sure that I had a good home support system because the journey was going to take a lot of time away from my family and community groups or whoever I was part of. The kaupapa (proposal, project) was quite a big thing and they had to understand that I might not be as available, I might not be able to devote as much time to other kaupapa. Maybe even to the point where I tried to still manage fulfilling kaupapa Māori by doing this project because I needed to keep myself associated with both the rainbow community, and within my Māori community. I had to maintain that sense of connection so that they understood that I wasn't leaving them.

Welby: That's interesting. A criticism that you sometimes hear about deeply subjective research is that the 'singular self' is a very Western, idealised position. So how, when we come from more collective cultures, do we deal with this? It's interesting because three Māori scholars working with heuristic, practice-led inquiries have questioned the singular nature of the self (Paora, 2023; Pouwhare, 2020; Williams, 2024).

Tangaroa: I think it has to do with the practice of immersion. The research journey requires me to be in the self, but also somewhere else. I am part of a community, and it is part of me. My community is with me. Also, the institution itself introduced me to so many people of different ethnic groups, and different religious beliefs. They all contributed to this PhD in some way. My contribution to the academy relied on the support of other people. I thought that was quite a massive thing because now the networks and the relationships that I shared ensure that, if they need anything culturally, I can be there to help, I know I can support them.

There, are, of course, other forms of support the researcher receives from family, friends, and other professionals. Students studying psychotherapy are required to be in their own personal therapy, which provides a forum in which they may well discuss the impact that their research is having on them. Another participant (who isn't a psychotherapy student) also discussed the benefit of such support:

Elizabeth: During my research, I chose to get therapy, which ran parallel with the inquiry. What the therapist gave me was really good, because the project entailed a big personal shift, and she had studied grief. So, she is a place I go to every fortnight for an hour, and I find that comforting and 100% supportive, which is really good given everything that is going on. She asks me the right questions; she asks about my history and being distracted. She introduced me to the work of Robert Neimeyer (2015), who I absolutely love. We have wonderful talks about growth and building narratives.

Responding to some of the other participants, Welby acknowledged the reality and impact of the context of their lives:

Welby: You know, you've got complex things going on in your world. There are kids to care for; there might be a teaching commitment; or there might be crises. So, the heuristic journey isn't some discrete thing. It sits in the context of a complex life ... a protean life that's always moving, always changing.

The supervisory relationship

Our discussion about this encompassed a number of factors or qualities.

Love, warmth, and trust

One of the students put this poignantly (talking to and about Welby):

Tangaroa: I always assumed my relationship was with you as a *koro* (grandfather): someone who protects the space, clears the pathway, and asks where you are. I've always seen that your grandparents, whoever they may be, have this role; to love you and to ensure that you feel safe to be who you are. That's what allowed me to immerse myself more within a heuristic approach. On the one hand, you articulated my thoughts and fed back to me what I was trying to understand... [and, on the other hand] you allowed me to discover my own way of interpreting this heuristic approach.

Elizabeth: It [the relationship] feels very loving. That sounds strange, but that's how it feels. This is a great place to come to when something new appears alien. So, you feel welcomed in and comfortable enough to explore and experiment and take risks: you can be really risky and know that it's safe, and you know safety when you see it.

Keith related this observation to the origin story of heuristics (at least as we have it from Moustakas):

Keith: That's great. I'm thinking about the history of heuristics, certainly from Moustakas, which came from his experience of loneliness in relation to his daughter (Moustakas, 1961), which he himself linked to love (Moustakas, 1970, 1972). We know that the heuristic method came from this experience, and it was only on reflection that he identified concepts and phases of heuristic inquiry (Douglass & Moustakas, 1985; Moustakas, 1990). So, this approach was born out of a difficult experience and struggle – and a loving relationship.

Responding to this, another participant talked about the importance of relationships:

Anna: This form of research requires more: more relationships, and more partnership. In the final version of my dissertation, I ended up writing a poem about my experience with the raw data, about hope and psychotherapy as a supervisee student, and I ended up with a poem because I couldn't disguise this data enough... you know, sift it all. It was so relational and so much about shame and being known and being seen. I didn't anticipate that about heuristics. So, I see something in my research about warmth: the warmth and openness of supervisors, which was hard to come by. This was crucial in order to meet my raw data, and to be seen as part of the transformation. Without that warmth and trust, I don't know if it [the dissertation and the transformation] would have occurred.

The journey, space, and time

Welby: Hossein talks about the journey of the birds (see Chapter 3), as a journey towards illumination. Tangaroa, you talk about heuristic inquiry as a journey between te kura huna and te kura tūrama; that moves back and forwards between the realm of the known and the explicit, and the realm of the esoteric (see Chapter 2). That's a journey across space and time that happens without a road map. How do you resource such a journey?

Tangaroa: Work. That's the fuel on the journey. If you stop doing anything, then you're just sitting there stagnant. So, it requires you to constantly be digging, digging, digging. When people talk about heuristic inquiry, the concept of the journey is massive. Work and reflecting are necessary for transformation.

Anna: Yes. There's some kind of journey that sits underneath it. A journey into darkness to get something out. It's transitional. There are transitional states. Sometimes, you know, we can do research and it's not transitional.

Derek: I think the journey is almost like going through a portal, to a place where you can safely have a conversation where you can talk with a supervisor about vision, and they can give them the safe space – a space that is more than physical space. The portal is something to pass through to a new thinking space.

Welby: So, this is interesting. You talk about darkness and portals and seeking safety. Why is safety so important to a heuristic inquiry?

Derek: Because there's so much uncertainty, there's so much personal doubt that goes with this and you never know how your ideas are valid – and you can spiral, right? This safe space is important because you are connected to the study and it's really personal to you. It's something that you have been examining and thinking about for a long time; something that you want to explore. The portal takes you into the dark because you are entering another world, you are reaching into discovery.

Welby: This makes me think about the darkness that comes before the light. So, in this unknown space, how do you know when to start believing in the project?

Luke: Hmmm. In my project, in which I was investigating the way that I view my father, I got to a point where I realised that everything had to be up for grabs. You can't really unpack the concept of your father without sort of unravelling your own DNA. So, even the self has to be up for grabs… everything… even getting to the point where you question your own conception of the self. You just have to go wherever it goes. Spiritually, it's like going back several generations. I found my whole person and what that meant… every dimension of selfhood. I did not expect that to happen.

Tangaroa: Across space and time I wrestle with myself unravelling and often this feels spiritual, I go into the dimension of the soul. It's one of the things that we understand as Māori: the dimensions of the self that sit outside of the cognitive and the rational. We are used to talking about the spiritual as a way of experiencing knowledge. In some cultures, this has traditionally been confined to theological academic inquiry, but somehow heuristic inquiry appears to make some space for that, and that has been an interesting thing to go through. Within a heuristic inquiry, spiritual knowing pops out calmly and it's disproportionately common. I was reading something the other day, where they were saying that your spiritual sense gives you an understanding of the mysterious and therefore you are more capable of going into the unknown because you've already got this affinity, or past understanding of the realm. It's not an interruption. Perhaps it's a dimension of the tacit, not just about things that are explicit and empirical.

I used Robert Pouwhare's (2020) Pūrākau methodology as an example. He uses a tree as a metaphor for it. I am the tree that sits in the realms of *Te Kura Tūrama* and *Te Kura Huna* (the realms of explicit and tacit or esoteric knowing, respectively). I know that tacit knowledge is hidden within the roots of the tree so, even though I can't consciously explain it, I know it's there and I know it resources the study. A dimension of this tacit knowing might be spiritual. As a researcher I draw the nutrients from the roots, into the body of the tree: I draw the knowledge from the realm of the unknown or what's hidden into the realm of the known and explicit. I think heuristic inquiry is an evolutionary process in which the tacit and explicit are constantly being combined to enable a researcher to work their way through something. Without the tacit the tree can't grow, but nor can it grow without the explicit. You need a supervisor who knows that this is the position you are working with. Your supervisor needs to have more than an intellectual empathy with the *kaupapa*. They need to have some feeling for the dimensions that you are working with.

Keith: I agree. Your experiences of supervision remind me of mine. While my academic supervisor for my doctoral project was very academic, and both supportive and challenging, he wasn't heuristic. I didn't realise the impact of this until I got to my viva (voce)/oral examination/defence of the thesis. The two examiners I met there had a good knowledge of heuristics and encouraged me to go deeper into my thesis. My recollection of the exam was that it was really good supervision. Although I passed with minor amendments, their feedback and encouragement was transformative, and, as a result, I rewrote large parts of my thesis (Tudor, 2010). What I take from that experience and from what you're saying is that the supervisor needs to be authentically alongside the student/candidate on their journey in space and time, and they need to encourage their supervisee to go deeper; to stay with it (whatever the 'it' is); to explore and discover more (even if that's scary); and to express and synthesise more.

Challenge

Derek: There is a deep challenge in heuristic inquiry. In my thesis I was exploring a notion of divine inspiration. Six hundred years ago Bonaventure (Hayes, 1996) wrote about a progressive order of cognitive insight that lifts you up to divine knowledge. His first foundation is doing, the next level is sensing, and his third level is thinking. I'd always felt that I can 'do', and I can 'sense', but I need a supervisor who will help me to think by asking deep questions. Questioning helps me to go deeper and with this depth my enthusiasm grows for the topic. My supervisor would say, 'I'm going to feed back what you just said… Is this what you mean?' Then he'd say, 'Now give that back in a simpler, clearer way.'

Welby: This could be helpful. We need to respond to what different people need: some might need to do more work, while others might need to heighten the level of sensing that they are bringing to the material (like the tacit or the poetic). The thing is that the levels of engagement and a candidate's responses or questions are all important. As a supervisor you have to be constantly thinking about difference, so you need to be moving between different emphases, depending on the project and the nature of the person undertaking the research.

Tangaroa: You also have to hold to high personal standards. You need a supervisor who believes in you and expects you to rise up. I remember once realising that I could lose it all because I walked into an appointment for supervision 15 minutes late and poorly prepared because I wasn't paying attention to my commitments. Well, my supervisor was disappointed in me, and he goes, 'I think we need to consider you finding another supervisor.' I was really shocked. I realised that I was not being consistently committed and how much was at risk here. This journey was a relationship. It was possible to lose a big thing: not just the mentorship, but the time to speak and think together. I'm pretty sure I never showed up late after that. Almost the opposite. That's mutual respect: respect for the question, respect for excellence, and respect for everybody on the journey.

These points appear to echo points made by Welby (Ings, 2011) regarding the importance of the supervisor's feedback and style of questions, as well as the importance of creating an environment for risk-taking.

Although it is clear that the supervisory relationship is key to supporting heuristic research, our discussion also identified some qualities of the two parts of this relationship (i.e., the person of the supervisor, and that of the researcher/student/candidate).

The person of the supervisor

In referring to the person of the supervisor, we are echoing Carl Rogers' (1961/1967a) ground-breaking work on the person of the therapist (i.e., that they are a real person and not someone simply fulfilling a role, and, moreover, someone who is contactful, authentic, valuing, empathic, and reflective). Our discussion highlighted three main themes: the importance of holding boundaries, being a witness, and supervisors being willing to share their experiences.

Holding boundaries

Anna: Following our first supervision, meeting regularly was helpful. We talked about the topic, and how we could work collaboratively with each other, but my supervisor always insisted that the project was mine, and I had to make sure that I believed this. Initially, I didn't because I didn't know where it was going.

Elizabeth: I needed a supervisor who was attentive to institutional requirements because, with a heuristic inquiry, it's really easy to get off track or forget where I was because I could get so far down into something that everything else disappeared. So, I needed to have the security of knowing that, while I was digging down, I would be reminded of things like meetings, catch ups, timetables, and schedules. I found the six-monthly progress reports required by the university helpful because they made me draw things together and bring my discoveries forward – which was important because the chance of getting and being lost for long periods of time was so great.

Being a witness

Luke: You sort out the research question and you grapple with that, and then you get sent off into immersion. This was quite a personal thing. I almost felt myself keeping you [Keith] out of that process to a certain extent: I would go away, and I'd do that, and I'd get lost in it. I remember that part of the process which evolved for me was that I spent a lot of time doing this and not writing; then, about halfway through the year, I took a week off to go out of town and just make a start on getting it all down on paper. For a week I sort of slipped into this weird kind of trance and it all fell out: basically, the whole 10,000 words just fell out, just came out of me. Then I was ready to sort of pull you in and, at this point, you were like the first witness to this personal thing. It was incredibly personal, but it was necessarily a lonely journey – but then your role became pivotal: being able to put this [draft] in front of someone and have them say this is this, and that is that. This was the moment when you were able to witness what I'd done, and I was able to calibrate it in relation to that.

Being willing to share their experiences

Elizabeth: It was important to me to have a supervisor who shared their own experiences. It created empathy and understanding, and it felt like recognition. The safety issue was very important, especially if you are involved in artistic practice because you are so exposed, and it is a totally new world that you're going into. You are coming to terms with the methodology, and scoping existing practice and literature, but concurrently, you are working through interior meaning and high levels of personal exposure. It feels safer when you have a supervisor you can see has been doing similar things in their own practice.

Derek: I loved the sense of shared excitement. I would take artistic risks, go into uncharted territory and my supervisor would get excited too. It was something shared, but also an ongoing human connection that gave me strength. I felt that there was a witness to, and an investment in, my courage.

Keith: So the supervisor's enthusiasm and excitement seems important. I wonder if this relates to an identification with the focus of inquiry? This is one of Moustakas' (1990) concepts which is clearly crucial for the researcher but, I think, also for the supervisor. While it's not the same identification, I think there needs to be some. I can't think of a heuristic project with which I've been involved that I haven't had an association or connection. Nevertheless, it's a good question: does the supervisor have to be connected to the topic, or is it enough for them to be connected to the person?

A few days after the meeting one participant sent us the following, which summarises a number these strands:

Alana: I would come to supervision feeling overwhelmed, busy, full, sometimes stuck, unsure, and feeling like I might not be doing it right. My supervisor would offer tacit knowledge and intuition, holding the uncertainty and the 'not knowing' with openness, interest/enthusiasm, understanding, and curiosity. This, in turn, elicited enthusiasm in me and sparked a light for the dying fire, leaving me feeling like I was on the right track. I would leave with a whole lot to write and new inspiration and enthusiasm. With regard to timekeeping [in the context of time-limited study] – my supervisor would tell us approximately where we should be, helping us to track where we were. He also challenged my pre-scribed way of writing by pointing out when my approach wasn't heuristic, and, by doing so he protected the method.

Finally, Elizabeth acknowledged the commitment this requires from the supervisor:

Elizabeth: Many people I've spoken to about supervision have said that it's quite isolating and you don't actually get much time with your supervisor, but that's not been the case for me. I've had everything and more. Yeah, that's an incredible commitment.

The qualities of the supervisee

Finally, a couple of the participants in the discussion touched briefly on the qualities that heuristic research requires of the researcher. Anna, who utilised Sela-Smith's (2002) heuristic self-search enquiry in her own exploration of hope (Kingi, 2024) and had been very influenced by Sela-Smith's ideas, commented:

Anna: I think it depends on how much emphasis you put on transforma-tion. I appreciated Sela-Smith's work on this and, similarly, found the work very transformative personally. I think the transformative element of heuristics is really, really important, but hard. Sometimes down there, in the darkness of the unknown [of the enquiry], there are no rules, and that is scary. You need a certain strength to do this kind of research.

Elizabeth: You have to be ready to take on a heuristic inquiry. I carried my self-doubt into the project with me, but I knew what it was. With this approach it's also about trying to sort your shit out, and exploring an idea of a return to identity. In a way the approach helped me to understand the process and also to heal: insight and healing together. It's a challenge because you must be ready to be looking in while you are looking out.

Keith: These are great points. Relating this to supervision, I'd suggest that we [supervisors] need to ask ourselves whether the student is emotionally capable of the work? Are they self-reflective enough? Will they go wherever they need to? Are they willing to go deep – and/or wide – to ask the questions, and to reflect on the answers?

This last theme reflects the point Ings (2011) makes about the importance of the student's emotional readiness, not least, in facing and working through resistance. As Sela-Smith observes: 'the researcher may unconsciously resist the actual personal problem and consider something less threatening' (2002, p. 65).

Further findings

In this last section, we (Keith and Welby) reflect on these themes, re-view the existing literature (summarised on pp. 184–187), and identify future directions for research.

Douglass and Moustakas state that 'Self-experience is the single most important guideline in pursuing heuristic research' (1985, p. 46). This suggests that facilitating the student's self-experiencing is the single most important guideline for supervision of heuristic research. Such facilitation is not always easy because it involves both supporting and challenging the student (as a number of the co-participants in the discussion acknowledge). This focus on self-awareness echoes Merry's proposition that the primary goal of supervision (in the context of his writing, of clinical supervision) is 'increased self- and other-awareness' (2004, p. 189). We particularly appreciate his reference to self and other as it resonates with our interest and concern about heuristics (i.e., that self-experiencing always takes place in a context and is often about or related to context). Joubert and Raeburn (1998) define mental health promotion as fostering both supportive environments and individual resilience, a perspective that we consider encapsulates the role of supervision of heuristic and other autobiographical research.

All of the participants acknowledged the significance of context (personal, family, community, institutional) and some spoke specifically about the importance of having supportive environments (i.e., Tangaroa and Elizabeth). This is not only a social and cultural perspective and value we also share, it's also directly related to what Welby refers to as the vulnerability involved in such research (Ings, 2014, and p.195). Given the emphasis in heuristics on identifying with the focus of enquiry, indwelling, self-search, self-dialogue, self-disclosure, transformation, resistance, surrender, and inward reach, such research cannot be impersonal; indeed, it demands vulnerability from the student and, therefore, care from the supervisor.

From this, we consider a number of features of such supervision:

- That the supervisor's 'negative capability' (as noted by Yerushalmi, 2019) needs to be complemented by positive engagement with the student and their work. In this sense, we view supervision of heuristic projects as curating both the project and the person.
- That the supervisor needs to hold the integrity of the heuristic process (as noted by both Akbar and Alana), part of which is to provide structure within which the student can explore a certain breakdown and disorganisation (as noted by Derek, Luke, Tangaroa, and Alana). This echoes what

Merry (2004) says about the creation – or co-creation – of some order from chaos, though we don't necessarily agree that this is more important than being empathic. As Ings puts it: 'if such an inquiry is to develop in an uncompromised manner the supervisor and the candidate need to accept both its instability and the time and resource implications this can pose' (2011, p. 76).

- That, at some point, the necessary 'inward reach' (identified and promoted by Sela-Smith, 2002) needs to be balanced by outward reach, and the subjectivity of the research examined with regard to its more general application to others and, for instance, a discipline (Auckland University of Technology, 2023). This is the external dialogue and exchange to which Merry (2004) refers. Aziz puts this well: 'The thesis is subjective. It would be impossible to realise in any other way. Because of this it is also biased, *but out of that bias comes a voice that seeks to relate*' (2009, p. 67, our emphasis).
- That it demands more of the supervisor, personally, in terms of their engagement with both the project and the student; emotionally, in, for instance, as Ings puts it, 'being a shoulder to cry on' (2014, p. 689); and in terms of resources, especially time. It is important to note, however, that the academic supervisor of heuristic research does not take on the role of a therapist or create dependency. In this context, we agree with Merry (2004) when he writes about identifying and strengthening the student's internal supervision. For us, it's more about being a real (authentic) person, and a humane (and humanistic) human being.

One of our initial interests in exploring heuristic supervision was the extent to which the supervision of heuristic research is in itself heuristic or is more consistent and effective if it is. Although some participants identified certain qualities of the supervisor which we can link to heuristic concepts such as intuition (mentioned by Alana) or self-disclosure (implied by the theme of supervisors being willing to share their experiences (p. 195)), the issue or question of the congruence or fit between heuristic research and heuristic supervision was not significant. Clearly, the phases of heuristic research do not need to parallel those of the supervision of an academic research project; neither do all of the concepts of heuristic research, specifically those identified by Douglass and Moustakas (1985), Moustakas (1990), and Sela-Smith (2002), need to be present in the supervisory relationship, although we think that it would be interesting and fruitful to see which of them are. Nevertheless, we would suggest that the experience of undertaking heuristic research prepares the supervisor to be able to accompany the student through their indwelling, self-search, self-dialogue, and the full journey of their research project.

References

Auckland University of Technology. (2023). *Postgraduate handbook* 2023. https://tinyurl.com/y6ksjk2b

Aziz, L. (2009). *Gilgamesh, the hero of Mesopotamia* [Master's thesis, Auckland University of Technology]. Tuwhera Open Access Theses & Dissertations. https://hdl.handle.net/10292/813

Douglass, B. G., & Moustakas, C. (1985). Heuristic inquiry: The internal search to know. *Journal of Humanistic Psychology*, *25*(3), 39–55. https://doi.org/10.1177/0022167885253004

Freeth, R. (2004). A psychiatrist's experience of person-centred supervision. In K. Tudor & M. Worrall (Eds.), *Freedom to practise: Person-centred approaches to supervision* (pp. 247–266). PCCS Books.

Hayes, Z. (1996). *On the reduction of the arts to theology. Works of Saint Bonaventure, 1*. The Franciscan Institute of St. Bonaventure University.

He, Y. (2023). *Experiments on nonlinear extreme waves in complex configurations* [Doctoral thesis, The University of Sydney]. Sydney Digital Theses. https://hdl.handle.net/2123/31573

Ings, W. (2006). *Talking pictures: The creative utilisation of structural and aesthetic profiles from narrative music videos and television commercials in non-spoken film texts* [Doctoral thesis, Auckland University of Technology]. Tuwhera Open Access Theses & Dissertations. https://hdl.handle.net/10292/346

Ings, W. (2011). Managing heuristics as a method of inquiry in autobiographical graphic design theses. *International Journal of Art & Design Education*, *30*(2), 226–241. https://doi.org/10.1111/j.1476-8070.2011.01699.x

Ings, W. J. (2014). Narcissus and the muse: Supervisory implications of autobiographical, practice-led PhD design theses. *Qualitative Research*, *14*(6), 675–693. https://doi.org/10.1177/1468794113488128

Ings, W. (2018). Heuristic inquiry, land and the artistic researcher. In M. Sierra & K. Wise (Eds.), *Transformative pedagogies and the environment: Creative agency through contemporary art and design* (pp. 55–80). Common Ground Research Networks.

Joubert, N., & Raeburn, J. (1998). Mental health promotion: People, power and passion. *International Journal of Health Promotion*, *1*(1), 15–22.

Khattab, O., Potts, C., & Zaharia, M. (2021). Baleen: Robust multi-hop reasoning at scale via condensed retrieval. *Advances in Neural Information Processing Systems*, *34*, 27670–27682.

Kingi, A. (2024). *Glimmer: A heuristic self-search inquiry into a beginning psychotherapists' experience of hope* [Unpublished master's dissertation]. Auckland University of Technology.

Liu, H. (2004). *Numerical modelling of the rock fragmentation process by mechanical tools* [Doctoral dissertation, Luleå tekniska universitet]. DiVA. https://ltu.diva-portal.org/smash/record.jsf?pid=diva2%3A998896&dswid=3214

Mace, M. A. (1997). Toward an understanding of creativity through a qualitative appraisal of contemporary art making. *Creativity Research Journal*, *10*(2), 265–278. https://doi.org/10.1080/10400419.1997.9651225

Merry, T. (2004). Supervision as heuristic inquiry. In K. Tudor & M. Worrall (Eds.), *Freedom to practise: Person-centred approaches to supervision* (pp. 189–199). PCCS Books.

Moustakas, C. (1961). *Loneliness*. Prentice-Hall.

Moustakas, C. (1970). Loneliness and love. In B. Marshall (Ed.), *Experiences in being* (pp. 53–60). Brooks/Cole.

Moustakas, C. (1972). *Loneliness and love*. Prentice-Hall.

Moustakas, C. (1990). *Heuristic research: Design, methodology and applications*. Sage.

Neimeyer, R. A. (2015). *Techniques of grief therapy: Creative practices for counseling the bereaved*. Routledge.

Palfreyman, D. (2008). *The Oxford tutorial: 'Thanks, you taught me how to think'* (2nd ed.). Oxford Centre for Higher Education Policy Studies.

Paora, T. I. (2023). *Takatāpui: Beyond marginalisation: Contesting gender roles in kapa haka* [Doctoral thesis, Auckland University of Technology]. Tuwhera Open Access Theses & Dissertations. https://hdl.handle.net/10292/16962

Pouwhare, R. (2020). *Ngā Pūrākau mō Māui: mai te patuero, te pakokitanga me te whakapēpē ki te kōrero pono, ki te whaihua whaitake, mē ngā honotanga. The Māui narratives: From Bowdlerisation, dislocation and infantilisation to veracity, relevance and connection* [Doctoral thesis, Auckland University of Technology]. Tuwhera Open Access Theses & Dissertations. https://hdl.handle.net/10292/13307

Rogers, C. R. (1967a). *On becoming a person: A therapist's view of psychotherapy*. Constable.

Rogers, C. R. (1967b). 'This is me': The development of my professional thinking and personal philosophy. In *On becoming a person* (pp. 3–27). Constable.

Schön, D. A. (1983). *The reflective practitioner: How professionals think in action*. Basic Books.

Schön, D. A. (1987). *Educating the reflective practitioner: Toward a new design for teaching and learning in the professions*. Jossey-Bass.

Scrivener, S. (2000). Towards the operationalisation of design research as reflection in and on action and practice. In D. Durling & K. Friedman (Eds.), *Foundations for the future. Doctoral education in design* (pp. 387–394). Staffordshire University Press.

Sela-Smith, S. (2002). Heuristic research: A review and critique of Moustakas's method. *Journal of Humanistic Psychology*, *42*(3), 53–88. https://doi.org/10.1177/0022167802423004

Townsend, I. (2004). Almost nothing to do: Supervision and the person-centred approach in homeopathy. In K. Tudor & M. Worrall (Eds.), *Freedom to practise: Person-centred approaches to supervision* (pp. 225–245). PCCS Books.

Tudor, K. (2009). 'In the manner of': Transactional analysis teaching of transactional analysts. *Transactional Analysis Journal*, *39*(4), 276–292. https://doi.org/10.1177/036215370903900403

Tudor, K. (2010). *The fight for health: A heuristic enquiry into psychological well-being* [Unpublished context statement for PhD in Mental Health Promotion by Public (Published) Works]. School of Health and Social Sciences, Middlesex University, London, UK.

Tudor, K. (2017). The fight for health: An heuristic enquiry (2010). In K. Tudor, *Conscience and critic: The selected works of Keith Tudor* (pp. 143–168). Routledge.

Tudor, K. (2022). Supporting critical self-enquiry: Doing heuristic research. In S. Bager-Charleson & A. McBeath (Eds.), *Enjoying research in counselling and psychotherapy* (pp. 57–79). Springer. https://doi.org/10.1007/978-3-031-13942-0_4

Tudor, K. (2023). Critical heuristics: From 'I who feels' to 'We who care – and act'. In K. Tudor & J. Wyatt (Eds.), *Qualitative research approaches for psychotherapy: Reflexivity, methodology, and criticality* (pp. 115–132). Routledge.

Tudor, K., & Worrall, M. (2004). Person-centred philosophy and theory in the practice of supervision. In K. Tudor & M. Worrall (Eds.), *Freedom to practise: Person-centred approaches to supervision* (pp. 11–30). PCCS Books.

Tudor, K., & Worrall, M. (2007). Training supervisors. In K. Tudor & M. Worrall (Eds.), *Freedom to practise II: Developing person-centred approaches to supervision* (pp. 211–219). PCCS Books.

Wang, Y. (2008). *Mechanical properties and microstructure of laser sintered and starch consolidated iron-based powders* [Doctoral dissertation, Karlstads universitet]. DiVA. https://kau.diva-portal.org/smash/record.jsf?pid=diva2%3A5524&dswid=-5201

Williams, T. (2024). *Tangohia mai te taura - Take This Rope: Exploring Māori documentary-making approaches to elevate whānau narratives* [Doctoral thesis, Auckland University of Technology]. Tuwhera Open Access Theses & Dissertations. https://hdl.handle.net/10292/17323

Yerushalmi, H. (2019). Negative capability, heuristics and supervision. *British Journal of Psychotherapy, 35*(2), 290–304. https://doi.org/10.1111/bjp.12458

Zachrisson, A. (2011). Dynamics of psychoanalytic supervision: A heuristic model. *The International Journal of Psychoanalysis, 92*(4), 943–961. https://doi.org/10.1111/j.1745-8315.2011.00417.x

Facing Outwards

11

EPILOGUE

Welby Ings and Keith Tudor

The nature of the book

So, we reach the end of the book, and we would like to take you down to the beach one last time.

On the final night of the retreat, the moon was late rising, and heaven was a spectrum of stars. We had finished writing for the day and we lay in the long grass, listening to the ocean. We were tired. Collectively, we had spent an intensive time discussing, listening, connecting, thinking, and eating together. We were due to leave the next day with initial drafts of the chapters developed for what have become the contents of this book. Although we had arrived with individual understandings of heuristic inquiry, we realised the extent to which these had been shaped inside limited contexts. Initially, none of us had fully understood the breadth of heuristics as it played out across the academy and in diverse, professional fields. In these few days together, we had shown each other its connections to approximation, self-search, the development of fictional and semi-fictional worlds, healing and growth, spirituality, and Indigenous approaches to research.

As we lay on the bank, the air moved quietly through the grass, and we gazed upwards into an expanse of the known and unknown. In the stillness someone quoted Vincent van Gogh,

> Is the whole of life visible to us or do we in fact know only the one hemisphere before we die?… For my part I know nothing with any certainty, but the sight of the stars makes me dream.
>
> (van Gogh, 1888/1958, letter #506)

DOI: 10.4324/9781003507758-16

Dreaming and knowing… the visible and the invisible, the tacit and explicit, the calculated and estimated, the pragmatic and the discovered: the concept of heuristics spans wide dimensions of understanding. None of us left the retreat unaffected.

This had not been a conference with 20-minute deliveries in parallel sessions, with five minutes reserved for questions. It was not a symposium with submitted abstracts to flesh out in a chronological schedule that left you with little time for communal deliberation. The retreat had been something different, something closer to a contemporary understanding of scholarship: a gathering of people who care for knowledge and the pursuit of meaning, and who approach these things with a generosity of spirit, resourced by questioning, critical, appreciative minds.

This book has been a negotiation that has followed Kleining and Witt's (2000) view that discovery in heuristic inquiry relies on flexibility. As writers and editors, we remained open to new concepts, employing a maximum variation of perspectives, while seeking out similarities, themes, and patterns.

The book has not pursued a 'putting to bed' of debate. Instead, we see it as a contribution to a greater, evolving whole. The chapters offer thinking to a future that is still to take form. Accordingly, the book has purposefully embraced diversity. There are applications of heuristics that blend cultural, intuitive, professional, and academic ways of knowing, and creative ways of discovering that knowing. Such an expansive consideration has not been published before. We have treated the protean nature of heuristic inquiry as a strength, and cultural and professional syntheses as testaments to its relevance and potential.

So, in completing this project, we face outwards to you the reader, and beyond this, to different and diverse disciplines, professions, approaches, and cultures of knowledge. From this position, it is useful in closing, to reflect on some of the themes that have emerged in the book.

The nature of voices

The chapters contain distinctive voices. We encounter the clinical and the poetic, the personal and the objective, the sensed and the analytic. We have been careful to preserve this uniqueness. Nevertheless, we have presented the contributions using a uniform approach to citation, referencing, and translation.

In 1990 Moustakas described heuristic inquiry as 'a way of engaging in scientific search through methods and processes aimed at discovery; a way of self-inquiry and dialogue with others aimed at finding the underlying meanings of important human experiences' (1990, p. 15). Indeed, Braud describes it as 'the richest and most satisfying description of an important human experience' (1998, p. 47). As a system of inquiry, heuristics is growing, both in volume and diversity (Hjeij & Vilks, 2023), and Mihalache (2019) notes its application across an increasingly broad spectrum of research.

As many of the chapters in this book demonstrate, heuristic inquiry employs a plurality of voices. These include the voices of the researcher and those of participants (co-researchers), as well as accounts found in literature, art, and wisdom traditions (Mihalache, 2019). In addition, in artistic practice, voices also constitute a dialogue between the researcher and an emerging artefact (Ings, 2018; Paora, 2023; Ventling, 2018). Moustakas (1990) argues that such dialogue deepens and extends understanding. Irrespective of the disciplinary context, the challenge the heuristic researcher faces lies in insightfully probing such voices, critically examining 'all the collected data in creative combinations and recombinations, sifting and sorting, moving rhythmically in and out of appearance, looking, listening carefully for the meanings within meanings' (Douglass & Moustakas, 1985, p. 52). As editors, it has been important to us that some of these voices are those of the displaced and marginalised. These are perspectives that need to be discovered, re-discovered, presented, and re-presented, in and through heuristic research, if it is to have relevance in our diverse and plural world.

The problem of ethics

However, as heuristic inquiry continues to develop there are issues that require attention. One of these relates to the ethics of care and representation which Elizabeth Hoyle discusses in Chapter 5. Here, we think she makes a profound point when she states that, 'Although the study was afforded university ethics approval, I found it necessary to reach beyond these provisions' (p. 99). Her observation suggests that university ethics criteria and committees are generally more concerned with instrumental ethics (which are based on consequentialism) than with intrinsic (value) ethics (which are based on relationality) (see Cornell et al., 2006; Nash, 2011).

Clandinin and Connelly remind us that, when using personal experience methods, 'The researcher is always speaking partially naked and is genuinely open to legitimate criticism from participants and from the audience' (1994, p. 423). In a heuristic inquiry, self-reflection and self-exposure remain constant throughout the study. This makes the approach, 'an extremely demanding process… that should not be attempted lightly' (Hiles, 2001, p. 2). This is because it is necessary for the researcher to navigate discomfort with personal disclosure and self-exposure (Djuraskovic & Arthur, 2010; Etherington, 2004; Ings, 2011; Sela-Smith, 2002), to balance privileging personal experience over that of the other participants (Mihalache, 2019), and to remain attentive to the nature of vulnerability (Ings, 2011, 2013; Mihalache, 2019). Both of these issues are discussed in Chapter 9.

Currently, in most universities, institutional review boards and ethics committees place emphasis on the safety of participants, but they often frame these people as external to the researcher. However, with a heuristic inquiry, ethical care requires careful discussion between the supervisor and the candidate (Ings, 2011, 2013, 2023), and the supervisor, candidate, and institution (Mihalache, 2019). This is because there is potential for the researcher to experience trauma that might interfere with the self-analytical processes (Mihalache, 2019). In addition, in authoring the study, the researcher is exposed, and self-disclosure may potentially have negative personal and professional consequences (Doloriert & Sambrook, 2009; Ings, 2011, 2013; Mihalache, 2019; Tolich, 2010). In navigating this, we suggest that heuristic researchers think through questions about, and issues of, ethics in relation to themselves, especially if an institution's ethics approval process doesn't include them. This is because, as Maurice Hamington states in Chapter 6: 'Ethics is a negotiation between mind and body, between action and reflection. To leave out one or the other element is to truncate the concept' (p.112).

Method and methodology

In our introduction (Gathering in), we referred to the diversity of views within heuristic research as they relate to method and methodology. We did this in order to set the scene for the diversity of representation that would occur across subsequent chapters. All the contributors discuss the heuristic method(s) they adopted in their research, that is, the 'construction of methods and procedures to guide a collection of data (Moustakas, 2001, p. 280), and, in Chapter 5, Elizabeth Nicholl offers an example of the heuristic method conducted 'in harmony' (p. 122) with another approach, in this case, narrative analysis. As far as methodology is concerned, three contributions furthered this discussion. In Chapter 2, Tangaroa Paora presented his research from within a Māori worldview which, methodologically, 'sought a productive meeting place between *rangahau* (Māori research) and heuristic enquiry' (p. 26). In Chapter 3, Hossein Najafi employed heuristic inquiry through the lens of the Persian philosopher Shahab al-Din Suhrawardi's (1186/2000) Persian illuminationism, and offered a synthesis of the thinking of Moustakas (1990) and the Persian poet Farid al-Din Attar (1984). Finally, in Chapter 4, Derek Ventling discussed 'the nature and merit of heuristics as a working methodology of visual arts in practice-led artistic enquiry' (p. 70), a methodology which, given his interest the embodiment of spiritual awareness, allowed for – and required – 'constant dialogue between the intuitive and the physical' (p.78).

The danger of dogma

In his original work on heuristic research, Moustakas (1967, 1990; Douglass & Moustakas, 1985) identifies six phases of heuristic research: initial engagement (with the topic or subject of inquiry), immersion, incubation, illumination, explication, and creative synthesis. These were derived from Moustakas' reflections on his experience of loneliness (Moustakas, 1961, 1972). These were not presented as stages of an invariant sequence that had to be followed. In his book on heuristic research, he states: 'Six phases of heuristic research guide unfolding investigations and comprise the basic research design. They include: the initial engagement, immersion into the topic and question, incubation, illumination, explication, and cumulation of the research into a creative synthesis' (p. 27).

Unfortunately, these phases have been taken by some (researchers and supervisors) as necessary stages to follow, and thus, they have been adopted as something of a dogma. Indeed, Sela-Smith asserts that 'If any one of these phases is not completed with full integrity, heuristic research is not successfully accomplished' (2002, p. 63), but then, somewhat contradictorily, she states that 'Although the phases must be completed, the completion of the phases cannot be the focus [of the research]' (2002, p. 62). However, if we consider certain words in Moustakas' sentences, he describes his phases as 'guides' in a 'basic research design'. From this, we suggest that he is not proposing an absolute structure but rather a more flexible, advisory, foundational, and expansive approach. Earlier, we quoted a passage from one of his last chapters on heuristic research in which he explicitly refers to the researcher's 'construction of methods and procedures' (Moustakas, 2001, p. 280), which positions the heuristic researcher as a designer rather than a follower. The same applies to the concepts Moustakas and others, over the years, have developed that underpin the – or a – methodology for heuristic research. We are interested to note, that with no prompting or insistence from us, none of the contributors in this book 'followed' heuristic research theory but, rather, they each adopted a critical, reflective view and designed phases or approaches that were driven by the specific needs of the research question they were addressing. Again, we see this in Moustakas' later work in which he writes that 'The research question and methodology flow out of inner awareness, meaning, and inspiration' (2001, p. 278).

The challenge of trust

At the heart of effective heuristic inquiry lies the necessity of trust: trust between the researcher and participants (including themselves if they are a participant), between the candidate and supervisor, and between the researcher and the institution.

When considering trust between the researcher and participants, all parties must accept that the study is subjective, and contributors are vulnerable. One of the roles of the supervisor is to assess and assert this, and to help the applicant/student to consider themselves as a participant.

The trust relationship between the candidate and supervisor is complex because, while the researcher must be constantly monitored and assessed, self-interrogation, fear, and declaration must be simultaneously supported and questioned (Ings, 2013). In addition, the researcher must be able to separate a critique of their study from a critique of the self (Tolich, 2010). Such trust requires considerable supervisory skill or what Tenni et al. refer to as a 'professionally intimate supervisory relationship' (2003, p. 4). (This relationship is explored in Chapter 10.)

Finally, institutions need trust in the ability of supervisors to support the protean nature of heuristic inquiries. Firstly, a duty of care must extend to the effective management of time and resources. Because of the immersive nature of heuristic inquiry, these can be complex issues that require experienced, perceptive, and consistent monitoring (see Chapters 9 and 10). Secondly, all parties must be cognisant of the need for support systems both for the researcher and supervisor. This is because the approach, by its nature, may involve personal and professional transformation for both parties.

In closing

In 1990, Clark Moustakas described heuristic inquiry as a 'mystery' that 'summons' (p. 13). As researchers, this summons demands our experienced/embodied knowledge, but this knowledge is incomplete. Consequently, we are forced to forsake certainty, and engage with doubt. From this state we develop and exercise processes of insightful questioning (Frick, 1990; Mihalache, 2019).

Heuristic inquiry is not the companion of the pre-imagined. It is demanding and protean. It has developed over centuries under diverse names, and in diverse cultures and contexts, as a way of approaching inquiry where no established formula exists. It requires a preparedness to embrace the uncertain and the unexplored. Accordingly, it demands criticality, courage, and the ability to rethink the very nature of understanding. This ability, which lies at the very heart of scholarship, is perhaps best described by Werner Karl Heisenberg in his seminal work, *In Physics and Philosophy: The Revolution in Modern Science*: 'Whenever we proceed from the known into the unknown, we may hope to understand, but we may have to learn at the same time a new meaning of the word "understanding"' (Heisenberg, 1962, p. 201).

It is to this idea that this book makes a contribution.

References

Attar, F. ud-Din (1984). *The conference of the birds* (A. Darbandi & D. Davis, Trans.; Re-issue edition). Penguin Classics.

Braud, W. (1998). Integral inquiry: Complementary ways of knowing, being, and expression. In W. Braud & R. Anderson (Eds.), *Transpersonal research methods for the social sciences* (pp. 35–68). Sage.

Clandinin, D., & Connelly, F. (1994). Personal experience methods. In N. K. Denzin & Y. Lincoln (Eds.), *The SAGE handbook of qualitative research* (3rd ed; pp. 413–427). Sage.

Cornell, W. F. (Ed.), Hargaden, H., Allen, J. R., Erskine, R., Moiso, C., Sills, C., Summers, G., & Tudor, K. (2006). Roundtable on the ethics of relational transactional analysis. *Transactional Analysis Journal*, *36*(2), 105–119. https://doi.org/10.1177/036215370603600204

Djuraskovic, I., & Arthur, N. (2010). Heuristic inquiry: A personal journey of acculturation and identity reconstruction. *Qualitative Report*, 15, 1569–1593. https://doi.org/10.46743/2160-3715/2010.1361

Doloriert, C., & Sambrook, S. (2009). Ethical confessions of the 'I' of autoethnography: A student's dilemma. *Qualitative Research in Organizations and Management: An International Journal*, 4(1), 27–45.

Douglass, B. G., & Moustakas, C. (1985). Heuristic inquiry: The internal search to know. *Journal of Humanistic Psychology*, *25*(3), 39–55. https://doi.org/10.1177/0022167885253004

Etherington, K. (2004). Heuristic research as a vehicle for personal and professional development. *Counselling & Psychotherapy Research*, *4*(1), 48–63. https://doi.org/10.1080/14733140412331383973

Frick, W. B. (1990). The symbolic growth experience: A chronicle of heuristic inquiry and a quest for synthesis. *Journal of Humanistic Psychology*, *30*(1), 64–80. https://doi.org/10.1177/0022167890301004

Heisenberg, W. (1962). *Physics and philosophy: The revolution in modern science*. Harper & Row.

Hiles, D. (2001, October). Heuristic inquiry and transpersonal research [Paper presentation]. Centre for Counseling and Psychotherapy Education, London, UK. https://psy.dmu.ac.uk/drhiles/HIpaper.htm

Hjeij, M., & Vilks, A. (2023). A brief history of heuristics: How did research on heuristics evolve? *Humanities and Social Sciences Communications*, *10*(1), 1–15. https://doi.org/10.1057/s41599-023-01542-z

Ings, W. (2011). Managing heuristics as a method of inquiry in autobiographical graphic design theses. *International Journal of Art & Design Education*, *30*(2), 226–241. https://doi.org/10.1111/j.1476-8070.2011.01699.x

Ings, W. (2013). Narcissus and the muse: Supervisory implications of autobiographical, practice-led, design theses. *International Journal of Qualitative Inquiry*, *14*(6), 675–693 https://doi.org/10.1177/1468794113488128

Ings, W. (2018). Private properties: Heuristic inquiry, land and the artistic researcher. In M. Sierra and K. Wise (Eds.), *Transformative pedagogies and the environment: Creative agency through contemporary art* (pp. 55–80). Common Ground Publishing.

Ings, W. (2023). Stories from the mirror: Supervising students' graphic memoirs. *Journal of Writing in Creative Practice*. *16*(1), 31–49. https://doi.org/10.1386/jwcp_00044_1

Kleining, G., & Witt, H. (2000). The qualitative heuristic approach: A methodology for discovery in psychology and the social sciences. Rediscovering the method of introspection as an example. *Forum Qualitative Sozialforschung/Forum: Qualitative Social Research, 1*(1). https://doi.org/10.17169/fqs-1.1.1123

Mihalache, G. (2019). Heuristic inquiry: Differentiated from descriptive phenomenology and aligned with transpersonal research methods. *The Humanistic Psychologist, 47*(2), 136–157. https://doi.org/10.1037/hum0000125

Moustakas, C. (1961). *Loneliness*. Prentice-Hall.

Moustakas, C. (1967). Heuristic research. In J. Bugental (Ed.), *Challenges in humanistic psychology* (pp. 100–107). McGraw-Hill.

Moustakas, C. (1972). *Loneliness and love*. Prentice-Hall.

Moustakas, C. (1990). *Heuristic research: Design, methodology, and applications*. Sage. https://doi.org/10.4135/9781412995641

Moustakas, C. (2001). Heuristic research: Design and methodology. In K. J. Schneider, J. F. T. Bugental, & J. F. Pierson (Eds.), *The handbook of humanistic psychology: Leading edges in theory, research and practice* (pp. 278–289). Sage.

Nash, K. (2011). Documentary-for-the-other: Relationships, ethics and (observational) documentary. *Journal of Mass Media Ethics, 26*(3), 224–239. https://doi.org/10.108 0/08900523.2011.581971

Paora, T. (2023). *Takatāpui – Beyond marginalisation: Exploring Māori gender, identity and performance* [Doctoral thesis, Auckland University of Technology]. Tuwhera Open Access Theses & Dissertations. https://hdl.handle.net/10292/16962

Sela-Smith, S. (2002). Heuristic research: A review and critique of Moustakas's method. *Journal of Humanistic Psychology, 42*(3), 53–88. https://doi.org/10.1177/00267802042003004

Suhrawardi, S. al-Din (1186/2000). *The philosophy of illumination* (J. Walbridge & H. Ziai, Trans.). Brigham Young University.

Tenni, C., Smith, A., & Boucher, C. (2003). The researcher as autobiographer: Analysing data written about oneself. *The Qualitative Report, 8*(1), 1–12. https://doi.org/10.4 6743/2160-3715/2003.1895

Tolich, M. (2010). A critique of current practice: Ten foundational guidelines for autoethnographers. *Qualitative Health Research, 20*(2), 1599–1610. https://doi.org/10.1177/1049732310376076

van Gogh, V. (1888/1958). *The complete letters of Vincent van Gogh* (Vols. 1–3). New York Graphic Society.

Ventling, D. (2018). Heuristics: A framework to clarify practice-led research. *Journal of Design, Art and Technology, 3*(2), 122–156. https://doi.org/10.29147/dat.v3i2.88

INDEX

wonderment 54, 94; the valley of 59–60, 62, 63
Wood, J. 30, 147, 155
Worrall, M. 183
writing, embodied relational 3
Wu, Y. 152

Yazdi, M. H. I. 48
Ye, Y. 151
Yerushalmi, H. 184, 197

Yilmaz, S. 152–153
Yuan, L. 107

Zachrisson, A. 184
Zadeh, L. A. 146
Zaki, J. 117
Zheng, A. 143
Ziai, H. 47–50, 64
Zwanzig, R. 48, 53

Printed and bound by CPI Group (UK) Ltd, Croydon, CR0 4YY

07/11/2024

01785272-0007